Local Histories

Pittsburgh Series in Composition, Literacy, and Culture

David Bartholomae and Jean Ferguson Carr, Editors

Local Histories

READING THE ARCHIVES OF COMPOSITION

Edited by Patricia Donahue
and Gretchen Flesher Moon

Foreword by Mariolina Rizzi Salvatori

Afterword by Jean Ferguson Carr

UNIVERSITY OF PITTSBURGH PRESS

Published by the University of Pittsburgh Press, Pittsburgh, PA 15260
Copyright © 2007, University of Pittsburgh Press
All rights reserved
Manufactured in the United States of America
Printed on acid-free paper
10 9 8 7 6 5 4 3 2 1

Library of Congress Cataloging-in-Publication Data

Local histories : reading the archives of composition / edited by Patricia Donahue and
Gretchen Flesher Moon ; foreword by Mariolina Rizzi Salvatori.

   p. cm. — (Pittsburgh series in composition, literacy, and culture)
  Includes bibliographical references and index.
  ISBN-13: 978-0-8229-5954-0 (pbk. : alk. paper)
  ISBN-10: 0-8229-5954-2 (pbk. : alk. paper)
  1. English language—Rhetoric—Study and teaching—United States—History—
Sources. 2. Report writing—Study and teaching (Higher)—United States—History—
Sources. I. Donahue, Patricia, 1953- II. Moon, Gretchen Flesher.
  PE1405.U6L63 2007
  808'.042071073—dc22

2007016300

FOR MIKE AND MIKE

Contents

(This is not a) Foreword

Mariolina Rizzi Salvatori

> In the past, historians could be accused of wanting to know only about "the great deeds of kings," but today this is certainly no longer true. More and more they are turning toward what their predecessors passed over in silence, discarded, or simply ignored. "Who built Thebes of the seven gates?" Bertold Brecht's "literate worker" was already asking. The sources tell us nothing about these anonymous masons, but the question retains all its significance.
>
> CARLO GINZBURG

> The phrase, "return to," designates a movement with its proper specificity, which characterizes the initiation of discursive practices. If we return, it is because of a basic and constructive omission, an omission that is not the result of accident or incomprehension. . . . The barrier imposed by omission was not added from the outside; it arises from the discursive practice in question, which gives it its law.
>
> MICHEL FOUCAULT

IF IT IS DIFFICULT and contradictory to introduce one's own just completed work, it is even more difficult and contradictory to do so for a collection of writings by other authors, especially because their projects resist straightforward summary. I consider this difficulty a marker of the strength of this collection.

Thus, rather than forecasting for the reader what's to follow, and lessen the pleasure of experiencing firsthand the materials these authors introduce and the readings of them they construct, I offer here a series of observations—

meditations on how these chapters cast light on some of the most crucial problems of historical understanding.

As different as they are from one another in terms of approach, subject matter, institution being examined, orientation to the past, and style, the chapters in this volume are linked by a shared aspiration: they emerge out of and address what Foucault names "a basic and constructive omission" of preceding discourse, an omission, or a series of omissions, which, to use Ginzberg's words, have "passed over . . . discarded, or simply ignored" historical actions, agents, and agencies that have been crucial to "building" the discipline of composition studies.

In "Rethinking Intellectual History and Reading Texts," Dominick LaCapra argues that "the more distinctive issue in historiography is that of the relationship between documentary reconstruction of, and dialogue with, the past" (27). LaCapra's concern is that in a narrowly documentary conception of historical understanding, the emphasis on contextualization "becomes a detour around texts and an excuse for not really reading them at all" (14). As a corrective he suggests that historians learn from disciplines like literary criticism and philosophy "the importance of reading and interpreting complex texts—the so-called 'great' texts of the Western tradition—and of formulating the problem of relating these texts to various pertinent contexts" (25). As readers and teachers of literary texts, cognizant of major philosophical traditions, attentive to the epistemological assumptions of their work, the authors in this book do the kind of work LaCapra argues intellectual historians need to do "to reopen the question of the field's nature and objectives" (23). But they do this not only with "texts" that he would not acknowledge as "the 'great' texts of the Western tradition"; they also raise the question of "what is/counts as a document?"

Several iterations, "repeated returns," mark this collection: a number of primary texts, and (their) authors, are frequently cited, but each citation uncovers a different path to an obscured moment in the past, each return potentially opening a different archive. And so, through the narrative paths these essays trace, what we know as the history of the origins of composition studies shifts, undergoes expansions, complications, reversals, and revisions. In some of these returns, some authors point to the strategies and effects of the so-called "Harvard chapter" in the traditional history of American higher education, and make visible what in this or successive chapters could and could not be understood as evidence of learning. By returning to Harvard to direct our attention to institutions that made "Harvard" and its work possible, they constantly introduce modifications; by reanimating suppressed voices, they show ways of productively transforming discursive practices structured not to see (and to make others not to see), not to take into consideration, what might otherwise disturb a given version of history. In other words, each author's investigative project returns to moments that traditional and dominant historical narratives make no mention of, and pays "particular attention to those things registered in the interstices of [those narratives], [their] gaps and absences" (Foucault 135). What about the work done at this institution? What about the enabling function of strict composition rules for this kind of student? What about the political commitment and participation of . . . ? No less than Bertold Brecht's literate worker's question, these are radical questions. Simple, pointed, irreverent, seemingly naïve, they are questions that, before critical reflexivity came to trouble the serenity, the aplomb with which traditional history tells its story, would have been deemed inappropriate, incongruous, irrelevant. These chapters make it clear that these questions propel different kinds of quests. Each contributor looks for and scrupulously "reads" documents, artifacts (assignments, compositions, records of meetings, echoes of discussions and political debates) that discursive omissions have "ghosted" but not fully obliterated. Each carefully avoids totalizing claims and conclusions, attentive to the limits of understanding that the lack of preservation (an implicit judgment on their value) of the materials under scrutiny sets up for its investigation. Each raises cogent questions about what constitutes legitimate proof, what "makes" a document: that is, what kind of research, contextualization, assessment, interpretation turn a catalogue, a memo, an assignment, a portrait into legitimate and legitimizing evidence. Implicitly, but persistently, each author raises questions about the now-in-vogue category of "ephemera." (What, after all, makes something "ephemeral"? Is ephemerality a property of an artifact's materiality? Of traditional value judgments? Of the care for and investment in that object? Of memory?)

In the chapter that concludes this collection, Patricia Donahue calls attention to the iteration of a gesture each contributor has been asked to make: by listing and foregrounding the documents they retrieve from oblivion and interpret as texts, the authors take responsibility for what they are doing and why, fully cognizant of the implications of this act. Repudiating traditional historical hubris, this gesture is a reminder to themselves and their readers of the (inevitable and constructed) fallibility and partiality of all historical accounts. Listed and located, their documents can be returned to by others and be expanded, enriched, modified, and interpreted to tell different, thicker, stories—each essay's incipit potentially a "transitive beginning." And something else bears noticing about this important structuring feature of the collection: each incipit is the place where the authors pay tribute to the work of the guardians and tutelary spirits of the materials they have assembled—the librarians, *Lares* of the archives. It is a tactful and generous gesture, one that acknowledges and leaves a record of those feelings, emotions, passions, and personal investments that have fuelled and guided the articulation of these "Local Histories."

Acknowledgments

THIS PROJECT REPRESENTS the fulfillment of a dream deferred. It was over fifteen years ago that the two of us, each year at the CCCC conference, began to share our concerns about the relative invisibility of certain kinds of institutions (especially small private universities, liberal arts colleges, junior colleges, and small public universities) in the historical discourse of our discipline. A little later we were fortunate to meet Tom Amorose and Paul Hanstedt; conversations with them eventually led to the formation of a special interest group for small colleges and plans for two different kinds of projects. One would survey general pedagogical and administrative issues; the other would examine gaps in the historical record. The first project reached fruition in the form of a special edition of *Composition Studies* (2004). The second project is to be found in these pages, in which a number of very capable compositionists, archivists, and scholars have turned their attention to the institutions in which they work, excavating from within their dusty archives important documents that will help illuminate and inflect current historical narratives in new and intriguing ways.

We owe the greatest thanks to our contributors, not only for their efforts and wonderful work, but for their good patience and humor. They understood the impetus for the book, met their deadlines, undertook their revisions with considerable good spirit, and tried not to ask us too many times, "When is the book going to be published?" To Mariolina Salvatori and Jean Carr, the writers, respectively, of our "non-Foreword" and "Afterword" we owe a special obligation. In her groundbreaking work on pedagogy, Mariolina Salvatori taught us what it meant to "documentify" a text and to bring history and pedagogy together in productive relationship. In a range of professional venues, Jean Carr taught us how to read nineteenth-century texts about history, reading, and writing. And in her work as coeditor of the Pittsburgh Series on Composition, Literacy, and Culture, she lent support to this project early on and inspired us to forge ahead when our energy lagged behind. They are the guardian spirits of this project. The careful and thoughtful anonymous readers suggested important revisions of the manuscript to bring it to its current form. And Deborah Meade, senior editor at the University of Pittsburgh Press, made a significant contribution to this project through her meticulous and energetic attention to the words on the page.

Patricia Donahue would also like to thank Lafayette College for much appreciated sabbatical support and her colleagues for understanding that sometimes a teacher just has to stay home and write. Husband, Mike Garst, and father, Joseph Donahue, lent their love and gentle tweaking. Former students, like Karen Cera and Heather Bastian, provided constant reminders of why such work matters. The bichon frises, Lily and Isabelle, remained steadfast in their devotion.

Gretchen Flesher Moon thanks colleagues at Willamette University for their enthusiasm for historical research of this nature, and for their support of collaborations spread between Oregon and Pennsylvania. Brisk early morning walks with Fritz and Jeb (dogs of no discernible breed, but of great curiosity) made long days poring over the manuscript physically bearable. And that Mike takes pride in my work and encourages me matters above all else.

Local Histories

1

Locating Composition History

Gretchen Flesher Moon

All of historical work, then, is provisional, partial—fragments we shore against our ruin. We are trying to make sense of things. It is always a construction. It is always tottering.

ROBERT J. CONNORS, "Dreams and Play"

BOTH ARCHIVE and archaeology have their etymological roots in the Greek *arche*, whose principal meanings are: beginning, origin; and first place or power, sovereignty. The archive has descended from *archeion*, the residence or office of the magistrates where public records were kept; archaeology studies that which is *archaios*, ancient, in human material culture. The archival researcher (we have no archivologist) digs through boxes of files, slips of paper, bound volumes with pages and pages in different hands, books richly illuminated by tiny marginalia, now sometimes in microfiche, on magnetic tape, in file servers and Web sites; the archaeologist sifts through what is buried, in graves, in landfills, in the recycled walls and built-over rubble of ancient cities, under volcanoes and floods. In the *archeion,* we catalogue the history of decisions—laws and decrees and elections—and their issue—judgments, sentences, tax assessments, rosters—and these are things that matter. In the burial grounds, we catalogue the artifacts that memorialize human activity—water jars, spoons, arrowheads, dolls and figurines, coins, jewelry, buildings, roads, obscure objects of beauty and desire—also things that matter.

The college archive preserves what has mattered to its teachers, administrators, and students. When one works in the archives, one finds not only the official records of enrollment, curriculum, and achievement, but also—often uncatalogued, undigested, uninterpreted—personal copies of books, notes, and papers that mattered to those who read and wrote in that place, at particular moments, on unique rhetorical occasions. Such items may be—most often, in fact, surely are—collected intermittently and without the kind of annotation that would help the researcher in the archives to assess confidently how typical —or not—were those moments and occasions at that place. Similarly, one cannot always trace the provenance of archival materials. Just who *did* deposit Box 643?

In dealing with historical artifacts as fragmentary and discontinuous as those in composition's archives, the authors of this volume have also paid attention to what we do not have and thus cannot read. We have finished essays, but not the assignments that generated them. We have lists of textbooks, but no explicit accounts of how they were used. We have the papers of a few students: were these students "representative"? Were these students' papers preserved by accident, or because they pleased the instructor who saved them, or because they showed the range of performances in a given class? As Connors reminds us, from the archives, provisionally, in fragments, one constructs histories.

The chapters in this volume construct local histories by drawing on a wide range of archival documents, including, but not limited to: faculty meeting minutes, personal letters, student literary magazines, alumni magazines, yearbooks, course catalogues, reports to the trustees, class notebooks, student essays, unpublished lectures, and mission statements. This book's contributors attempt to reconstruct how students—variously inflected by class, race, and gender—have learned to write at different times, in different places, with different teachers, textbooks, and curricula, and how teachers, also at different times, in different places, have developed pedagogies, built curriculum and programs, and contributed to the emergence of a discipline.

Each chapter in this book tells a story. Kathleen A. Welsch locates composition history in Mahala Jay, a nontraditional student, married and twenty-two years old when she began at Oberlin, who, with her husband, began again at Antioch three years later when they learned that as a woman, Mahala could not read her graduation paper in public. Kenneth Lindblom, Will Banks, and Risë Quay set the story that Albert Stetson's professional essays tell about himself as a teacher against the epistolary narrative from the letters of Abbie Reynolds and her brother John, and conclude that Abbie's version of the story is much sadder than Stetson ever knew. Jeffrey L. Hoogeveen projects the history of curricular change in composition at Lincoln University, the oldest historically black university in the United States, on the screen of the contemporary civil rights movement events, which united its faculty and students for an extended moment between 1969 and 1974. Each arising from a particular place and time, these stories ground us in the specific and discrete circumstances of local writers, teachers, classrooms, and institutions that are diminished, forgotten, and lost.

The writings in this book can, and should, also be read as stories that connect to, disconnect from, comment upon, and contradict one another in many ways, ways that resist the construction of a unified narrative of the discipline. In her reflections on the 1988 CCCC, "Octalog: The Politics of Historiography," Sharon Crowley writes, "There are so few histories of rhetoric and composition studies in print that those which have been written and published so far have become much more authoritative than I imagine their authors ever thought they might be" (Newkirk 39). It is not our aim in composing *Local Histories* to construct a single narrative of composition history but rather to extend, challenge, complicate, and thereby enrich the narrative as it has thus far developed. From these local histories, one might begin to tease out several potential alternative histories. Composition's almost universal common feature —the first-year composition course—has encouraged the discipline to think of its history as the history of that course only, a history commonly believed to have begun at Harvard. In fact, the chronological primacy of Harvard in offering a course in English composition is challenged by Patricia Donahue and Bianca Falbo's archival work on the career of Francis March at Lafayette. The disciplinary primacy of freshman composition is challenged by all of the contributors, generally, and specifically by Heidemarie Weidner's work on Butler University and Julie Garbus's work on Wellesley College. Beth Ann Rothermel and Patrice Gray both find that while elitist motivations affected the Massachusetts normal schools, faculty and students also resisted them in important ways. On the other hand, William DeGenaro, perhaps surprisingly, extends the narrative: he argues that the junior college movement, in its origins, resulted from the same elitist motivations that inspired the entrance examinations in writing at Harvard. In so doing, he challenges an equally powerful myth about disciplinary origins and institutional character: the myth of the two-year college as "democracy's college," an institution historically and ideologically committed to egalitarian and democratic values.

Local histories complicate the notion of students: not exclusively young, white males, not exclusively among the New England elite—but also women, even a married couple in their twenties, even midwesterners. They complicate the notion of teachers: not exclusively either rhetoricians or literature faculty, but generalists as well as specialists. Weidner and Garbus write about powerful women professors with innovative pedagogies. These histories complicate the notion of institution: not only the emerging university of colleges and divisions and departments, but colleges, normal schools, two-year colleges, and historically black colleges and universities constitute composition history. Indeed, Francis March's story of reading and writing suggests that the history of literature vs. composition—which even at the beginning of the twenty-first century has less explanatory power and descriptive accuracy at liberal arts colleges than at research institutions—is rich, nuanced, and complex. The local histories at Antioch College, Butler University, Wellesley College, and Lincoln University chart a history of teaching by generalists with a liberal ideal.

The chapters within also propose an argument for the flourishing of lively and diverse rhetorical practices:[1] the oral presentation of papers (Welsch); the cultivation of conversation (Weidner); the flourishing of literary societies (Welsch, Weidner, Garbus, Rothermel) and debating and dramatic clubs

(Rothermel, Gray); political activism (Hoogeveen). They propose alternatives to the prevailing late-nineteenth-century fixation on correctness: Weidner reads "accuracy of expression" in the practices of Catherine Merrill and her own student and successor Harriet Noble as a much more rhetorically complex problem than simply the grammatical and spelling correctness dictated by Illinois State Normal's Albert Stetson (Lindblom, Banks, and Quay). There is also evidence of imaginative and innovative pedagogies, engaging peer responses and multiple revisions (Weidner), service learning (Garbus), community-based research (Fitzgerald), writing across the curriculum (Donahue and Falbo, Weidner, Rothermel), and student-centered language (Rothermel).

IN ADDITION to their narrative components, this volume's chapters can be read as analyses of particular types of institutions. Composition's dominant historical narratives have located history in major research institutions whose institutional missions, teaching philosophies, intellectual ethoses, attitudes toward students, and student bodies are not universally shared by other kinds of institutions. The first four chapters locate history in liberal arts colleges. Kathleen A. Welsch's "Thinking Like *That*" reads the compositions Mahala Jay wrote at Antioch College in the 1850s; Patricia Donahue and Bianca Falbo reconsider the teaching of reading and writing from the example of Lafayette College in the 1850s; Heidemarie Weidner studies the careers of the first two holders of the Demia Butler Chair established in 1869 at Butler University; Julie Garbus analyzes the pedagogy of Vida Scudder, whose career at Wellesley College spanned forty years, from 1887 to 1927. These institutions share a peculiarly American faith in learning as conducive to—if not constitutive of—moral improvement and a related dedication to lives of service for the greater good, here manifest in the students' writings as well as in a much wider range of rhetorical practice by both students and their teachers. Even so, their histories are different in important ways. For example, Antioch, Butler, and Wellesley are all dedicated to the equal education of women, but the social positioning of women—and consequently their rhetorical positioning—changed significantly between 1853 when Mahala Jay matriculated at Antioch and 1927 when Vida Scudder retired from teaching at Wellesley.

The next four chapters locate composition history in normal schools, two in the Midwest and two in Massachusetts. Until very recently, normal schools have been nearly erased from the narratives of composition. Yet their stories inform the stories of composition in the public elementary and secondary schools, whose graduates fueled, and whose teachers would bear the blame for, fresh outbreaks of literacy crises. Normal school students were assigned complex subject positions; made to feel somehow inferior, more suitable for training than education, but also responsible for transmitting the culture's values, or at least for enforcing its standards. Lindblom, Banks, and Quay conclude that the ethos of the Illinois State Normal University positioned working-class teachers in opposition to working-class students, and they locate that ethos in a rule-bound writing pedagogy that taught Abbie Reynolds that she could not write. Similarly, Beth Ann Rothermel finds that at the Westfield Normal School, the rhetorical curriculum narrowed toward the end of the nineteenth century, focusing on "how to speak and write correctly" rather than offering a broader and more complex program. In the archives at Fitchburg Normal School, forty miles from Harvard University, Patrice K. Gray reads Helen Bradford's understanding of her own positioning in a normal school: "This school is not a seminary or an institution where women can receive the higher education, but it is here that they can imagine what higher training would be and the joy it would bring them." Kathryn Fitzgerald does not read that particular tension at the Platteville Normal School in Wisconsin, but, attempting to follow a set of forty-four papers back to the assignment that gendered and engendered them, she cannot always hear the writers'—especially the female writers'—voices. It seems they were silenced by the demands for conformity to dominant subject positions concentrated in the genre of "student writing." However, in a few examples, Fitzgerald reads rhetorically deft manipulations of genre by which writers were able to simultaneously adopt and undercut the prescribed conventions of the assignment. Moreover, both Rothermel and Gray argue that even while external forces were narrowing the rhetorical curriculum in normal schools, a variety of extracurricular rhetorical practices greatly enriched students' educations. William DeGenaro locates composition history in the problematic rhetoric and ideology of William Rainey Harper, the "father of the junior college." In reading Harper's papers and books, DeGenaro not only follows the trajectory of first-year composition, but parallels it to the particular discourse of "service," which subordinates general education and lower division courses to academic specialization and research. He acknowledges the same anti-democratic impulses that Lindblom, Banks, and Quay find at Illinois State Normal and reads the anti-aspirational rhetoric of discouragement that Rothermel and Gray detect in the Massachusetts normals during the same period. Like them, he recognizes the resilience of both two-year colleges and first-year composition to resist those discourses.

Finally, Hoogeveen locates composition history at a historically black liberal arts university. Focusing particularly on the years 1969 through 1974, he traces the alliance of students and faculty in calling for a curriculum and pedagogy across all humanities departments to equip them for the rhetorical demands of leadership in the civil rights movement. Hoogeveen, like DeGenaro, proposes parallel historical tracks, in this case, between the history of composition as a system of knowledge and the civil rights movement. The response he reads in the Lincoln University English Department's archives is less inspiring: some members of English respond to these calls as a literacy crisis, just as many other colleges and universities were doing, and issue warnings about appropriate diction clearly meant to ban Black English Diction. Just as Composition was beginning to define itself as a discipline with a special field of knowledge, the English Department began insisting on its expertise and ownership over the new course to be taught by colleagues across the curriculum.

THE CHAPTERS in this book are also studies of the archival materials—and the writers who produced them—that constitute their primary sources. A list of archival sources (which almost always require a researcher to be physically present and to hold the materials in her hands, although some archived materials are now available on line) appears at the end of each chapter, to identify the exact materials used, and to illustrate the kinds of materials one might find in an archive.

Among the artifacts that memorialize a college's life, teachers' assignments and students' writing are strangely rare. Garbus reminds us that even now, college students keep very little of their own writing, that teachers must necessarily clean house of accumulated student writing from time to time, and that college archives still have little interest in preserving boxes of student writing that will be reproduced annually. Connors's explanation—that their creation in single copies or in only enough copies for the students in a class renders them unavailable to archivists for saving—makes sense ("Dreams and Play" 20), but he also implies that papers written in the first-year composition course simply have little value to their writers ("Writing" 58). While this lacuna in the record is problematic, the contributors to this volume locate composition history both through and across the curriculum and find several specimens outside freshman composition for analysis. Welsch has seven complete essays written by Mahala Jay between 1851 and 1856, and quotes extensively from them. Fitzgerald has forty-four unmarked papers, and both the fact that they were saved and the occasion she deduces for their composition testify to their significance, to the writers, and to the teacher. Gray draws on a collection of student theses from 1897 to 1910, and Rothermel alludes to a Westfield State Normal School student essay. These examples are not many, but they offer corroboration, and correction, to the idealizations of student writing projected in textbooks and pedagogical treatises.

Students' notes and notebooks, analyzed extensively by Garbus and Rothermel, are even rarer than finished papers and perhaps even more valuable to historians in approximating what students have really learned about writing and the teaching of writing. The normal school students Rothermel writes about were, after all, learning to be teachers; they carefully made notes about the goals and methods of rhetorical instruction for younger students as they were being trained. But, as anyone also knows who has ever looked over students' notes or collected "exit cards" recording "what I learned today" and "what I'm confused about" or "what is still a mystery," what is said or taught can be very different from what is heard or learned or read. Thus, Garbus comes to question some of Vida Scudder's personal assessments of her pedagogy because students' notes represent a somewhat different pedagogy. Weidner has found in Colin King's 1879–1883 diary of his Butler University education a very important record of the regular practices of peer review and revision in Catherine Merrill's courses. Similarly, in personal letters to family and friends, such as those read by Garbus, Lindblom, Banks, and

Quay and Welsch, students write candidly about not only what they're learning, but also how it feels to them. From Abbie Reynolds's letters home, for example, Lindblom, Banks, and Quay educe not only the errors-obsessed pedagogy described in Albert Stetson's curricular and pedagogical essays, but an overarching harsh and demoralizing composition pedagogy that students experienced at Illinois State Normal.

Another kind of archival source contributes to this more richly nuanced historical account of teaching and learning writing: an institution's occasional and celebratory pieces. Documents like Maud Goodfellow's "Historical Sketch and Lists of Former [Fitchburg Normal] Faculty and Students" (Gray), Herbert Sedgwick's "Record of the Class of 1886" typescript prepared for the [Westfield Normal] class semi-centennial" (Rothermel), Hilton Brown's "In the Heyday of the Literary Society" published in the *Butler Alumnal Quarterly*, and *Quarterly* editor Katherine Merrill Graydon's biography of Professor Catherine Merrill (Weidner) are epideictic; they do not pretend to be objective or analytical. But they offer insights into what students remembered and valued about their schools and their teachers, things that mattered. At Fitchburg in 1909, "The Faculty Meeting" skit's authors captured "a sense of the lived experience of this academic community that is impossible to discern in the official documents alone" (Gray).

Just as the skit documents the "lived experience" at Fitchburg, several of the authors in this volume reconstruct rhetorical education by looking more widely at the extracurriculum. Welsch knows more about Mahala Jay's reading during college than the college catalogue can tell her because she has also read the minutes of the Alethezetean Society, of which Mahala was a member. Rothermel has read issues of the Westfield student periodical, the *Normal Exponent*, from 1897, which add texture to the picture of turn-of-the-century thinking, academic life, and writing. The records of the school's nineteenth-century literary society, the *Normal Philologian*, record a wide range of rhetorical activities—dramatic readings, discussions, debates, extemporaneous speeches—on topics related to their vocation as teachers. In the yearbook, the *Tekoa*, she finds records of the debating and drama society active in the 1920s and 1930s, Delta Omicron Alpha—the Daughters of Athena, and learns that the 1929 topic was "equal pay for equal work." While an earlier issue of

9

Tekoa clearly relishes the pure fun of dramatic enactment, one also suspects that these young women, whose life work is increasingly defined as women's work and whose formal education as defined outside the institution by the state Board of Education is increasingly restricted and mechanistic, were passionately and intellectually engaged in their more serious 1929 topic.

Teachers' formal writings are surely as complex in their negotiation of various audiences, purposes, and subjectivities as student writings are. Essays on teaching matters, reports to supervisors and boards, even course descriptions represent ideals. If they do not, perhaps, perfectly match practice, they probably at least reflect a teacher's philosophy and intention. Or maybe they represent what a teacher thought the board or other colleagues needed to read, or expected to read, or wanted to read. Or they might, as Hoogeveen suggests of one faculty member's memos, belie political purposes quite contradictory to those stated. Thus, this volume—and several of its chapters—argues for a complex layering of institutional, teacher, and student documents. Donahue and Falbo reveal how the diary kept by Lafayette College valedictorian James Boyd between 1853 and 1859 includes his reflections on how his reading informs his writing. His papers are not preserved in the archive, but the diary discusses them at a tellingly self-conscious remove. Weidner shows how student Colin King's diary confirms that Catherine Merrill's pedagogy is represented in her course descriptions. Thus, when Weidner reads an 1872 committee report to the Butler Board of Commissioners quoting Professor Merrill on the need for "much more attention paid to the English language and literature," she is able to reconstruct Merrill's definition of good writing from a close reading of her course descriptions, as well as her published essay on Shakespeare, letters she wrote to friends, and an admiring letter from a newspaper columnist on her graceful style. These same materials permit Weidner to speculate about the influence on Merrill of the works of Genung and Newman, which Merrill might have known although neither authored Butler University's prescribed rhetoric text. Lindblom, Banks, and Quay present Albert Stetson's essays on grammar and spelling, prepared for an annual Teachers' Institute at Illinois Normal, which express not only his philosophy of language but also his classist assumptions about his students, assumptions that seem also to have been expressed in his teaching to Abbie Reynolds.

Official institutional documents—annual reports, course catalogues, faculty minutes—have formed the underlying structure of composition's historical narrative. All of the contributors to this book weave documents from teachers and students over the warp of the official record. But as Donahue and Falbo illustrate so strikingly, even these most public records contain information about composition's histories that has not yet entered the historical narrative. As composition's historians read, and read closely, the reports and catalogues and minutes of more institutions, the richly layered local histories will compose an ever richer, ever more complex historical narrative.

Finally, the archival materials for these local histories wrestle with the definition of the archive. DeGenaro discusses at length the problem of retrieving archival materials from an institution—or even a class of institution—that has not maintained an archive or, as in the case of many two-year colleges in their early years, even had a building of their own in which an archive might have been kept. DeGenaro argues that there are, however, primary sources from which we may construct a history of composition for the two-year college: in the locally published teacher narratives and essays published in small journals, or by in-house printing, or in conference proceedings. In such materials, he reads the narrative in which teachers, administrators, and the movement for specialization and science in the university position two-year colleges in general and composition in specific as service institutions. And, working on a historical period within living memory of some of his colleagues, Hoogeveen includes in his "archive" the ongoing memorial reconstruction of text that lives in conversation, allusion, gossip, and faculty chat.

CONNORS REPEATEDLY reminded his readers as historians to face their own prejudices. We necessarily read the past from where we stand now. We are indignant on behalf of young women students whose rhetorical education was carried on in a separate sphere. When we find evidence for writing instruction diffused throughout an undergraduate education by the generalists who presided over American colleges in the nineteenth century, even as departmentalization was developing, some composition historians will applaud an antecedent of writing across the curriculum while others will bemoan the implication that teaching writing requires no special knowledge. And we necessarily read from the perspective of the landmark histories written in the last fifty years, narratives that have located composition history at Harvard and University of Michigan and defined current-traditional as a system of beliefs and practices. Most composition scholars, including the authors of this collection, would probably, following Connors, name Albert R. Kitzhaber the author and originator of composition history and have learned from him and from the second generation of composition historians he inspired.[2] In the final chapter, Patricia Donahue reflects on Kitzhaber's exemplarity as a historian and on the ways that his work has taught the discipline to seek and find beginnings.

Local histories of composition test our theories about the influence of popular textbooks, innovative teachers, dominant pedagogies, and landmark curricular reforms. They challenge the dominant narrative of composition history, located in primarily elite research institutions, disrupting its apparent simplicity as the myth of origin and proposing alongside it a complicated and discontinuous array of alternative histories. We hope that this book will inspire our colleagues to find their ways into and around their own institution's archives and to produce many more local histories; each chapter's headnotes and self-reflective comments are intended to support new work. What S. Michael Halloran wrote in 1990 will remain true for several more decades: "What primary materials exist—textbooks, student manuscripts, diaries, lecture notes, college calendars and catalogues—have not been given the attention they deserve. . . . Much scholarship remains to be done before we can be confident of the story of writing instruction in America" ("From Rhetoric" 155). These chapters illustrate not only the variety of archival materials that document composition's histories, but the ways of reading that produce these histories. And, we hope, they serve as exemplars of an explicitly reflective critical practice.

Notes

1. The scholars whose archival work has been outside the university—in primary and secondary schools and in the "extra-curriculum" of writing groups, women's groups, literary societies, and the like—have, of course, already begun this alternative history

and their influences are noted throughout these pages: Arthur Appleby, Catherine Hobbs, Shirley Wilson Logan, Sarah Robbins, Lucille Schultz.

2. Connors called Kitzhaber the grandfather of composition history. As the essays repeatedly indicate, we, the grandchildren, are all enormously indebted to the work of the second generation, including (and here one inevitably risks omitting branches of the family tree) Katherine H. Adams, James Berlin, John Brereton, Jean Ferguson Carr, Stephen Carr, Robert Connors, Sharon Crowley, Wallace Douglas, S. Michael Halloran, Winifred Horner, Nan Johnson, Susan Miller, James J. Murphy, Stephen North, David R. Russell, Mariolina Salvatori, Donald Stewart.

‒⟨ *2* ⟩‒

Thinking Like *That*

THE IDEAL NINETEENTH-CENTURY STUDENT WRITER

Kathleen A. Welsch

MAHALA PEARSON JAY was an untraditional nineteenth-century college student in many ways. She was twenty-two years old, did not come from money, and did not imagine the college experience as an opportunity to mix with social peers. Married in October 1849, she entered Oberlin College in February 1850 with her husband to pursue higher education in preparation for a life mission of teaching. Many in their religious Society of Friends, in keeping with the general public sentiment of the times, expressed opposition to their plans, but Mahala and Eli received strong family support and encouragement. Not only did Oberlin espouse a philosophy of marriage—the "joining of two active partners, both dedicated to bettering the world around them"—compatible with their own (Seidman), it also appeared to offer the educational opportunities sought by both. Mahala and Eli held high expectations for coeducation: they anticipated that Mahala would receive an education and academic experience

Archival materials referred to in this chapter are held by Antiochiana, The Olive Kettering Library of Antioch College in Yellow Springs, Ohio; The Arthur S. and Kathleen Postle Friends Collection and Archives, Lilly Library, Earlham College, Richmond, Indiana; and the Oberlin College Archives, Oberlin, Ohio.

commensurate with Eli's. The reality at Oberlin, however, did not meet their expectations. Women at Oberlin—as elsewhere in society—were still perceived as appendages to men and prohibited from participating in public forums. When school officials informed the Jays in their third year that Mahala would not be permitted to participate in the public reading of graduation papers along with her male classmates, they withdrew and matriculated in the first class at Antioch College in Yellow Springs, Ohio, in 1853. Under the supervision of Horace Mann, they believed "the place accorded women in that institution would be equal to that given men" (Beede). Thus, Mahala (now twenty-five) and Eli (now twenty-six) began their college educations again at the first-year level and were among Antioch's first graduating class in 1857.

Mahala does not represent the social class, geographical area, curriculum, institutional setting, or (for the most part) gender commonly encountered in discussions of nineteenth-century, Harvard-style, student writers. Similarly, the Harvard model may have been the prototype for many nineteenth-century composition-rhetoric courses; however, it represents just one configuration among many. Student writers in nineteenth-century America may have shared textbooks, theme topics, essay formulas, and cultural narratives in common, but they did not write out of identical contexts. In *The Emergence of the American University*, Veysey distinguishes between academic institutions in the East and those in the West when he writes that, unlike the exclusivity found in eastern schools, the student population in schools west of the Alleghenies "encouraged the widespread belief that inclusiveness and quality were reconcilable goals" (100). The difference also manifested itself in the form of student motivation and attitudes regarding the pursuit of higher education. Helen Horowitz reports that students who came to "college off the farms [in the West were] filled with seriousness and impatient with what appeared to them to be the childish silliness of many college students" (64). As evidenced by their letters to the editor in student publications, serious students rejected the extracurricular fraternity life as well as the sophomoric mentality of many of their peers (68). Students in western institutions approached studying more conscientiously because they tended to perceive higher education as a means of achieving life goals and improving class status. For Mahala, there was an additional responsibility—demonstrating through her academic performance the intellectual equality of women with men.

Narratives about nineteenth-century composition-rhetoric at schools outside of New England are largely absent from the historical record as are narratives about strong, dutiful, invested student writers. Only recently have historians (e.g., JoAnn Campbell, Donald Stewart, Charles Paine) begun to draw student writers and teachers into the conversation as revealing players and contributors to the history. One cannot, for example, continue to dismiss Richard Whately's *Elements of Rhetoric* (1832) as simply unproductive or cast it as the villainous impetus of true rhetoric's degeneration into thoughtless prose and artless, mechanical exercises without exploring the richer, more complex narrative of how educators and students struggled daily to use such a text—how they imagined it as useful in their attempts to teach writing and compose essays within the confines of academic, social, and cultural discourses. To understand the history of ideas associated with nineteenth-century composition, its evolution, adherence to seemingly unproductive pedagogy, rigid rules and expectations, and seemingly lackluster student writing, we need to imagine individuals like Mahala who enacted them. What academic, social, and cultural circumstances motivated her, formed her values, and influenced her understanding of composition-rhetoric? How did she imagine herself invested in the cause of higher education through the essays she wrote?

Investigations that imagine individuals as products and participants of their nineteenth-century world; that explore the historical, social, and cultural contexts; and consider the ethnologic behind the "contextual influences that converge in the classroom" (Jolliffe 263) transform student writers like Mahala from one-dimensional background figures to individuals who can teach us differently than theories, methods, and rhetoricians have. A contextual exploration allows us to consider a different kind of question than we have been taught to ask: "What was it like . . . to *think with these ideas?*" (Paine 36, italics original). Mahala no more wrote in an academic vacuum than students do today; the context of her time provided her compositions with a logic reflective of her historical moment as well as her choices as a writer. Her essays are an opportunity for us to consider what it was like to think like that—a conscientious and dutiful, female student writing compositions at a small, liberal, midwestern college in the 1850s.

Through a close reading of five of Mahala's essays, I explore how Mahala's historical, social, and cultural influences converged with academic expectations and the rules of rhetoric outlined in Whately's *Elements of Rhetoric*—the "most widely used rhetoric text in American colleges between 1835–1865"—and Samuel Newman's *A Practical System of Rhetoric* (1839), which "supplement[ed] Whatelian argumentative rhetoric with other modes" (Connors, *Composition* 61). The college bulletins of both Oberlin (beginning in 1838) and Antioch (beginning in 1866) list Whately's text as the primary text for the course in rhetoric; therefore, Mahala's writing at both institutions was guided by Whatelian principles.[1] I am invested in a reading of these materials that works to understand them rather than evaluate them as wrong-headed. Although Mahala's essays may not reflect the type of student writing we value today, her attention to writing as a serious mental activity rather than mere preoccupation with correctness represents the kind of student writer nineteenth-century textbooks frequently describe. Her work presents us with the occasion to reconsider what we have come to expect of nineteenth-century student writing as either unengaged (Connors, "Personal") or resistant (J. Campbell "Controlling"; "Real")—and to read it as the work of a writer in context.

STUDENT LIFE AT ANTIOCH COLLEGE

Antioch College, unlike Oberlin, promised a "new direction" in its employment of female faculty, admittance of women to the same course of study as men, and decision to allow the sexes to study classical languages together. Despite this contrast, however, Antioch as guided by Horace Mann (1853–1859) still adhered to Victorian convictions—specifically, in the case of female students, to the cult of true womanhood. Mann's commitment to women's full intellectual development was tempered by his preoccupation with their moral development in a coeducational environment. Even though women and men studied the same curriculum together, the purpose of their education differed. Where men were exposed to the rigors of competition, in-depth study, and opportunities for extracurricular learning, Mann was committed to an institution that shaped pure and morally upright women who were studiously prepared for the female sphere of life and feminine careers (Rury and Harper 490).

Mahala was no shrinking violet on matters concerning the value of women, as her departure from Oberlin and some of her essays indicate. She was, however, a product of her time in her adherence to Victorian beliefs. As a member of the first generation of women to attend American colleges, she negotiated the competing demands of "a social world that expected women to be of service to family and community and an academic world that valued individual intellectual performance over all else" (J. Campbell, "Real" 768). But unlike the female students discussed in Campbell's work, Mahala did not perceive her position between these two worlds as one that silenced her or inspired her to mock academic writing requirements ("Real"); nor was she moved to criticize her professors' lack of response to issues raised in student essays ("Controlling"). Helen Horowitz suggests that serious students "sought to succeed in the classroom" and looked to professors as mentors rather than to their peers (62).

Mahala chose appropriate avenues (both academic and extracurricular) to voice opposition to issues and practices regarding the education of women. When the college faculty denied the Alethezetean Society's petition to meet as a coeducational group, for example, Mahala not only resigned her position as president of the female branch, but resigned from the organization altogether (Rury and Harper 495). Despite this boldness, she was still very much of her time. As a married woman, Mahala was not required to live in Antioch's female residence hall because she lived in her husband's house under his supervision. Eli was unarguably the head of the household and Mahala accepted that without question. Their great-grandson, Jay Beede, explained their marriage this way: "Mahala did not wear the pants in the family, but she most definitely had a pair of her own."

Students at Antioch were characteristically different from their counterparts in the northeast: the mean age in the first four classes was 21.6 years; they came from middle and lower class origins with "well defined goals of life and work"; and the women were independent and unconventional in their lifestyles (Rury and Harper 492). Yet like other nineteenth-century colleges and universities, Antioch students were bound to the institution in a filial role. Mann explains this relationship in the *Antioch College Bulletin:* "When students enter college, they not only continue their civil relations, as men, to the officers of the college; but they come under the new and special obligations to them. Teachers take on much of the parental relation towards students, and students much of the filial relations toward teachers. A student, then, is bound to assist and defend a teacher as a parent, and a teacher is bound to assist and defend a student as a child" (45). The early classes at Antioch were also weighted with the additional responsibility of establishing the character of the institution. The quality of their individual and collective conduct was expected to shape public opinion of the school as well as erect "standards of conduct which their successors [would] observe and imitate" (51).

Mahala, although married and possessing a strong personality and clearly defined life goals, did not imagine herself beyond the parental influence of the institution. For her and Eli, the pursuit of college education was, as Mann defined it, "the highest of all earthly purposes" ("Address" 44) and it provided the rigorous mental and moral discipline necessary for their life mission as teachers.[2] She did not imagine her education in individual terms; that is, what she alone gained from it. The instructive, corrective, moralistic language of the college community reminded all students of their duties as members of society preparing to enter the professions. The ethnologic of the college demanded more than mere adherence to its paternalistic standards; it also demanded that students transform institutional ideals into real behavior through appropriate student-teacher interactions, diligent study, and compliance with the honor code.

The values and expectations governing student behavior were not confined to defining outward actions. Early nineteenth-century education was preoccupied with issues of culture, and reading and writing were perceived "as a means of acquiring social refinement and social (or ethical) values" (Woods 380). In a course like Antioch's "Rhetorical Exercises," then, cultural values and expectations were just as much a part of the lesson as rules of rhetoric. The latter shaped students' rhetorical practice while the former shaped their subject choice and the manner in which they wrote about it.

RHETORICAL EXERCISES

Mahala's essays are products of required "Rhetorical Exercises" at both Oberlin and Antioch, where the curriculum and pedagogy followed the nineteenth-century philosophy of mental discipline and character education. Although

Connors would have us believe that nineteenth-century textbook topics and assignments produce unengaged, impersonal student writing ("Personal"), Mahala's essays are anything but—even though she offers no personal disclosures about her life or interests. Her investment in her work and the individuality of her writing are inflected in the ways she selects information, interprets a subject, includes quoted material, and chooses words and turns of expression. Within the context of nineteenth-century composition-rhetoric, she illustrates what Samuel Newman describes in *A Practical System of Rhetoric* as the "intellectual and moral habits" of the "good writer": the ability to gain the attention of the reader, display "valuable thoughts and just reasoning," and employ sentiment that rouses the readers' sympathy (13). Newman explains, "the foundations of good writing are laid in the acquisition of knowledge,—in the cultivation of the reasoning powers,—and in the exercise and proper regulation of the imagination, and in the sensibilities of the heart" (14). This passage indicates how the development of the writer's mind was imagined as the primary aim of nineteenth-century composition-rhetoric instruction, but is not simply preoccupied with an abstract theory of mental development or issues of correctness and form. It defines qualities of writing—attention to audience, logical presentation, and evocative strategies—that require action of writers if they are to be successful. It also places value on quality of thought and control over presentation. Ideally, Newman's theory requires writers to develop a certain mental discipline that leads to the realization that thoughtful choices and specific acts of attention are the work of a writer.

The ideal of Whately's *Elements* is correctness: of argument and arrangement, of managing the passions and influencing the will, and of style. However, the management of the writer's passions as a means of swaying a reader's will—the use of language as an instrument of correct reasoning—is the characteristic which distinguishes Whately from other rhetoric texts of the time. The "'linear adjunct theory of persuasion'" to which Whately subscribed "argues that for action to be produced, both the understanding and will must be addressed" (Berlin, "Richard Whately" 15). Mahala's essays demonstrate an understanding of this concept as she weaves her knowledge of cultural commonplaces, academic narratives, social values, individual convictions, and skill in expression into appropriate arguments aimed to influence readers. She is the kind of able and knowledgeable writer Whately ideally imagines can avoid error through an "attentive study of the precepts." Her essays are exercises in the execution of Whatelian textbook lessons on argument and style as she "pursue[s] a connected train of thought with power and correctness" (Newman 17).

It would be easy to read the following essay—"Composition Writing: What the aim and what the end?"—written by Mahala in 1852, as the clever maneuverings of a smart student who knows that repeating commonplaces regarding duty, education, and the value of writing (in elegant prose, no less) will gain her the instructor's approval and a good grade. It would be equally tempting to read it as the work of a resistant student mocking an academic exercise. But as Mahala and Eli's courtship letters reveal, her explanation of writing's value is not a predictable repetition of nineteenth-century assertions. Both she and Eli believed that appreciation of God's works, both material and mental, depended on "Intellectual culture and Moral elevation"; this was the right foundation for bringing oneself "into harmony with the soul of [God's] works" and becoming "capacitated to fill the station designed for a human being to occupy." For someone who held to such a philosophy and imagined teaching as her life mission, Mahala's essay is a moral and intellectual exercise in developing the harmony and capacity that will fit her for her station in life. To read the essay from either of the aforementioned perspectives would misrepresent her work. Likewise, Mahala's essay does more than showcase her ability to write well; it also demonstrates her understanding and articulation of educational principles colored by her passions and convictions.

Composition Writing: What the aim and what the end?

Shall we hold these meetings week after week, term after term, Yes! Year after year, and still feel in our hearts no answer to the inquiring. "What this aim or what this end?" Shall composition writing be always a task imposed, and shall it never become a privilege to be enjoyed? Shall we be told that it is for our own good that this duty is enjoined upon us, and shall we sincerely believe it, for the reason that, we cannot question the motives of those who enjoined it, while we feel sure that our compositions can do no one else any good? Even in this our feelings may lead us into error.

The earnest effort to fulfill known duty, may itself, provoke some halting sister to emulation. The idea which we have caught and clothed in our language, no matter how common place it may be may yet strike a cord in the mind of the hearer which will set in motion the whole machinery of that mind, shall vibrate to a thousand reproductions of that thought, in as many new forms, in as many beautiful and instructive variations: like to the tiny raindrop, that, falling on the surface of the placid water, uprises the little wavelet, which sets into motion another wave, and that, again, another till wave after wave is circling on and widening as they go. Yet the advantages arising from this exercise will, doubtless, be chiefly our own. As Dr. Dewey has said of labor, and its productions, "The act of creating is better than the thing created."

While here, in the nursery as it were, we do not expect to write "thoughts that breathe, and words that burn," but it is not an end worth the pains, and may we not hope, while here, so to cultivate our faculties for thinking, and so to improve in the art of composing, that, with more mature minds we may think such thoughts, and clothe them with such words? And what part of our education do we think would be more useful? What acquirement more available for good, than easy and forcible diction? Think you, that, of all the laborers in the great field of human improvement, there is one who has accomplished so much for the cause of universal enlightenment, in so short a time, as has Mrs. Stowe with her gifted pen? And who knows, that, in some of our all to reluctant essayists, the germ of a future Mrs. Stowe in literature, is not developing.

We can hardly cherish a more exalted aspiration than that of becoming good, efficient writers. If our purpose is to labor in the worlds broad mission field, for the advancement of truth; when we consider the powerful influence reading has over the mind, the facility with which books and papers are multiplied and circulated, and the vast number of minds with which an author may come in contact through his writings, we can but choose the pen as the most efficacious instrument with which to labor.

If we are ambitious to obtain a reputation, if we wish to leave behind us an undying name, who of mankind, and especially, of <u>woman</u>kind, lives so long, or in the hearts of so many as does the good and the gifted author? In fine, if we would develop the most exalted capacities of our minds, if we would cultivate our highest intellectual powers, it is in writing we find the surest, the most adequate means.

Some writer has said, that, the conception of any original idea, the giving birth to a thought purely one's own, was man's nearest approximation to the creative power; and if this be true, does not he, who invests a grand conception, with the ardor, and the inspiration of a noble soul, approach nearest the power of bestowing immortality upon his creations?

Though we know, that to "gifted spirits" only, belongs the power to vibrate the cords of the human heart, so that the pulsations may be felt through time; yet have not we, all, power, if we choose to use it, so to play upon those strings, as to effect good in our own day? And though, in the galaxy of talent, as among the heavenly hosts, all cannot be stars of the first magnitude, yet as we think not that the smallest visible star speaks less its Creator's power, or answers less the end of its creation, than the greatest, so also, should we look on the productions of ordinary minds. And if in these exercises, we learn to use the talent for writing intrusted to us, to the best advantage, while we employ well the power it will bestow upon us, we shall never fell that these meetings have been all in vain.

Oberlin College, August 2, 1852

In Whatelian form, Mahala opens with an "introduction corrective" as she presents the manner in which the subject has been misunderstood and misrepresented (Whately 204). As an astute reader of the academic community, she offers the "negative testimony" of a common student argument against seemingly useless exercises. This uncontested opening argument allows her to make an appeal "to this circumstance, as a confirmatory testimony . . . especially [since those acquainted with the matter] are likely to be unwilling to admit the conclusion" (88). Her introduction follows Whately's instruction in presenting propositions: it establishes the fact that students do not see the value in composition writing, accounts for why this is so, and presents the consequences that result from this belief (58). In order for her argument to successfully influence the will of readers, she draws on real experience and passions associated with the subject in a controlled manner. The opposing voices of students and teacher in the essay are not pretentious; they present a familiar student complaint and the culturally anticipated, paternalistic response. One can imagine a nineteenth-century teacher or a textbook author presenting a similar narrative—one in which the "unreasonable" student's opposition is an example of inappropriate behavior. By using cultural narratives and moral instruction, Mahala represents common sentiment in a manner aimed to influence the reader's will as well as establish herself as a writer of good principle, good sense, good will, and "friendly disposition towards the audience" (223).

From the beginning of her essay's second paragraph, Mahala specifically addresses female readers as she aims to persuade them on the benefits of writing. We see this in her uncommon move to openly include women in her argument (rather than assume their inclusion through the universal "he") and to consider the particular value writing has for women. She refers to the inexperienced writer as a "halting sister," turns to Stowe as an example of a writer "who has accomplished so much for the cause of universal enlightenment," implies that women may emulate Stowe when she suggests that "the germ of a future Mrs. Stowe" may develop from a reluctant writer, and inquires "who of mankind, and especially, womankind, lives so long, or in the hearts of so many as does the good and gifted author?" As a dedicated academic, Mahala is conscious of "the powerful influence reading has over the mind, . . . and the vast number of minds with which an author may come in contact." It is no accident that she uses inclusive language and addresses women directly since she herself is so aware of the power of words and their longevity. Part of the strength of her essay's argument comes from her enactment of the power of writing.

In her essay "Influence of Female Character" (1851), Mahala's explanation of the influence of female character negotiates cultural narrative and individual conviction. As part of her argument, Mahala reconstructs the traditional narrative regarding women not simply because it is expected of her, but because she believes and lives it. In a letter to Mahala in 1847, Eli compliments her desire to pursue education: "'[I]t is encouraging to behold occasionally a noble that is desirous of fulfilling the object of existence here. And more encouraging still is it if that soul is found in the ranks of Woman. For to the gentle influence of the softer sex does the world look with earnest hope for its redemption." Mahala's essay reflects this belief that the female virtues of social refinement and affectionate persuasion are a civilizing influence. Mahala sees woman's true power in her moral and intellectual sensibilities. She uses what Tonkovich calls "the enablements of writing" as a means of promoting woman's empowerment (180) (also evidenced in Mahala's "Composition Writing") while maintaining the social and intellectual norms of the "neoclassical practices in which [she] had been trained and whose practice accrued . . . so much respect and profit." So even as Mahala proposes a new view of woman and presents her as the true agent of "Universal Reform," she does not let go of "the old ways of thought, the old patterns of meaning, the old system of exclusion" (181). Mahala is not a radical abandoning revered tradition; she sees herself as a reformer exercising persuasive power in an appropriate manner. Again, her essay is an enactment of her argument as she demonstrates appropriate female influence through writing: "Woman's influence when used aright, will foster every true virtue, will press forward every true reform."

Influence of Female Character

Influence is commonly understood to be power which is manifested only in its results. Doubtless everything possesses this silent power, in some degree, Female Character, of course, included. What its influence is and what it should be, it certainly becomes females to know. We cannot doubt that he who formed the female mind, designed that it should exercise a powerful influence over the character and destiny of the human race. Else, why had he made it so potent an instrument for good, or for evil? why had he compensated with persuasive power, the physical weakness of woman?

The world acknowledges the influence of the Female Character, in many things, especially in the refinement of society. Man, restricted to the society of men, inclines to rudeness and coarseness. He becomes negligent in his habits, careless in his manners, and indifferent to that delicacy of feeling and sentiment, so delightful in the intercourse of human beings with each other. The presence of woman insensibly restrains this tendency. As has been remarked by another, "the presence of one female will change the vulgarity of the drunken revel, into the refinement of the ballroom."

We may not depreciate this power, which our sex wields over the character of the human race. We may not undervalue the worth of this influence, applied to the progress and development of society. But it is perhaps just, to remark in this connection, that woman confined to the company of her own sex, inclusively, degenerates in the noble attributes of character, and becomes over fastidious and effeminate. Nature seems to have designed that the sexes should exercise a reciprocal influence, that man should enoble, and woman refine.

Maidens have all heard of another species of influence, which they involuntarily exercise, the influence of the personal attractions. Such as the delicate hand, the slender waist, the bosom's voluptuous swell, auburn locks, or golden ringlets, fair brows, carnation lips, and diamond eyes, and of the bewitching power of the modest blush, the fascinating smile, and the low sweet music of their voices. Oh yes! They have heard of these, and have been told that, endowed by Nature with such exquisite attractions, they need no more to make their power infinite. Infinite over what? Over the other sex, to be sure. Where <u>else</u> should they wish to exert and power? "There," says a vitiated Public opinion, "is the proper sphere of your influence, young ladies." "There," says the flatterer, "you are omnipotent, and what more could you wish, what more could you have? They who rule the hearts of men, rule the nation" But should they believe it? should they lay this "flattering unction to their souls"? Indeed, it is not flattery, but degradation. They who, in this estimate of Female Character, and of its influence, discard the worth and attraction of her <u>mind</u>, degrade her below the rank of human beings, and place her on a level with the humming-bird and the butterfly.

But there is another appropriate field for the exercise of the peculiar power of the Female Character, and one where it is greatly needed— that of Universal Reform. In past time Reformers urged their plans by physical force, and the sword was their great executive. But now it is generally conceded, that little good can be expected from reforms secured by violence, and reformers are learning to appeal to the more rational and humane means, of argument, persuasion, and kindness. These means it is woman's privilege to apply with peculiar success. The drunkard and the criminal are much more effectively won back to ways of virtue by her gentleness and kindness, than by the more rigid policy and colder arguments of man. The unfortunate daughters of degradation find in her forgiveness and counsel a much stronger inducement to return to the path of rectitude, than in the harsh condemnation of their brothers. The wayward child that rebels against its sterner father, is subdued by the tears of an affectionate mother. The boy that will contend with his brother about a trifle, will not refuse the gentle request of his sister.

Other, also, than criminal reforms, receive efficient aid from the influence of the female Character. Woman's influence when used aright, will foster every virtue, will press forward every true reform. By a virtuous life, a kind disposition, a noble and worthy purpose, she may make error appear more false, truth more truthful, right more sacred, and virtue more attractive.

Oberlin College, July 15, 1851

This narrative of female influence focuses on the ennobling qualities and possibilities of woman and refutes the competing narrative of influence through beauty, rather than mind or character. Again, Mahala's introduction is corrective in order that she might dispel expectations of triteness and "serve to remove or loosen such prejudices as might be adverse to the favorable reception" of the argument (Whately 204). However, it is not only the aim of her introduction to be corrective but the entire essay, especially as she addresses the degrading "species" of woman's influence. She challenges the narrative that woman's primary interest is men, that her major concern lies in influencing men, and that her power to influence comes from her physical attributes rather than her mind. While a writer may control the will of readers by appealing to reason through the presentation of facts and examples, the feelings she desires to evoke are not under the control of the will. As Whately states, "No passion, sentiment or emotion, is excited by *thinking about* it, and attending to it; but by thinking about, and attending to, such objects as are calculated to awaken it" (216). The writer may state her conclusion plainly from the start, but must then, through the process of argument, steadily draw readers' attention to the point to be proven in order to awaken sentiment (219). Mahala's passion on this subject is evident in the content and tone of her argument; however, she is a woman of "well regulated mind" who, in Whatelian style, practices rhetoric on herself. Through the rational crafting of her argument, she submits her emotions on this issue to her rational will.

There is no personal writing, as it is understood today, in Mahala's essay—no relating of personal experience or using herself as an example even though she is a model for the argument. Consistent with protocols governing the relationship between writers and readers, she maintains a level of objectivity as she assiduously attends to correctness of arrangement, structure, and grammar. Even in moments of expressing personal conviction, she keeps her distance from subject and audience by using the universal "we," presenting generalizations, and turning to the words of others rather than to personal experience or the personal "I." Yet her writing is still her own in the nineteenth-century sense that it represents what she knows. The subjects about which she chooses to write are governed by the cultural narratives and the discourses associated with them. It is not "original" thought that makes the essay hers, but her choices in presenting the narrative, selecting information, interpreting facts, choosing language, quoting others.

It would be inaccurate and unfair of contemporary readers with twenty-first-century expectations to read Mahala as unoriginal, impersonal, or parroting empty platitudes. Her essays enact the nineteenth-century theory that successful writers are those who possess a "rich fund of thoughts. The storehouse of the mind must be well-filled and he must have command over his treasures, which will enable him to bring forward, whenever that occasion may require, what has been accumulated for future use" (Newman 16–17). But as Mahala's essays reveal, what one chooses to fill the storehouse with and bring forward later directly reflects the individual's interests and level of intellectual engagement. Her essay, "What are the Advantages of Studying the Latin and Greek Languages?" (1855), for example, could surely be read as the type of nineteenth-century topic that generates little student interest and insipid writing. But that is too easy a reading; the challenge is to read it as a product of a particular historical context and a particular student's investment. For Mahala, the subject is more than an exercise in generalities. Consider her context: Antioch is an institution under the supervision of the renowned educator Horace Mann; as a member of Antioch's first class, she carries the burden of establishing academic standards for students who follow; a knowledge of Latin and Greek are prerequisites for admission and included in the freshman and sophomore curricula; she is an exceptional student of Latin and plans to teach. She has a vested interest in this topic even if it is not of her own choosing.

What are the Advantages of Studying the Latin and Greek Languages?

[PARAGRAPHS 1 & 2]:
This question, perhaps every student of these languages has asked himself, at some time in the course of his study; but doubtless the satisfying answer to his inquiry has often come late if ever. If this were not the case how could we account for the circumstance of so many after having

commenced the study of these languages, leaving it off, or at least desiring to, even though they do not purpose to give up their course of study?

Until recently, indeed, the treasures of literature and science were, as it were, shut up in these languages, and every one who aspired to a liberal education studied them of course, it was a matter of necessity, its advantages beyond question, for it was the only means of access to the then known fields of knowledge. But this absolute necessity no longer exists. The most valuable writings in these languages have been carefully translated, and besides we have a modern literature as noble and as rich as the classical, more pure, and imbued with sentiments more accordant with the spirit of Christianity, and the vast fields of science now open to us, were almost unknown to the ancients, and are ours, as well in the language in which they are set forth, as in the right of research and discovery. Other reasons then, than the imperative one of necessity, must be adduced for the study of these languages at the present time.

As in her essay on composition writing, Mahala opens by anticipating student doubts on the value of studying these languages. However, the length and depth of each paragraph, as well as the entire essay, reflect her development as a writer and a student. The essay is controlled by the reasoned voice of someone who respects the academic process and understands the value of studying classical languages as part of it. Following Whatelian precepts, her tone is both fair and logical as she considers the validity of the opposition's case that these languages no longer need to be included in a liberal education. She presents the "testimony of adversaries" in two key arguments against studying the classical languages: "the most valuable writings in these languages have been carefully translated" and "a modern literature as noble and rich as the classical . . . were almost unknown to the ancients, and are ours." She is prepared, therefore, to cite other reasons for studying these languages.

[PARAGRAPHS 3 & 4]:
The question whether their study should be made an essential part of a liberal education, has of late been often discussed, and not unfrequently answered in the negative. Without venturing an opinion upon the merits of this question, or the kindred one of what proportion of time should be devoted to classical attainments, some advantages arising from the study of Latin and Greek may be pointed out. These advantages are of

two kinds, the one relating to the discipline of the mind, the other, to the acquisition of knowledge.

With reference to the first, it may be premised that the thing to be attained in mental discipline, is the development of the whole mind, the training of all its faculties to discharge fully and harmoniously their respective functions. Therefore that study which brings into requisition the greatest number of these faculties, which demands the vigorous and normal exercise of the nearest all the powers of the mind, is but adapted to purposes of mental discipline. How, in order to master Latin or Greek, it is indispensable that the attention be fixed, that memory, judgment, and constructive ingenuity be called into simultaneous and powerful action; and at the same time those powers will be incidentally trained which other departments of learning, as geography, history, poetry, and eloquence, especially exercise. By the great regularity of the structure of these languages, the idea of law is suggested, and the mind, disciplined to considerable of the exactness derived from mathematical studies. Being thus free, to a great extent, from the tendency to cultivate one set of faculties to the exclusion of the rest, but still requiring severe mental exercise, precedence, for a means of discipline, over every other single department of learning, has been conceded to the study of the classic languages, by almost, every one competent to express an opinion on the subject.

Antioch College, June 11, 1855

The advantages Mahala suggests position her squarely within the nineteenth-century academic narrative, not simply because she can reproduce it but because, as a dedicated academic, she participates and believes in it. What she writes about the advantage of developing mental discipline sounds like the familiar voices of educators writing in periodicals, textbooks, and teacher training manuals Latin and Greek offer the opportunity to acquire knowledge that might be lost through translation, provide insight into Greek and Roman culture, and increase students' vocabulary and facility in English. In short, the study of these languages leads one to what Eli defines as "the business of life." He writes to Mahala in 1847: "May we never cease to obtain the mental culture, which will give us enlightened minds"; and again in 1848: "Does not reason lift the veil and mental science point to the object of our lives? And should we not listen to its voice and comply in youth with it requisitions? O, let not those who ever expect to build a truthful superstructure spend their time in laying a wrong foundation." From a distance of years removed, Mahala's argument for studying classical languages may sound like an exercise in pleasing the professor when, in reality, it presents deeply held personal convictions.

Another example that students' intellectual powers were valued more than personal experience is Mahala's 1856 essay "The Harvest Moon," which draws on established narrative and a "storehouse" of acquired knowledge rather than the personal. It is easy for us to imagine a subject like "The Harvest Moon" as full of possibility for descriptive writing, personal reverie, or at least illustration based on personal observation and associations. Not so for the nineteenth-century student for whom such possibilities wouldn't occur. From reading Mahala's essay, one would think she had no more knowledge of this natural phenomenon than what she had learned from a textbook. One could say that she begins poetically: "The heavens, the starry heavens, have been the wonder of man ever since Adam first gazed up among their shining hosts as twilight faded from the hilltops of Eden; and time and the advancement of science have not in the least diminished their charms." The rest of the essay, however, is limited to a detailed explanation of the history and science of the harvest moon.

Among the simple yet interesting of celestial phenomena is that called the Harvest Moon. About the time of the autumnal equinox, the moon when near the full rises several nights in succession not far from sunset, instead of fifty minutes later each evening as the mean amount of its daily separation from the sun. From the circumstance that this phenomenon occurs about the time of harvest in England it received the name of the Harvest Moon.

Without seeking for a scientific explanation, Fancy invests it with many imaginary charms; she sees the full moon lingering in her wonted course, staying her accustomed speed, that she may smile on the laborer at his protracted toil, that she may rejoice with him over the rich harvest which he gleans from the productive earth. She ascribes to her a benignant care for man's comfort and pleasure not knowing that this seeming care is the result of an arrangement inwoven in the constitution of the planetary system, from its very foundation, an arrangement by which the motions of several planets do not take place in the same plane. In the case before us, the phenomenon of which we speak results from the inclination of the earth's axis to the plane of her orbit. For this plane or the ecliptic, very near which the moon's orbit lies, being oblique to the equator cuts the horizon at different angles in different parts, and the angle is the smallest near where the plane crossed the equator. At the time of the autumnal equinox the sun at its setting appears at that point in the heavens where the circles of the ecliptic and celestial equator intersect, and the full moon rises in the east at the same time at their opposite intersection; And since at this point the ecliptic makes but a small angle with the horizon, the moon, though she has advanced her usual distance in her orbit will be not far below the horizon at sunset on the following evening, and consequently will rise only a little later than on the preceding evening, and thus until the moon has passed some distance beyond the vernal equinox the time of her rising varies on successive nights much less than the mean amount, and hence the beautiful phenomenon of the Harvest Moon.

The essay demonstrates not what Mahala personally thinks or imagines about the harvest moon but what she knows about science, astronomy, superstitions, religious beliefs, and principles of rhetoric. This should not be surprising given her educational context and her extracurricular reading. The October 20, 1854, minutes of the Alethezetean Society record the following titles as just some of those submitted for approval by the group: Ackerman's *Natural History*, Coate's *School Physiology*, *History of Spanish Literature*, Schmitz's *History of Greece*, Comstock's *Geology*, Davies's *Surveying*, and *Class Book of Nature*. During the same year, Mahala and Eli presented the society with, among others, *Visit to Northern Europe*, *Life of Joseph Addison*, *Thompson in Africa*, and *The French Revolution of 1848*.

Mahala's lack of descriptive, imaginative writing is not indicative of an inability to produce such writing. There is more than enough evidence throughout her essay that she's quite adept with words and images—not just words and knowledge. She describes superstition throwing "her cloudy mantle over the minds of earlier observers," "man blindly labor[ing] to read the destinies of nations and of individuals among the stars," and "heavenly hosts mov[ing] onward in their appointed course." Although her sentences do not reflect her presence through personal pronouns or personal experience (qualities contemporary readers may equate with good student writing), *her* selection of information, its presentation, individual turns of expression and ways of understanding are the closest she comes to creating something akin to personal writing.

In "Personal Writing Assignments," Connors examines rhetorical practices in American colleges during the period that Mahala was a student. He describes the type of subjects illustrated in Mahala's essays as "completely, utterly, relentlessly impersonal," "creaking abstractions" which produced "very poor writing" (170–72). He asserts that the impetus to shift to more personal composition topics grew out of a sense of frustration and a "concerted disgust" with the "old abstract rhetorical assignments" that had little if anything to do with what students actually knew from *experience*. Yet Mahala's essays reveal that the expository essay *is* personal when personally inflected. But without contextual information that allows us to see her investment, her beliefs and life circumstances, we might find ourselves in agreement with Connors's conclusions.

Of all the essays written by Mahala from 1851 to 1857, only one fits the category of a "personal" writing assignment in that the assignment specifically invites students to compose an essay based on their own interests and experience. Yet it is the only composition topic to which Mahala expresses open resistance, impatience, and a degree of disgust. Her negative reaction is the opposite of what Connors describes; personal writing assignments are supposed to be more appealing and easier for students to address than the old abstractions. Unlike her other essays, however, "Some Account of my Studies during Vacation" (1856) is uncharacteristically unfocused and appears to end in mid-thought rather than proceed to a formal conclusion as do all of her others.

Some Account of my Studies during Vacation

[PARAGRAPH 1]:
These are the words of the subject given us for our first essays, and I place them at the head of my paper, though aware that they are not exactly applicable to anything I have to write. I am not, however, going to offend against the instructions we received when the subject was an-

nounced, namely; that it was not intended that we should tell of misspent time, and make our essays a lamentation over what we had failed to do. My idea of a vacation is incompatible with my idea of study, and I would almost as soon think of writing about my recreations during recitations, as my "studies during vacation," I would never undertake to harmonize the two ideas, practically, to any considerable extent, unless compelled to, by necessity. So far as pertains to books, I look upon vacation as a season for miscellaneous reading, for which term-time affords to little leisure.

This topic is inconsistent with Mahala's philosophy of education as the exercise of mental discipline and does not relate to any academic narrative with which she is familiar. Where is the intellectual challenge in an assignment that asks her to write about two subjects she sees as incompatible with each other as well as incompatible with her image of herself as a student? Where a contemporary reader might see an invitation to write a personal essay as liberating or full of possibilities, for Mahala, it lacks the rigorous mental challenge she has come to expect of a subject or herself as a writer. All of her other essays illustrate nineteenth-century "good writing" as grounded in the acquisition of knowledge, arrangement of argument, exercise of reasoning, and management of emotions. An essay based on personal experience is incompatible with this method of writing; it does not require extending thought beyond the self. Compelled by the necessity of having to complete the assignment, she attempts to compromise by discussing what she has read. After all, vacation is "a season for miscellaneous reading, for which term-time affords too little leisure," and books, at least, are associated with school and academic concerns.

Throughout "Studies during Vacation," Mahala's discomfort with attempting the serious work of a student within the framework of a personal narrative is evident; she is more adept at reflecting on major themes and historical figures. An account of her reading "that beautiful work of Madame de Stael, 'Corrine or Italy'" is the only personal experience she deems relevant to the assignment. But even here she falters, admitting that she hadn't read this book as part of a course of study. She was more interested in "knowing the fortunes of the heroes of the story" and only later "re-read with a care that could improve [her] knowledge of the [French] language." "Such were [her] studies during vacation"; but by third year student standards, her essay is far from complete. The reader has a sense of Mahala groping for what to write since an "account of the magazine and newspaper literature," "poetry and other miscellaneous reading" would be "less profitable to the class." Instead, she attempts a discussion of two books but offers only a perfunctory synopsis of each.

While "Studies during Vacation" is the only essay in which Mahala openly reveals personal information, the manner in which she struggles reveals more about her than the actual content of the essay. We witness a student who is practiced in and excels at writing attempting to do the work of a good student, but within the confines of a topic that resists what she has learned about good writing. It does not allow for the kind of distance between writer and subject to which she is accustomed. Even when she interjects her point of view regarding the contradiction in "studies during vacation," she directs her reader's attention outward and away from herself through a discussion of books. By foregrounding the books, she achieves a degree of distance and objectivity and moves in the direction of presenting acquired knowledge from sources. She also creates distance between herself and readers by relating information she considers "profitable to the class" rather than that which might simply appeal to readers' curiosity (which magazines and newspapers she prefers). Mahala's work in this composition illustrates more clearly than others the careful negotiation required of a student when discursive demands converge in incompatible ways.

HOROWITZ REMARKS that learning about serious students in the nineteenth century is particularly difficult. Conventional sources focus on larger campus events, and written records produced by students reflect the mentality of the fraternity men who controlled them. She writes: "In the nineteenth century the sober students had no clear public voice" (68) and so their story has remained obscure. The same can be said of the history of composition: sober students who represent the ideals of their time—like Mahala Jay—have not been accorded a place in the history because they are not easily found in existing records. Mahala's essays offer us the opportunity to watch a serious student writer at work, establishing her own position while maneuvering among cultural narratives and the demands of academic discourse. Attending to the *manner* in which Mahala engages in the work of composing—that is, combining ideas and information in ways that mark her as an educated and moral individual; arranging an essay in terms of organization, expression, and style; adhering to curriculum requirements at a specific institution; negotiating the competing narratives of society and academe; following the precepts of good writing presented by professors and textbooks—teaches us more about nineteenth-century student writing than only attending to *what* she writes. Her work illustrates the way in which nineteenth-century composition-rhetoric instruction aimed to represent a set of practices and narratives that—given the quality of the writer—might inflect the personal rather than produce the personal.

The pleasure in reading Mahala's essays is experiencing her mind at work on the page, actively engaged in negotiating the discursive maze of assignments, rhetorical precepts, cultural narratives, Antioch's vision of the exemplary student, and her own view of herself as a student and future teacher. She teaches us to read nineteenth-century student writing as a cultural artifact connected to an agenda beyond the boundaries of the academy and rhetorical theory.

Notes

Locating nineteenth-century student writing is like searching for a needle in a haystack: it requires perseverance, creativity, precise inquiry, and the sharp vision and comprehensive knowledge of a special collections librarian to find it. I am indebted to Nina Myatt, Acquisitions and Technical Services Assistant at The Olive Kettering Library, for pointing me in the right direction and assisting me in identifying the finer contextual details of Mahala Jay's educational experience at Antioch.

1. Crowley, too, reports on the predominance of Whately's text in rhetoric curricula in the 1850s and 1860s and on Newman's departure from British authorities in his consideration of invention (*Methodical* 57). Furthermore, the 1853–1855 *Antioch College Bulletin* identifies Newman as the primary text for the English Composition course in Antioch's Preparatory School. Whately is listed in the 1866–1867 *College Bulletin* as the primary text for the second-year college Rhetoric course. However, given that Rhetoric courses in the 1853–1855 bulletin are listed as "Rhetoric, Logic and Belles-Lettres" and that Horace Mann visited Whately in England during his wedding trip in 1843, one may assume that although not listed by title or name in the bulletin, Whately's text was

at least available for students if not required for "Rhetorical Exercises" during the college's early years.

There is no record at either institution of the specific assignments to which Mahala's essays respond.

2. Mahala and Eli's courtship letters describe education in a similar manner—as a means of rising above "mental imbecility" through the development of enlightened minds capable of seeing the work of God in all things, both mental and material.

Archival Sources

Beede, Jay (grandson of Mahala and Eli Jay). Telephone interview by author. June 24, 1994.

The following items are in the Antiochiana, Olive Kettering Library, Antioch College, Yellow Springs, OH:

Alethezetean Society minutes. September 29, 1854.

————. October 20, 1854.

Antioch College Bulletin. 1853–1855 (single issue).

Jay, Mahala. "Composition Writing: What the aim and what the end?" Unpublished essay. 1852.

————. "The Harvest Moon." Unpublished essay. 1856

————. "Influence of Female Character." Unpublished essay. 1851.

————. "Some Account of my Studies during Vacation." Unpublished essay. 1856.

————. "What Are the Advantages of Studying the Latin and Greek Languages?" Unpublished essay. 1855.

M. A. J. B. "Life Sketch of Mahala Jay."

Mann, Horace. "Address of the president of Antioch College, to Its Students." *Antioch College Bulletin.* 1855–1856. 43–48

The following item is in the Arthur S. and Kathleen Postle Friends Collection, Lilly Library, Earlham College, Richmond, IN:

Jay, Mahala, and Eli Jay. Courtship letters. 1847–1848.

The following item is in the Oberlin College Archives, Oberlin, OH:

Seidman, Rachel. "A Generations Experiment: Oberlin Womanhood, Coeducation, and the Ladies' Board of Managers, 1835–1879." History honors thesis, Oberlin College. 1987.

_৩ 3 ৫_

(The Teaching of) Reading and Writing at Lafayette College

Patricia Donahue and Bianca Falbo

THIS ESSAY OFFERS a partial narrative of the teaching of reading and writing at Lafayette College in the nineteenth century. Such a narrative is partial because our archive is fragmented and incomplete: the shards are dispersed; excavations are ongoing. We have placed "The Teaching of" in parentheses to emphasize that the challenge faced by compositionists in inferring from early historical "documents" (texts that have been assigned evidentiary force) a pedagogical practice of reading and writing is considerable. Moreover, for compositionists like ourselves, the relationship between composition and teaching is one of powerful interdependency. This claim is controversial: some compositionists consider it a reason why our discipline has been debased

This chapter is based on archival materials from the Special Collections Library at Lafayette College. Francis A. March was a prolific writer—the author of more than 190 books and articles. Unfortunately, relatively little of his writing about teaching survives (such as lecture notes, assignments, etc.). This circumstance, though disappointing, raised some interesting questions for us: what constitutes the "history" of a course? a "record" of teaching? In the absence of direct "evidence," what sorts of materials might usefully contribute to our knowledge of a figure like March? In addition to writing by March (especially his textbooks and his work on the means and ends of literary study), our sources for this chapter also include the journal of James P. Boyd, a student at the college during the early years of March's career (1855–1859). Finally, in tracing the history of composition (from localized and dispersed practices to the "English Composition" course first taught in 1858), we relied on Lafayette College catalogs.

within the profession at large ("Teaching? Sounds like *education*"). For us, however, it is a *sine qua non* of our work both as teachers and as scholars.

While we share with other contributors to this collection the "archival angst" that inflicts historians as they struggle to locate documents and discern their importance, our project focuses on a widely celebrated figure about whom a great deal has already been written. Francis A. March, a philologist of international renown, served on the faculty at Lafayette College, in Easton, Pennsylvania for about fifty years in the nineteenth century. In literary historiography, it is widely assumed that March was responsible for introducing the teaching of Shakespeare into the American college curriculum (in a course in the English language); it is also widely accepted that March was granted the first chair in the English language (and comparative philology) in this country. Whether or not March deserves the title of "father" of English literary study is moot; the truth will not be known until the story of every college and university in the nineteenth century is told. But a considerable body of lore has accumulated around March, transforming him into one of the most resilient of pedagogical stereotypes, the "great teacher."

Our archival work rescued us from potential superfluity by revealing another side of March, a side that had gone unrecognized, or perhaps could not be recognized, until the narratives of disciplinary emergence and construction in composition studies had achieved a certain level of complexity. Our recuperated March is a Janus-like figure. Not only a teacher of reading, he is also a teacher of writing, as committed to one as he is to the other, able to consider the relationship between reading and writing in terms not of logical priority and privilege but of mutual reciprocity and reinforcement. Aware that we risk a charge of "presentism" in making these claims, we nonetheless assert that the figure of March we have reconstructed through our archival work is a teacher for whom pedagogy appears to be a theoretically inflected praxis; he is, in short, an early compositionist.

COLLEGE CATALOGUE AS ARCHIVAL SOURCE

It is widely acknowledged that a major obstacle in the reconstruction of nineteenth-century pedagogy is the paucity or dispersal of primary materials. One does the best one can, flexing the imagination in feats of creative renaming.

And if one is lucky, serendipity strikes. Such was the case when William W. Watt, a retired member of the English Department at Lafayette College and the author of *An American Rhetoric*, a widely used composition textbook, suggested to one of us in conversation almost fifteen years ago that college catalogues might provide valuable information about curricular change and pedagogical shifts. Modern college catalogues are primarily tools of self-promotion, but in the nineteenth century they sometimes contained educational policies and pedagogical specifics, such as writing assignments. They were almost always carefully preserved.

Our research on March led us to the catalogues of Lafayette College. Eventually affiliated with the Presbyterian Church, Lafayette College was founded by the city of Easton, Pennsylvania, and named for the Marquis de Lafayette "out of respect for the signal services rendered by General Lafayette in the great cause of freedom" (Lafayette College Charter, Article 1).[1] The college's unusual mission is spelled out in the trustees' second annual report, published October 7, 1833: "to bring the higher branches of education within the reach of youth in the humbler walks of life, even where indigence has traveled:—To elevate the standard of common school instruction—To secure health of the student—To promote the feeling of honorable independence—And, to cement the extremes of society together and so promote the permanent well being of the happiest nation of the world." Lafayette College, unlike elite schools like Harvard, was built to serve first-generation students preparing for middle-class professions.

Roughly twenty years after Lafayette College was established, this spirit of pragmatic preparation inspired the addition of two new courses to the curriculum, each of which emphasized English, although in different ways. The earlier course (the one often frequently referred to in histories of English departments, such as Gerald Graff's) was English Literature, which first appeared in the 1853–1854 college catalogue as a requirement for second-semester seniors.[2] English Composition first appeared in the 1858–1859 catalogue (and retained this title until 1891) as a requirement for freshmen in their second and third term. If catalogue dates for English Composition are reliable, the Lafayette College writing course predates by almost twenty years the 1874 establishment of the Subject A course at Harvard (while Harvard offered a writing course before the establishment of "subject A," it was a rhetoric course, not a composition course).

Because Harvard is so strongly identified with the origin of composition as a discipline, our discovery of the Lafayette course was, frankly, a "Eureka" moment. At first, we speculated as to how exciting it would be to argue in the professional literature that histories of writing be rewritten to accommodate this information. However, very little is actually known about the composition course at Lafayette College; Harvard's position as disciplinary origin is too deeply entrenched to be easily challenged; and, as Donahue discusses elsewhere in this collection, Harvard's designation as origin serves numerous ideological purposes.

Yet it continues to strike us as peculiar that no one who has participated in the public representation of Lafayette College has ever taken note of the English Composition course. Were we really the first to make this discovery? If so, then those who have written about the history of writing at the college —like William W. Watt, who referred us to the college catalogues in the first place—must have had a reason, conscious or unconscious, for ignoring this information or deeming it irrelevant. In fact, rather than present the history of writing at Lafayette College in somewhat originary terms, despite its complex and circuitous development, Watt presents it as a duplicate of the Harvard model. In a piece entitled "Freshman English and Variations," published in the *Lafayette Alumni Quarterly* (April 1964), he offered the following rendition: "English 1–2 [the two semester composition sequence taught for many years] has changed significantly since the autumn of 1906, when James Waddell Tupper, a slender black-haired Canadian with a Ph.D. from Johns Hopkins, first began to promote literacy and rebellion by carrying out the Trustee mandate 'to put into practice the methods of instruction in Freshman composition now in vogue at Harvard University'" (5). The story Watt tells here is, of course, the Harvard story: Harvard is postulated as the creator of composition, with its teachers and students proceeding with missionary-like zeal to "seed" it elsewhere. While it is an appealing tale, and certainly a familiar one, it evidences several problems. Watt's suggestion that the relocation of an instructional method from one site to another is a relatively uncomplicated matter strikes us as facile: even if Lafayette did at one point borrow the "Harvard method," it would inevitably have transformed it into the "Lafayette way of teaching 'Harvard Style.'" Moreover, his history eradicates almost fifty years of instructional practice: specifically, the teaching of writing by March and others during the so-called "March years." It is possible that Watt elided March's contribution to English composition to preserve and exalt March's reputation in literature. Although Watt authored a composition textbook, he did not see himself as a "compositionist"; in fact, the term would have struck him as peculiar and clumsy. As a Shakespearean and a Miltonist, his disciplinary alliance would have been with March, the literary teacher, not March, the writing teacher.

When the college began in the late 1830s, the curriculum was classical, with the exception of engineering courses.[3] Students of comfortable means who aspired to careers like law received considerable training in mental discipline. Students of the "humbler classes" also benefited, acquiring the credentials necessary for entry into middle-class careers such as teaching. The very first mention of writing instruction at Lafayette College (which predates the mention of English Composition) appears in reference to future teachers: as stated in the college catalogues, students preparing to teach were provided with extracurricular opportunities in composition (no other details appear). Prospective teachers were not the only students to receive instruction in writing, however. All Lafayette students, by virtue of requirements in rhetoric, acquired significant practice—if not instruction—in writing.[4] The fact that this requirement was a floating signifier of sorts—some years it was required of seniors, some years of juniors—is evidence of the "generalist" thrust of the classical curriculum.

In using the term "generalist," we allude to Gerald Graff's analysis of the division between generalists and specialists that began to emerge in American higher education in the early mid-nineteenth century. As Mariolina Salvatori and Patricia Donahue discuss in their essay, "English Studies in the Scholarship of Teaching," Graff (like others) makes it clear that English Literature did not become a course in its own right and a subject in which a scholar could specialize until the adoption of the German university model in the 1870s (the first research university, Johns Hopkins, was established in the United States in 1876). Salvatori and Donahue point out that the establishment of this new course posed new pedagogical challenges for teachers, which they often responded to by grafting old pedagogical practices onto a new subject area. The pedagogy that transpired was thus an adaptive one. They go on to explain: "The archival materials Graff presents make visible how these new pedagogical responsibilities, along with the importation of the German model of academic specialization, soon led to, or perhaps dramatically foregrounded, a split between, as he calls them *generalists* and *specialists*" (72). Graff characterizes the generalists as employing a "casual impressionistic, effusive approach to literature," while specialists were those researchers, primarily philologists, "who promoted the idea of scientific research" (55). To this distinction, Salvatori and Donahue add:

> Graff's archive casts light on the bifurcation of teaching and research at a moment when the role of the English professor being in flux, the relationship between teaching and research could have been dialectically articulated, each provided the motivation for and the test of the other. Faced with unprecedented institutional demands, however, specialists seized the moment to privilege research (understood as discovery) and practice teaching as dispensation. Generalists, on the other hands, seized the moment to denounce the irrelevance of philology (and later of psychology, sociology, and history) to the appreciation of literature. As they tried to cling to the notion of a teacher's talent and natural inclinations, they unwittingly contributed to the diminished institutional and disciplinary status of teaching. (73)

When a teacher's professional expertise became dependent on his or her ability as a researcher, inevitably research assumed priority, and teaching became regarded as the mere effect of research knowledge (a "teacher" was authorized to teach a subject simply by virtue of having studied it).

This division is apparent in the emergence of composition instruction at Lafayette College, which made its appearance in the form of an extracurricular opportunity for prospective teachers. Rhetoric was originally a subject not for "specialists" but for "generalists" (which accounts for its curricular shifts—whoever wanted to teach the course taught it, at whatever level).

In the college catalogue of 1892–1893, some thirty-five years after Lafayette introduced English Composition, this statement is attributed to Francis A. March: "For training in speaking and writing English correctly every student is required to hand in two themes in every term of his college course. Many of them are read in class and criticized as time allows. In this work professors of all departments take part. It is desired that students in each department shall write on subjects connected with it in the words and phrases current among experts, and know the precise meaning of these words and phrases. In these matters, the professors in each department are authorities." In the absence of material evidence we can only offer as conjecture the idea that English Composition would have emerged before the advent of academic specialization. When specialization eventually took hold, no department would have existed within which writing instruction could be situated. An argument in favor of widespread discipline-based writing—as represented above—might have been a way to solve the problem. In other words, before 1891, in a generalist academic program, a course in English Composition could be offered without undue concern about who would teach it and where it would be taught. After 1891, such questions would become critical. Watt notes, for example, that James Waddell Tupper was hired in 1906, an event that might have been in response to pressure to hire an "expert" who had taught at Harvard.[5] What implications might this have had for the teaching of reading and writing, literature and composition?

THE TROPE OF THE GREAT TEACHER

On the third floor of Lafayette's Pardee Hall, near the English Department office, hangs an enormous portrait of Professor Francis A. March compiled from several photographs in the college's archives.[6] Professor March is seated beside his desk at the head of a classroom. Legs crossed, arms folded, he stares directly out at the viewer, his formidable pose balanced by the friendly gleam in his eye. He appears, in short, as the epitome of the great teacher—of literature. For this representation of March is all about reading: On top of his desk, as well as every other surface in the room, there are stacks (and stacks) of books. There is writing on the chalkboard behind him—a list of what might be essay topics (e.g., "Compare Venus and Adonis"), but these are so faint as to be barely legible. March's reputation as a wise and learned teacher is clearly identified with all of those books. Although there are other images of March on campus, this one is the most widely recognized and reproduced. It is the image by which most at the college remember him.

Francis Andrew March (1825–1911) is a figure who looms large not only in the history of Lafayette College, but who occupies a prominent place in the history of English as a discipline.[7] March, who taught at Lafayette from 1853 to 1906, was a respected scholar with an international reputation. Self-trained as a philologist (there were no graduate programs in the subject in American universities at the time), March was the author of more than 190 articles and books on a range of topics in philology, literature, pedagogy, and spelling reform. He was twice elected president of the American Philological Society (in 1873 and again in 1895) and the only American honorary member of the London Philological Society (for whom he helped coordinate American contributions to the Oxford English Dictionary). His *Comparative Grammar of the Anglo-Saxon Language* (1869) was a highly respected work well into the twentieth century, as was his *Thesaurus Dictionary of the English Language* (1902) which he compiled with his son, and which is only fairly recently out of print. March served from 1891 to 1894 as president of the Modern Language Association, which in 1984 established a prize in his name. Today, however, March is probably most famous for being one of the first—some say *the* first—to teach English "like Latin and Greek"—that is, to apply to English literature methods used in the study of classical languages.[8]

While March's role in the development of a curriculum in English literature has been well documented (Graff refers to him as a "pioneer"), March's importance is bifurcated and slanted in one direction. The March privileged in the available disciplinary histories is the March who taught reading, who taught literature, who imported to Lafayette College in 1855 the pedagogical experiments he conducted while at Leicester Academy from 1845 to 1847. The "other" March, the one who could as easily be identified a progenitor of composition, is virtually erased, even though an examination of his "method," as represented in the course catalogue, his textbooks, and other published writing shows his deliberate effort to integrate the practices of reading and writing in the teaching of literature. This omission is in part due to how philology has been represented (really misrepresented) as dull or pedantic (a characterization, itself, that, as Mariolina Salvatori has documented in *Pedagogy*, has its roots in late nineteenth-century debates about the status of pedagogy as art or science).[9] Such representations have become part and parcel of our disciplinary history—a history that has insisted, as well, on the "rise" of literary study as a departure from the study of rhetoric. Characterizing March's contribution as a "curricular abnormality," for example, Frederick Rudolph describes how "March wrested English Literature away from the old rhetoric tradition, with its stultifying emphasis on form and rules, and took to it some of the concern with thought, criticism, and esthetics that had characterized the uses of literature in the literary societies" (140). Rudolph recapitulates a familiar kind of story in which the "origins" of literary study, here "the uses of literature in the literary societies," are not the same as the origins of composition studies.[10] As we will discuss, however, March did not "wrest" English Literature away from rhetoric, so much as he helped situate it within a curriculum where rhetoric was firmly established.

A different image of March and the significance of his contribution to the discipline emerges if we examine what he wrote about his method for teaching English literature. In fact, we are reminded that he taught writing as well as reading. This is evident from the first "official" record of March's influence on the Lafayette curriculum, which appeared in the catalogue for 1860–1861: "The English Language is studied in the same way as the Latin and the Greek. The works of Milton and Shakespeare are made the basis of instruction in the rhetorical laws of English composition, and in the principles of epic and dramatic art. Select passages from them are thoroughly analyzed, the grammatical and historical etymology of every word discussed, and the text made the ground work of general philological instruction" (16–17). It is not hard to imagine how this passage, cited often in descriptions of March as well as histories of the discipline, has contributed to the story of him as a "pioneer" in the study of literature. Here, literature serves as a vehicle for composition. Students learn how to write by carefully analyzing what they read. But another way to understand the significance of this passage is that it describes an effort to integrate reading and writing—it acknowledges, in other words, that writing comes from reading (and reading comes from writing). This is a very different image of writing than the disembodied one depicted in March's portrait, in which great writing lies entombed between the covers of books to which specialists, like March, provide access.

Evidence that March thought otherwise is readily apparent in much of his writing about the study of literary texts. In the preface to his *Method of Philological Study of the English Language* (1865), for example, he advises teachers: "The habit of investigating and writing out results makes the full man and the exact man at once; it divests composition of ninety-nine parts of its horrors, and it quickens thought ninety-nine times as much as beating the brain for original brilliancies. If, however books are not to be had, the teacher should give the needed facts and thoughts in a lecture, and the students should take notes and rewrite" (iii). Notable not only for its insistence on the relationship between reading and writing, this passage is also interesting for its characterization of writing as a vehicle for thinking. Indeed, March's ideas here sound like arguments in our own day for process writing. In context, however, his proposal for integrating reading and writing actually speaks to practical concerns, namely that English is usually taught by a rhetoric teacher: "Many college professors wish to teach English, but can not get time for it. The Professor of Rhetoric, into whose hands this study oftenest falls, usually controls the writing of the classes, or some of them. Would not a weekly written exercise embodying answers to the questions in this book or to others like them, continued for a term or two, and followed by an examination, do something toward a thorough study of the English language and of English literature?" (*Method* iv).

The above passage is not a prototype for a course in writing, or even an argument for the importance of writing over reading. Rather, March recommends writing be used to teach literature, and that it be taught by the person already responsible for writing instruction (one who "usually controls the writing of the classes").[11] Thus, literature here is imagined not as a departure from rhetoric, but part of the same curriculum.

In fact, during his career March devoted considerable energy toward establishing a comprehensive curriculum in English that, beginning early on, included practice in writing as well as reading. In an address to the National Education Association on "Methods of Teaching English in the High School," for example, March outlined four "principal direct uses in studying

English." These were: "1. to understand what is said in that language; 2. to speak it well; 3. to write it well; 4. to master English literature" (240). Writing was central to this curriculum: "The student in the high school should write much, I mean write often and write carefully. Every day he should have to write something. It is an old saying, To study without pen in hand is to dream; and year by year, with the growth of the press, grows, also, the relative importance of skill in writing" (241). By "skill in writing," March meant that students had to "be trained in the very kind of writing which they are to need" (241). But he also advocated the use of writing "in connection with the study of classic authors." In response to "representative passages," he explained, "a written analysis should be handed in, special attention should be paid to the relations of the clauses and sentences to each other, and the basis in the nature of thought for each mode of expression should be pointed out, as far as may be" (242). In addition, he recommended "weekly essays on assigned topics," including:

> the life of the author, his contemporaries, his works, the particular work studied, an outline of such parts of the work as are not to be gone over in the minute analysis, giving the number of times certain leading grammatical forms occur in each passage, and explaining the reasons for the different proportion in which such forms are found in different passages. Essays on such topics as these, with subordinate points more or less fully mentioned, should be so managed that the life and times of the author may be understood, and his work seen in its true relations as a representative work. (242)

Writing was never marginalized, at any level, in the English curriculum imagined by Francis March.

Upon March's appointment as Professor of the English Language, the curriculum shows evidence of increased attention to the English language. The sophomore rhetoric course drops out briefly in 1856–1857, and those students instead read Richard Chenevix Trench's lectures *On the Study of Words*.[12] The catalogue also describes "daily exercises in declamation and composition" for sophomores and juniors, and declamation of "original compositions" for seniors. While this is not the first mention of "composition" in the catalogue, these and other changes point toward an increase in the kind and number of academic exercises and practices that use writing after March's arrival.[13] The 1857–1858 catalogue specifies "written" debates for sophomores and juniors. Rhetoric reappears in the third term for sophomores, who in addition to Trench, study William Chauncey Fowler's *English Grammar*.[14] A course in English Literature for seniors was established by March when he started his teaching at Lafayette as a tutor (the course appears in the catalogue in 1853–1854), but in 1857–1858, juniors read Milton's *Paradise Lost* and study Anglo-Saxon. The rhetoric course for seniors reappears, but instead of Campbell, they use Richard Whately's text. In 1858–1859, juniors in the third term read Shakespeare's *Julius Caesar*.[15] These changes mark the beginning of the sustained attention to reading and writing that, though now forgotten, distinguished March's long career at Lafayette.

THE FIGURE OF A LAFAYETTE STUDENT

James P. Boyd (1836–1910), better known in his adult life as a prolific author of biographies, histories, and textbooks, was a student at the college from 1855 to 1859.[16] During his time at Lafayette, Boyd (like most students) joined one of the campus literary societies, and his academic record was strong enough for him to graduate as class valedictorian. He also recorded his experiences—almost daily—in a journal, a portion of which the college has in its archives.[17] The kinds of literacy experiences recorded in Boyd's journal have not, typically, been the focus of institutional histories of literacy instruction—partly because such histories tend to be written about students as subjects rather than writers,[18] and partly because, having been composed by students (rather than "legitimate" authors), such artifacts tend not to be preserved. Boyd's journal is valuable not only because it provides a rare glimpse into student life during the early years of March's career, but also because it serves as an account of the range of ways in which reading and writing could be said to have been understood as mutually related practices.[19]

One kind of evidence for such understanding is provided by Boyd's accounts of the assignments he has to prepare. For example, Boyd writes on

January 27, 1859, "here I am without a composition and the time for reading it at hand." As was typical for the time, written compositions were declaimed. Writing, that is, inevitably culminated in reading. Consequently, reading was also part of Boyd's writing process beforehand. In several entries, for example, Boyd describes himself writing at the last minute, and he laments the fact that he has left himself no time for rereading and revising his composition. "Have this evening experienced the evil effects of procrastination," he writes in that same January 27 entry. Having been distracted from writing by "visits from several friends," he later reflects: "How very important it is to not only get amply ready but to get ready in ample time. How much better might those performances be, which are gotten up at one's discretion (as regards tone) and upon which he will have time to ponder after they are written before he reads them than those hastily prepared which must be only a collection of thoughts fumbled together in a confused mass without the symmetry of arrangement."

As they were for March, reading and writing for Boyd are described here, and elsewhere in the journal, as related activities: A better "performance" of his writing, Boyd reasons in the entry above, requires time for "ponder[ing]" (presumably through reading one's own writing) and rewriting. The idea of "performance" is important here not only as a historical detail (student compositions were written to be declaimed; students understood reading, not just silently, but also aloud, as a necessary part of the writing process) but also for what it suggests about the relationship between the practices of reading and writing and the performance of a self. Notably, Boyd frames his writing about procrastination with an aphorism (or imitation of one) that likely comes from his reading elsewhere. As he does throughout the journal, in this passage, Boyd constructs a self not simply through recording in writing his observations but also through reflecting in writing on his writing. Boyd's journal entries, like his written compositions, are "performances," rehearsals of a self that is continually under revision, a self impossible to conceive without reading and writing—and reading one's own writing.

A later entry, another on the evils of procrastination, conveys as much, and argues that improvement in writing (through reading) leads to self-improvement: "Have an essay for Thursday morning and have not yet written a word. O my thievish ruinous habit of procrastination! . . . My productions never get proper reviewing from me and scarcely a correction after once uniting with ink. This is wrong. Time should intervene between the writing and reading or speaking. You may then read and correct and notice errors and improve yourself by observing the defecting points." In revising his writing, he improves himself. Throughout the journal, reading and writing are, for Boyd, the means to such self-improvement. For example, Boyd writes frequently about what he reads. Often this writing reflects his efforts to improve his understanding of a text, as it does in this entry: "Have just finished my lesson on the Constitution. How valuable a study to become acquainted with not just the structure, but with the principles of those men who framed it and with the spirit of the time which gave it birth" (Jan. 29). At other times, Boyd uses his writing to evaluate the "style" of an author: "Commenced reading the 1st Vol of Goldsmiths Miscellanies. Find them very good so far. The subjects are rather of a light kind treated in rather a philosophical manner. . . . He enters into the minutiae of everything with a warrantable exactitude, yet his style is not monotonous. There is still enough vivacity and variety of expression to command interest and dispel tediousness. He is sufficiently fluent. His language is choice. His expressions rather classical. In him the students find much to admire little to condemn. I read him more for his style, than for information" (Jan. 30). Of Alexander Hamilton's *Eulogies on General Green,* which he reads for pleasure, Boyd notes, "it was well written, plain and concise" (Feb. 20). In all of these examples, Boyd uses writing to process reading. Moreover, as the two latter examples suggest, what he learns by writing about his reading might, in turn, be used to improve his own compositions.

What Boyd's journal helps make visible, then, is how reading and writing during the March years were considered mutually related practices not only in school, but much more generally, for acculturation. Boyd uses what he learns in school about "good" writing (and speaking) to evaluate the "style" of the lectures and sermons he hears in town as well as what he reads for leisure. Although we have no examples of Boyd's compositions, there is writing in the journal to suggest that he explores in writing the "styles" he encounters and finds worthy models. Imitation (in writing of what he read or heard) was for Boyd, as for nineteenth-century readers and writers in general, a vehicle for literacy acquisition. That is, the kind of anxiety about "original" thought that, at an earlier moment, would have excluded Boyd's journal from the historical record was, in fact, understood very differently in Boyd's own day. "Originality" was certainly valued, as Boyd notes when he describes an "interesting time in Society" upon hearing "an oration on the subject of 'Cultivating ones own thoughts and opinions and not depending upon other opinions and judgments'" (February 24). But the means to "originality" in thought or composition included imitation, not as a dead end, but a means of understanding.

This understanding refocuses attention on a literacy practice like imitation that figured prominently for students in March's day, and reminds us of the range of literacy activities (reading, writing, listening, speaking) and sites (classroom, literary society, public lecture, sermon) that such a practice implicates and crosses. In being so reminded, we are invited to reflect and reconsider gaps in our institutional history.

RESITUATING MARCH

The inclusion of a figure like March—a figure whose work was widely known and who worked at an institution like Lafayette dedicated to undergraduate education—enlarges the parameters of the history of composition. The celebration of March as a "pioneer" of literary study hides from consideration his nuanced attention to writing and the interaction between reading and writing, and distorts the range of his contribution to English study—his advocacy, as he put it, of "the abundant use of writing" ("Methods of Teaching English" 244). At the same time, it inspires the raising of new questions. What is at stake in the construction of a figure like a "great teacher"? How might March function as a locus for a certain mythology and historiography? Finally, the presence of March at Lafayette College in the nineteenth century underscores the fact that significant curricular and pedagogical innovation in composition can occur anywhere reading and writing are taught and practiced, but only if our assumptions about what constitutes proper evidence for such innovation are reexamined. If March was indeed a pioneer in literary study, it is because he provides an early example of the use of writing to teach reading.

Perhaps this facet of March's contribution has been ignored because the record of evidence is so hard to read. His was a highly specialized expertise and is, therefore, subject to being misread, misconstrued, misrepresented. In fact, as a philologist, March was ideally positioned to understand the importance of an individual's relationship to his (or her) own language. In his writing March claimed that a thorough understanding of the master works of literature was every student's "birth right," and—as such—had to be carefully conducted. This belief fueled his interest in developing a curriculum in English from the earliest levels.

Perhaps even more importantly, though, the "new" March has been ignored because our ways of reading his contributions are implicated in the stories constructed about the rise of literary study. In making available examples of March's writing about teaching, we hope to complicate the notion that he saw himself (or for that matter, was seen by his contemporaries) as only a teacher of literature. Rather, March reminds us that any claims about the origin of literature as distinct from composition are suspect, and that the history of English is, indeed, a story of reading *and* writing. The story of reading and writing instruction at Lafayette College, like so many stories of the nineteenth century that rely on archival materials, makes us think twice about the modernity of certain disciplinary theories and practices, such as the equation: "to read is to write is to read is to write." Such equations are only modern (or more accurately postmodern) in their recuperation of an already established praxis whose origin has been forgotten. In our effort to reestablish still another point of provisional beginning, our work on March has led us to ask what happened in composition pedagogy to make it posit reading and writing as in any way separable.

Notes

We are indebted to college archivist Diane Shaw and her assistants Ellen Kristen Turner and Emily George. We would also like to thank Paul Schlueter, who shared with us not only his library but his own bibliographic research on Professor March. And, finally, our thanks to Mariolina Salvatori for her insightful comments on an earlier draft of this chapter.

1. The state of Pennsylvania granted Lafayette College a charter in 1826, but a lack of funds kept the school from opening its doors to students until 1832. The first sen-

ior class graduated in 1836. Today Lafayette College is a private liberal arts college with a nearly invisible religious affiliation (Presbyterian), situated in Easton, on the east coast of Pennsylvania, on the border of New Jersey.

Americans' enthusiasm for the Marquis de Lafayette resulted in many cities and streets bearing his name, but ours is the only college named after him. Lafayette's second American tour in 1824 included stops in cities in every state of the union.

2. Because some issues of the catalogue are missing, it is unclear when this happens.

3. We learn from the college catalogue that in the years 1833–1836, that program consisted of the following courses:

Freshmen: Latin, Greek, and Mathematics

Sophomores: Latin, Greek, Mathematics, and Evidences of Christianity

Juniors: Latin, Greek, Mathematics, and Evidences of Christianity, Moral Philosophy, Mental Philosophy, Natural Theology, and Rhetoric

Seniors: Latin, Greek, Mental Philosophy, and Rhetoric

4. The increasing emphasis on writing in rhetoric courses is related to a social shift in the importance of "silent discourse." In the 1850s, with innovations in transportation and technology increasing the distance between communicants, the "rhetorical function" of writing increased. However, writing as a material practice would have had other functions as well, a story which is less well documented.

5. In the catalogue of 1906, under the Department of English Language and Comparative Philology, the following description appears:

During the Freshman year, a new course is being presented in the theory and practice of English Composition. The theory is taught throughout the year in lectures and recitations, and the practice obtained in daily themes, some of which are written in the classroom under the eye of the professor. Longer themes are prepared at intervals of a fortnight, and regular consultation hours are appointed at which each student is required to discuss his work with his instructor.

In 1908, the first year that courses in the department are identified in the catalogue by number, a remarkable change is made in the college catalogue, lasting only one year. A three-term writing course is described in detail, and its readings and assignments are included. In the first of these terms, the following texts were assigned: Shakespeare, Macaulay (*History, Essay on Boswell*), L.B.R. Briggs (*School, College, and Character*), Stevenson, Thoreau, and Green (*A Short History of the English People*). During this term, five essays were required, assigned at approximately two weeks intervals (from October 5th to November 30th). The first four essays were to range from 500–1,000 words; the final essay could be as long as 2,000 words. The five assignments were:

I. Who I am and why I came to Lafayette

II. How to make or do something

III. An exposition on a subject selected with the approval of the instructor

IV. An expression of opinion

V. A Biographical portrait

During the second and third terms (January 25 to May 17), outside readings included: Tennyson, Homer, Stevenson, Kipling, G. P. Barker (*Specimens of Argumentation*), Lincoln (*Letters and Speeches*). Two textbooks were also required: Gardiner, Kittredge, and Arnold (*Manual of Composition and Rhetoric*) and Nutter, Hersey, and Greenough (*Specimens of Prose Composition*). The following assignments, six of them in total, were to be submitted approximately one month apart or every three weeks:

VI. Brief or Introduction to Argument

VII. Brief of Argument (2–3 pages)

VIII. Argument (1–1500 words)

IX. Description (500–1000)

X. Narrative (500–750)

XI. Narrative (750–1500)

6. The college's archives has three photographs of March in the same pose and setting, taken after the latter part of his career (we have dates for two of them, ca. 1894 or 1895 and 1907). Except for the fact that he's a little older in each one, the other noticeable differences have to do with the writing on the chalkboard. In one of the photos it appears to be topics for discussion or writing for a philosophy class (March taught a range of subjects at the college), and (more to the point for our purposes here) the other shows diagrammed sentences.

7. March, who earned both a BA (1845) and an MA (1848) from Amherst College, came to Lafayette as a tutor in 1853, after a lung infection forced him to abandon his law practice in New York City. The 1855–1856 catalogue identifies his position as "Adjunct Professor of the English Language." In 1857, the board of trustees appointed March to a new position: Professor of English Language and Lecturer in Comparative Philology. The claim that this position was the first of its kind in the country seems to have originated with college president G. Wilson McPhail.

8. This phrase, "to teach English like Latin and Greek," is frequently quoted in contemporary histories and appears to have been widely circulated in March's own day.

9. As Salvatori's *Pedagogy: Disturbing History, 1819–1929* demonstrates, although the emergent art/science binary was fraught, by the early twentieth century, teaching had come to be considered more art than science. Graff's earlier history recapitulates this distinction when he describes March as typical of early teachers who "copied the methods long used to teach the classics" (38).

10. March himself admits that his belief in the value of literary study was, indeed, influenced by his own participation in one of Amherst College's literary societies. But

as he explains, and as the records of Lafayette's two literary societies (The Franklin and The Washington) reveal, participation in these extracurricular clubs included writing as well as reading: "Our exercises were Orations, Essays, Poems, and the like, written performances which were carefully given out at the beginning of each administration, by the Presiding officers, so as to bring all the members on every term. . . . Then we had a critic, who read a written critique on the last meeting" (March, Letter to Mr. Geo. R. Cutting). James Boyd (1836–1910) writes frequently about his literary society activities in ways that suggest cross-pollination among a range of popular and school literacy activities.

11. It is possible that March imagines a place for writing in the rhetoric classroom, but "the classes" might refer to the teaching of writing in a more general sense.

12. Trench's book was tremendously popular (at least nine British and at least twenty-five American editions). The college would later award a prize for the best essay based on this book.

13. By "academic" we mean to distinguish between writing assigned, taught, and or evaluated in the classroom, and writing conducted in other venues since Lafayette's literary societies included many kinds of written exercises. These societies, their contests, and publications, the student newspaper, and other college prizes for essay, debate, and speech contests, were all part of the larger culture of writing at the college.

14. Fowler was the son-in-law of Noah Webster; March had studied with both men while a student at Amherst College.

15. College lore credits March with being the first in the country to teach a Shakespeare course to undergraduates. In fact, to our knowledge, he taught individual plays, rather than a course, and as March himself explains, some plays work better than others:

   . . . of all the plays of Shakespeare, "Julius Caesar" is best fitted for class study. The story is familiar, the characters are well known. The unity of the play is easily seen in respect to its controlling course of thought and feeling, and the development of character and events. The relations of subordinate characters and events to this central current are easily thought out. There is much declamation, and long-continued, striking dialogue, which give occasion for the study of rhetorical art. The language throughout is simple, and, for Shakespeare, bears the application of school grammars, dictionaries, and rhetorics remarkably well. The versification is also very regular and simple. ("Craik's English of Shakespeare" 303)

16. Boyd's publications include *The Military and Civil Life of General Ulysses S. Grant* (1884), *Wonders: In the Two Americas* (1886), *The Story of the Crusades* (1892), and the *Bible Dictionary and Analytical Concordance* (ca. 1897). Versions of Boyd's *Bible Dictionary* were still being published at the end of the twentieth century.

17. The copy of Boyd's journal in the college archives is actually a handwritten transcription by one of Boyd's descendents. The entries begin on January 22, 1859, and

conclude on July 27, 1859, with Boyd's graduation, but this manuscript is possibly (almost certainly, likely) excerpted from a longer document whose whereabouts are, unfortunately, unknown.

18. Important exceptions include Lucille Schultz's *Young Composers* (1999).

19. While Boyd cannot be made to speak for all students, he does frequently speak about other students, including interactions with them in classes, at literary society meetings, and other cultural events.

Archival Sources

The following college catalogues, circulars, and reports are in the Special Collections library at Lafayette College, Easton, PA:

Catalogue of the Officers and Students of Lafayette College. 1841–1842; 1844–1848; 1853–
    1859; 1892–1893.
Circular of Lafayette College, Easton, Pennsylvania. 1851–1852.
*Circular, Containing the Triennial and Annual Catalogues of the Officers and Students of
    Lafayette College, with the Course of Studies Etc. for the Academical Year 1852–53.*
Lafayette College. Fifth Annual Report, The College of Laws and Course of Studies. 1836.

Other items in the Special Collections library:
Boyd, James P. Diary. Unpublished ms. 1858–59.
Lafayette College Charter. 1826.

The following item is in the Amherst College Archives, Amherst, Massachusetts:
March, Francis Andrew. Letter to Mr. Geo. R. Cutting. April 20, 1871.

ꞈ 4 ꞈ

A Chair "Perpetually Filled
by a Female Professor"

RHETORIC AND COMPOSITION INSTRUCTION AT
NINETEENTH-CENTURY BUTLER UNIVERSITY

Heidemarie Z. Weidner

COMPOSITION HISTORIES HAVE largely been seen in one of two ways—golden age or golden textbook. Indeed, Robert Connors has argued that textbooks probably best mirror actual classroom practice, and that other materials will only be useful "after the major currents of the age—important figures and theories—have been mapped out" ("Historical Inquiry" 15, 11). Butler University's composition history complicates these stipulations and argues for a reevaluation of scope and method when writing the history of composition. Albert R. Kitzhaber's groundbreaking dissertation about rhetoric in American colleges was based on evidence from large institutions—Harvard, Yale, and Michigan. Butler University compellingly shows that the nation did not always follow Harvard and that composition historians must research

Based on evidence found in Butler University's Rare Books and Special Collections Irwin Library, my narrative incorporates the perspectives of the university's administration, its faculty, and its students. Sources include (1) official documents: board minutes, presidents' reports, university catalogues, enrollment and tuition ledgers, library records, and newspaper releases and advertisements; (2) faculty documents: reports to the board, minutes of faculty meetings and committees, lecture notes, letters, journals and memoirs, and publications (textbooks, collections of essays); and (3) student materials: diaries and reminiscences, notebooks, essays, theses, manuscripts, the student literary paper (somewhat comparable to today's student newspaper), literary society minutes, and alumnal publications.

a variety of institutions to compose a broader picture of writing instruction in the nineteenth century. Additionally, composition narratives must be based on a broad inquiry, one that includes archival sources that represent the perspectives of the official college, of instructors, and of students: presidents' reports, board and faculty minutes, university catalogues, instructors' lecture notes and diaries, faculty publications, student themes and journals, student magazines, and alumni memoirs.

I spent much of the summer and fall of 1990 in Butler University's Rare Books and Special Collections, reading anything that might shed light on the university's beginnings. Butler's interdenominational and coeducational aspects intrigued me. Perhaps this institution's story might counter Kitzhaber's narrative of rhetoric's decline during the second half of the nineteenth century. Sustained by cheerful assistance of the archivist, I read handwritten minutes of board and faculty meetings, studied catalogue after catalogue, discovered lecture notes, student themes and diaries of both students and instructors, browsed through publications of the literary societies, and cross-referenced discoveries with one another and contemporary textbooks. Each day I immersed myself deeper into the lives of Butler's faculty and students, a kind of time travel that became eerily real when upon leaving the library I startled over seeing the sights of twentieth-century Indianapolis. As my research came to an end, I unwillingly said good-bye to the many students and faculty members who had wandered in and out of my days (and nights!), with whom I had rejoiced at graduation or whose passing I had mourned.

The researcher's personal involvement constitutes one of the major differences when working with primary sources. Another outcome of such intensive multiple-source studies is the web of intertextuality that gradually brings to life an entire period. Infrequently at first, then more often, connections appear almost serendipitously: objectives in a catalogue are borne out by a student diary or supported by recorded observations of a faculty member; the heated discussions in a literary magazine contradict the melancholy assessment of student writing in a contemporary article; evidence of early peer evaluation, student-teacher conferences, and writing across the curriculum tells the researcher that not all pedagogical "innovations" of the twentieth century are truly new. Finally, such contextualized searches create histories that at times reflect, at times supplement, and at times complicate established historical narratives.

Nineteenth-century Butler University in Indianapolis, situated at what was then the western frontier, differed considerably from the eastern schools Kitzhaber examined in *Rhetoric in American Colleges, 1850–1900*. Harvard, for example, served students who generally came from families that had always attended college (Hofstadter and Hardy 51). Until the reform movement took hold, such institutions had seen knowledge as relatively static, a means to turn undergraduates into gentlemen. Education was "designed for the strengthening and adornment of the mind and not for immediate practical use or advancement" (12–14). Midwestern institutions, on the other hand, faced the incongruity between classical studies and the practical needs of their students. Less inflexible, more convinced of the necessity to adapt to rapid changes brought on by a growing westward expansion—and often forced by financial problems to adjust to their supporters' demands—they found it easier to choose curricular change, a decision which resulted in a dynamic, community-centered, and practical education. Among those institutions Butler is a particularly good example, for it contradicts Kitzhaber's dictum that denominational colleges fought "nearly all the new trends that were beginning to appear; coeducation, courses in laboratory science, higher standards of scholarship, all ran counter to their traditional ideals and mode of operation" (8).

Butler University, founded by the Disciples of Christ Church and with the financial support of Ovid Butler, a prominent Indianapolis citizen, opened in 1855. Proud of its "liberal and enlightened policies," the university advertised a "free popular education," admitting from the beginning every student, regardless of race, creed, or sex (BM 1861, 326; Burns 3; Waller 1). Butler emphasized an English education, with special attention to English language and literature when many other colleges upheld the classical curriculum. It also boldly supported women's higher education, in particular, by establishing the Demia Butler Chair, a professorship for women only.

PRACTICALITY AND UTILITY

According to Frederick Rudolph, curricula reflect what colleges consider "useful, appropriate, or relevant to the lives of educated men and woman at a certain time" (ix). Butler's board considered "practicality and utility" a logical stipulation for an institution preparing young people for the task of transforming a wilderness into civilization. Because such goals singled out English as a necessary foundation for all studies, the board ordered the faculty to "place first and as of primary importance, a critical and thorough study of the English language, including composition, elocution, rhetoric, belles lettres" (BM 1857, 230). In 1857, the board's directive constituted a considerable innovation. English as a medium of instruction had appeared at Harvard and Yale between 1756 and 1776 (Rudolph 38–39), but classical languages and their literatures still formed the "backbone" of a liberal education (140).[1] Not until the 1870s would Butler's approach enter the majority of colleges and universities. The prestige of Harvard and the forcefulness of Charles William Eliot, who in 1869 had addressed the neglect of a "systematic study of the English language," made English studies a national concern (qtd. in Rudolph 140).

Initially, some of Butler's board members discriminated against those "who [did] not wish to undergo the labor of the full classical course" (UC 1857, 14). Yet, board minutes from the 1870s continued to stress the work in English. For example, in 1872, Ovid Butler spoke eloquently about students' need for English literacy:

> Every graduate . . . should have a thorough knowledge of his or her own language and literature. . . . More time [must] be spent in learning and building up our mother tongue. We are living in a practical age. Men and women are not so much regarded for what they can as for what they *do* learn. It is well for them to understand the classics . . . but it is better for them to know more of the living present that when they go forth in the great battle of life they may be better prepared to meet its realities. (BM 1872, 449–52, italics original)

As late as 1889, the board minutes emphasized that the university's mission was different from that of schools in the East. President Benton, speaking about Bible Department students who had "only" an English education, reasserted that Butler could not model itself after eastern schools: "Our circumstances and needs are different, and our courses of study and methods must be adapted to the necessities of our young men who are preparing for the ministry" (BM 197). Such study involved rhetorical training: a blend of theory supplemented by practice in writing and speaking.

RHETORICALS AT BUTLER

Among the university's entertainments described by Lydia Short, one of Butler University's earliest women students, speeches, lectures, and sermons dominated.[2] Judging by Short's diary entries, Indianapolis society considered the arts of composing and delivering effective oral presentations marks of the educated person. Hence it is not surprising that Butler emphasized rhetoric and rhetorical exercises as "indispensable to a good education" (UC 1870–71, 42) and a natural outcome of the institution's educational goals. Butler's practice supports Nan Johnson's argument that "rhetorical education played a crucial role in bolstering . . . nineteenth-century liberal education, an enterprise which was committed to the development of an intellectually progressive and culturally enlightened society" (*Nineteenth* 16).

Students took one course in rhetorical theory, taught under such diverse departmental groupings as ethics, natural philosophy, and moral philosophy. Despite this hodgepodge of labels, the university's rhetoric instructors did not fit the picture of semi-illiterate country preachers turned rhetoricians. All had received extensive theoretical and practical training in the art of rhetoric —either as ministers or lawyers—and their instruction tended to balance theory with practice. As the lecture notebooks in Butler's archives show, the teachers of rhetoric followed Samuel P. Newman's advice about instruction. Unhappy with the recitation method, Newman suggested the use of "familiar lectures" and literary models to enrich the materials in the textbook (*Practical*, 1851, 5–11). One of Butler's early rhetoric teachers, George H. Hoss, later chair of Indiana University's English Department, explained his teaching philosophy: "We learn to write by writing and to speak by speaking" (UCIU 1874–75).

If practical concerns motivated the teaching of rhetorical theory, instructors made doubly sure that its principles were practiced throughout a student's entire college career. Prejudiced by Kitzhaber's narrative of decline, a twenty-first-century observer would be pleasantly surprised to have observed the energy and enthusiasm compelling theory and practice of rhetoric at Butler University. Rhetorical exercises took the form of declamations, essays, and orations. Declamations exercised the memory, while essays and orations incorporated the principles of rhetoric and critical analysis. The exercises ranged in frequency and complexity from the "once in two weeks" of the 1855–1857 catalogue (14) to the system devised in 1870 that grouped students according to their abilities (UC 1870–71, 41).

Instructors also ascertained that final versions of written work, after several revisions, were error-free, as the catalogue of 1870–1871 states explicitly: "Every student in the institution will be required to write and read, and after correction, carefully revise and re-write, three essays, of a length not less than three pages foolscap, during each term. . . . Errors will be marked and essays returned, and a succession of careful revisions required, until they are satisfactory to the one having charge of the class" (42). The term "correction" meant both the correction of surface errors and the advice to change an essay more substantially. Short and Colin E. King, a student whose diary is also part of Butler's archives, mention rewriting frequently in their journals. Although neither the length nor the frequency of writing assignments sounds impressive, apparently confirming Kitzhaber's conclusion that during the early nineteenth century little actual writing occurred (31–32), S. Michael Halloran notes the physical effort involved in writing with nineteenth-century tools (170). Furthermore, beginning with the 1870s, the rhetorical exercises were supplemented by writing in students' regular classes. Courses in rhetorical theory, natural history, psychology, and English literature asked for written critical analyses besides the usual recitation. Even the courses in classical and modern languages stressed "elegant English" in translation (UC 1876–77). As writing "invaded" classes in other disciplines, the content of those other disciplines began to influence the nature of rhetorical exercises, for students were encouraged to write "critical essays in subjects pertinent to their different branches of study" (UC 1884–85, 15). In the early 1890s, the blurring of objectives assigned to rhetorical exercises and content classes finally led to the disappearance of rhetoricals as a separate entity. But this process began in 1869 when Ovid Butler endowed the Demia Butler Chair, a significant development in the university's history and the beginning of a separate English department. Now rhetorical training became augmented by the courses in literature, criticism, and writing offered by its first two Demia Butler professors —Catherine Merrill, 1869–1883, and Harriet Noble, 1883–1895.

THE DEMIA BUTLER CHAIR

Named after Ovid Butler's late daughter Demia, the first woman graduate of Butler's classical course, the new chair was to be "filled always and only by a good and competent Female Professor," with "such Department and Studies pertaining to the Collegiate Course as may be most appropriately taught by Female Professors" (BM 1869, 188). Butler saw the creation of the new chair in line with the university's "original position and purpose to educate the sexes together" (BM 1869, 190). Following his proposal, the board agreed that "the Department of English Literature and such other studies as in the opinion of the Faculty may be most appropriately taught by Female Professors and in connection with English Literature shall be assigned to the said Demia Butler Chair" (BM 1869, 191).

Two ideas fuelled Ovid Butler's endowment: his consuming interest in a liberal education and his conviction that English serve as the foundation for such an education. Yet the mix and match of professors and courses at Butler University had not yet produced the thoroughness of instruction he envisioned. Only the creation of distinct departments, Ovid Butler argued before the directors of the board, would make it possible for every instructor, "by proper study and attention . . . to keep himself in advance or at least fully up to the requirements" (BM 1869, 207–9). The new English Department would create such an environment.

Catherine Merrill

In 1869, Catherine Merrill, the daughter of Samuel Merrill, State Treasurer and founder of the first publishing house in the Old Northwest Territory, was forty-five and a private teacher. She was also the author of the two-volume anthology, *Indiana Soldier in the War for the Union*, a collection of letters, conversations, and observations gathered from the men Merrill had nursed during the Civil War. Since many people knew Merrill, the university acquired in her not only a competent teacher but also a woman whose name would attract more women students. Indeed, shortly thereafter the board began to advertise her as a teacher and guardian to whom the "moral and educational wants and interests" of young women could be entrusted (UC 1870,

30). Merrill's duties included rhetorical theory, literature, and composition, and under her energetic leadership, the new Department of English increased its offerings dramatically. By 1876–1877, students took English throughout the four-year course: freshman and sophomores took composition, juniors had "English Classics"; and seniors studied "Rhetoric, Aesthetics, and English and General Literature." Students' reading lists were long: plays by Shakespeare; essays by Bacon; poems by Milton, Longfellow, Wordsworth, Dryden, Marvell; and novels, such as *The Vicar of Wakefield*. A recommended reading list stressed language, the history of literature, and taste: "Dwight's Philology, Muller's Science of Language, Sismondi's Literature of the South of Europe, Dunlop's History of Fiction, Schlegel and Hazlitt's Treatises on Literature, Kuyser's Religion of the Norsemen, History of Philosophy, the works of Morell, Lewes, and Cousin. Aesthetics—Taine's and Ruskin's works, and Cousin's True, Beautiful and Good" (UC 1870–71, 36). The connection between history and literature was typical of the time, the term "literature" until the 1880s still denoting a large variety of written discourses. Their inclusion formed part of nineteenth-century rhetoric's expansiveness, a characteristic criticized by Kitzhaber and other scholars.

Merrill combined the study of rhetoric and literature with frequent practice in critical analysis. She made it quite clear in her course objectives that such work awaited her students: "Theses will frequently be demanded of the Classes in Aesthetics, Literature and History of Philosophy, containing critical compendiums for the matters treated in the text-books. The principles of Criticism and English Composition will be thoroughly familiarized by daily exercises in composition during the study of Rhetoric and English Literature" (UC 1870–71, 36). Merrill's course objectives and her teaching load represented nineteenth-century rhetoric's multiple approach to the teaching of rhetoric. Informed by classical rhetoric, it added aesthetics, criticism, history of philosophy, and literature, subjects that helped develop aesthetic judgment and foster critical awareness. Increased practice, the "daily exercises," was a feature at Butler University long before Barrett Wendell's daily themes.

Merrill's least favored subject was rhetorical theory. In particular, she felt unqualified to teach the university's text, Alexander Bain's *English Composition and Rhetoric*. Her class of six—"one lady, five gentlemen—three of the latter officiating as preachers of the Gospel frighten[ed]" her. She wrote, "I am not at all at my ease, and I am afraid they think me inefficient, and draw from me the inference that women are unfit for such a position. It is awfully uncomfortable to think this, and I determine every day that I will *possess* my soul" (Graydon 349). On the other hand, Merrill was confident when it came to the practical aspect of rhetorical training. Once on the faculty, she regulated and directed the rhetorical exercises—essays and oral presentations— and insisted on a kind of writing across the curriculum where every instructor helped with the topics for, and evaluation of, the rhetoricals.

Naturally, Merrill's own writing habits influenced her teaching of composition. For her, writing and speaking were ways to create "one's own thoughts of poetry and prose" (Graydon 342). Strict with herself, she imposed equally high standards on her students' written and oral work. In particular, she felt that good writing required frequent revision and therefore much effort and time. Since she personally liked to read aloud what she had written, we may assume that she passed on to her students what she found helpful for herself. In grading students' assignments, she looked for what the rhetorics of her time considered "exemplary": a careful match between clear thinking and concise expression. She therefore "gave great attention to the writing of her students, correcting every theme . . . with great care. Every sentence must be exact in form, every word accurate and the best" (Graydon 385).

To achieve her goals, Merrill assigned much writing in her classes (UC 1870–71, 36). Like President Butler, she saw the need for increased instruction in English language and literature. A committee report from 1872 includes this statement by Merrill to the board members: "If the Honorable Board had read *Senior Examination Papers* in Preparitory [sic] Studies or in anything that requires English writing, the members of the same would agree with me in desiring much more attention paid to the English language and literature than is now given to these studies" (BM June 1972). We may glean Merrill's criteria for good writing from her description of two outstanding students, among them her successor, Harriet Noble: "They read carefully, observe closely, penetrate into motives, weigh causes and effects, think out a thought fully and take the trouble to fit words accurately to thoughts" (Graydon 388). It was this "accuracy of expression" (385) that Merrill now also applied to the recitations and to the periodic written examinations. As Merrill's objectives indicate, writing assignments followed a specific sequence (UC 1870–71, 36–42). Freshmen began with "filling out notes" taken during class lectures and practiced clarity in exercises based on E. A. Abbott's *How to Write Clearly* (UC 1870–71, 36–43). Abbott's "little book," later much appreciated by John F. Genung, "supplied sentences and paragraphs, so constructed that the rewriting of them will necessarily apply the principles learned" (*Study* 24). Freshmen also wrote "original compositions," and graduated to "themes on historical subjects," writing assignments they continued as sophomores. As juniors and seniors, students applied the principals of rhetoric and criticism to their own writing in the form of "critical essays" or "criticisms" (UC 1870–71, 36–42). According to Johnson—and judging by the examples found in Butler's student publication, the *Butler Collegian*—such criticisms were a "highly complex form of composition . . . analytical and evaluative in intention," in which the writer summarized the work and judged whether it might be considered "valuable, significant, or tasteful" (*Nineteenth* 212, 214).

Rhetorical training during the last quarter of the nineteenth century increasingly focused on written discourse, exploring inner spaces rather than public speaking's outer spaces. Butler composition classes under Merrill, however, continued to serve as a public forum where written essays became oral presentations. At the same time, these public readings increased the amount of practice in criticism. Class critiques continued a method of peer evaluation students knew from their rhetorical activities in the literary societies. In Merrill's classes, the procedure usually involved student A reading his or her paper, a critical evaluation of an assigned literary text or a comparison of a topic treated by two different authors, e.g., "King John's reign in Greene's History compared with John's reign in Hume's History of England" (King 63). During the same class period, student B read a critical analysis of A's essay, written after a study of the two texts about King John. Finally, the class discussed the relative worth of both the original essay and the critique.

Before class discussion students signed up for private teacher-student conferences. Popular today, such individual sessions were also recommended by Newman in *A Practical System of Rhetoric,* a work Merrill might have known. Newman suggested "a familiar mode of correcting the first attempts of students" (13). "If practicable"—and Merrill's classes were small enough

—"the instructor may with advantage read over with the pupil his production, and alone with him freely comment upon his defects and excellences. While in this way needed encouragement is given, the attention of the student is directed to that point where there is most need of improvement" (1851, 13–14). We may assume that Merrill was likewise concerned with individual guidance, but also wanted to spare students the humiliation of a rough draft read too early in front of their peers. Genung, who greatly influenced Merrill's successor Noble, speaks of students' writing ability as an unfinished process. All a teacher can hope to accomplish is "sowing seed for future harvests" (*Study* 14). Harsh criticism can only inhibit growth. In a lecture on rhetoric, Genung quotes a friend about the treatment novice writers demand: "Stimulus, more than criticism, is what the forming literary mind requires. . . . The criticism that is applied should be living criticism—by which we mean oral criticism, in which the criticized writer himself should share as respondent, while the writer's classmates, under stimulating and regulating direction from the head of the department, should take a principal part in it. . . . Infinitely better . . . it would be for college classes, if their rhetorical teacher should even, save in exceptional classes, never once *see* the essays of their pupils" (qtd. in *Study* 17).

Colin E. King, one of Merrill's students, recorded in his diary that he wrote several "criticisms" for Merrill and that fellow students critiqued the "criticisms" in writing. Only then did both writer and critic present their essays to the class. Following King's entries we can piece together such an assignment: "Feb. 6, 1880: Grafton gave me his Senior Literature Essay on Hamlet for me to write a criticism on. Feb. 8, 1880: I read Hamlet today. Feb. 9, 1880: I wrote a criticism on Mr. Grafton's Essay on Hamlet this afternoon. Feb. 10, 1880: I read my criticism on Grafton's Essay in English this morning" (48–50). King's entries about his commencement speech illustrate one of Merrill's objectives as stated in the university catalogue, "private criticism of the Professor" (UC 1876–77, 22). King spent two months on his commencement speech, selecting and abandoning topics (he discarded "The Poetry of Patriotism" and "The Statesman" for a more manageable and practical subject, "Andrew Jackson"), visiting the library and checking out books (Parton's *Life of Andrew Jackson*, 1861, and von Holst's *Constitutional and Political History of the United States*, 1881), reading and taking notes, drafting his speech, consulting with his father and "Miss Merrill," revising according to their suggestions, submitting the draft again to his English teacher, incorporating her "corrections" in yet another revision, finally copying the finished paper on "sermon paper," and then starting the arduous practice of delivery (King 221–28).

Merrill's pedagogy was innovative in another significant way. In 1869, with the endowment of the Demia Butler Chair, Butler's English Department anticipated developments at Harvard, where, in 1876, Francis James Child became "the first [documented] professor of English literature" (Kitzhaber 64). Before 1869, literature at Butler University—and generally elsewhere—had been ancillary to the principles of literary criticism as featured in Hugh Blair's *Lectures,* Henry Lord Kames's *Elements of Criticism,* and Alexander Bain's *English Composition and Rhetoric.* These texts interspersed biographical material with a few quotations from the actual works to demonstrate and practice critical analysis. Literature study often meant the reading of historical manuals, such as Backus Shaw's *Outlines of English Literature,* from which students memorized biographical and historical facts.

But unlike most of her contemporaries, Merrill considered the reading of actual literary works crucial to a liberal education (Kitzhaber cites Professor Lounsbury at Sheffield as being the first professor who insisted on the reading of entire works, 39). While students read literature in our sense of the word—fiction, poetry, and drama—on their own or in the literary societies, probably only Shakespeare was required class reading before Merrill's appointment (Short Braden 148). As the first Demia Butler Professor, Merrill was instrumental in fulfilling Butler's mission of teaching English literature, and her insistence on more literature in the upper years succeeded (Graydon 357). One student testified about the "discriminating taste for literature" Merrill's teaching instilled "in the minds of three generations" (Levering 376).

The texts Merrill selected belonged to the canon of nineteenth-century literary works thought best to model sound rhetorical principles. Students read Shakespeare's tragedies, analyzed so-called classical authors like Bacon, Milton, Johnson, and Golding, and studied Merrill's favorites, in particular personal literature such as letters, essays, and diaries.

If Merrill changed the content of literature classes, she also changed their method of instruction. Her biographer Katherine M. Graydon tells us that Merrill's introduction of the lecture system was considered a novelty and said to have influenced Andrew D. White's use of the same at Cornell University (380). Perhaps Merrill was guided by the "first American rhetoric specifically designed as a textbook" (Kitzhaber 55), Samuel P. Newman's 1830 *A Lecture on a Practical Method of Teaching Rhetoric*. It suggested teaching through the use of "familiar talking lectures" and argued for using a textbook as a tool or an outline only (4). "Familiar talking lectures," as Newman explained them, attempted a connection between a rhetorical principle and a student's experience of it. Likewise Merrill, for whom literature was a "criticism of life," saw all literary works "related to some phase of human experience" (15). This relationship, she felt, could be deepened and strengthened through talking and writing.

Just as Newman's way of lecturing was meant to unmask the "mockery of set questions" (*Lecture*, 1830, 5), Merrill's lectures, interspersed with "lively discussions," were intended to break the monotony of daily recitations. Students took careful notes and filled them out later at home as part of their composition exercises. The lectures' power often lasted long beyond a student's university years. Many former students reminisced of having kept the lecture notes, of reading them occasionally, or remembering the gracefulness of their style. The letter of a noted newspaper columnist in Indianapolis is typical: "When I wanted to do particularly well in making a dinner talk or writing an article, I reread pages of Miss Merrill's words . . . to catch the spirit of mellowness and beauty of her language" (qtd. in Graydon 381).

Harriet Noble

In 1883, Merrill retired from Butler University and returned to private life and private teaching, and Harriet Noble became the second Demia Butler Professor. Educated at Butler and Vassar, Noble was recommended by Merrill. Of Noble and a classmate, Merrill had written to a friend: "They talk delightfully because they read carefully, observe closely, penetrate into motives, weigh causes and effects, think a thought out fully and take the trouble to fit words accurately to thoughts" (qtd. in Graydon 388). In contrast to Merrill, Harriet Noble considered herself, and was considered by those who knew her, a feminist. Her rejection of societal expectations was reflected even in her outward appearance: Noble could see no redeeming quality in the fashion of her times. One of her students wrote: "In an age when small waists, many petticoats and tight shoes were restricting the average woman, Miss Noble wore made-to-order common-sense shoes and adopted a reform costume with straight lines, all the weight suspended from the shoulders" (BAQ 18, 1930: 101).

By the time of Noble's appointment, Indianapolis had changed from the frontier town of Butler's early years into a large, busy city. Having outgrown its earlier site and building, the university moved to its second location, Irvington, a "pleasant and healthful suburb . . . free from the temptations and dangers often surrounding college life" (UC 1891–92, 17). Although the old goals of "practicality and utility" still reigned at the new campus, they were now joined to the idea of "culture." Literary criticism, which in 1830 had been but one of Newman's five goals of rhetorical training (*Practical*, 1851, 4), had, over the ensuing sixty years, gradually overtaken the other four—philosophy of rhetoric, taste, language skills, and style (3–4)—and become the central focus of the educated person. The objectives of the catalogues of the 1890s years reflect the new emphasis: "Whatever man's vocation may be, he should be able to maintain literary interest for his own instruction and culture. . . . [Thus] the intention of this department is to develop in the student a knowledge and appreciation of the best in English thought" (UC 1891–92, 26). While rhetoric had directed its students outward, to benefit others, literary criticism emphasized the move inward, to benefit oneself. Butler's admission policies also demonstrated increased emphasis on literary pursuits. Under Merrill, freshmen needed to be "well-grounded in grammar and the elements of rhetoric" (UC 1876–77, 21); they studied critical appreciation of literature in the college years. Under Noble, catalogue objectives demanded the "study of both prose and poetry" and "criticisms" from the preparatory students (UC 1891–92, 26). In addition, subtle shifts occurred in the phrasing of writing assignments, now couched in elegant language with emphasis on style and cultivation of "an appreciation of their [poems'] beauties" (27).

While such developments might, as Kitzhaber discusses, have impoverished rhetoric, Noble's choice of textbooks demonstrates otherwise. In connection with a literature manual, she used Genung's *Practical Elements of*

Rhetoric and William Minto's *Manual of English Prose Literature, Biographical and Critical*. Both texts seem to counter the individualistic, introspective tendencies of the university catalogues. Genung stresses rhetoric as a practical and active art. It differs from other "contemplative" disciplines in that it is presentational, critical, and creative. For Genung, rhetoric means "skill and power," a combination that turns the student into an "originator, not a mere absorber, of thought and impulse" (*Study* 5). This practical aspect of rhetoric means that students can use rhetorical principles for the "actual construction of literature" (*Practical* xi).

Kitzhaber calls Genung's rhetoric "perhaps one of the most systematically ordered textbooks on rhetoric ever written" (65), and Noble's planned course of study, reflecting this order, seems to follow closely the one Genung outlined for Amherst College (*Study* 22–25). Noble's catalogue objectives contain many references to Genung's ideas, and her textbook, *Literary Art, A Handbook for Its Study*, shows signs of his influence. Like Genung, remembered by a student as "deeply conscious of artistic form" (Kitzhaber 65), Noble compared literature to other expressive art forms such as music or painting (14). Genung also featured the outline, which Noble called the "skeleton," prompting many jokes in Butler's *Collegian* about students' skeletons. Yet the idea of outlining did not originate with Genung. Newman mentioned "skeletons" in his discussion of style, arguing that teachers should direct a student's first efforts at writing to arrangement and to "a plan, or skeleton, stating the precise object he has in view, the divisions he proposes, etc" (*Practical*, 1851, 13).

While Genung's definition of rhetoric as creating and constructing countered the growing emphasis on stylistic appreciation, Minto's *Manual of Style*, the other textbook used by Noble, stressed the influence of purpose and audience on stylistic choices. Noble's choice of the Minto text challenges repeated claims made by Kitzhaber and his followers that rhetoric and composition instruction emphasized not purpose and audience but style for its own sake. Minto's *Manual* argues that style is not a general, solidified entity but an individual, fluid process. It offers "criticising upon a methodical plan" in order to discover the "varieties of good style." These varieties, Minto insists, depend on audience, purpose, and rhetorical principles, and "goodness or badness in style" can never "be pronounced upon without reference to the effect aimed at by the writer" (vi–ix): "Instead of aiming blindly at the acquisition of a 'good style,' the writer or speaker should first study his audience, and consider how he wishes to affect them; and then inquire how far the rhetorical precepts that he has learned will help him to accomplish his purpose" (vi–ix).

Noble contributed to her students' rhetorical growth through two seemingly contrary innovations: her system of prizes, meant to revive the interest in beautifully written essays (UC 1892–93, 36) and an emphasis on writing as an outgrowth of polite conversation. To develop conversation, Noble founded a club that met twice a month in her home for discussions of literature and current events (BAQ 4, 1915: 108). Undoubtedly, Noble was aware of the connection between conversation and writing that writers from Cicero to Emerson had stressed, a connection renewed in the 1990s by Shirley Brice Heath (195). The congenial atmosphere of friends and books that Nobel sought to promote when inviting her students into the privacy of her home could best foster Cicero's "canons for conversation," which serve equally well as "canons for writing."[3] Adaptation to context, attention to the feelings of others, and respect for one's audience—these were qualities demonstrated in abundance by the University's Demia Butler Professors. They provided a solid basis and rich nourishment for the education and growth of their students.

CONNECTING WITH STUDENTS

Ovid Butler's decision to fill the Demia Butler Chair with women professors placed most of nineteenth-century rhetorical education at Butler University in the hands of women. Before Merrill's tenure, rhetoric had consisted of lectures (given by male professors except for Merrill's first year at Butler) and rhetorical exercises supervised by the entire faculty. With the creation of the Demia Butler Chair and the establishment of an English department, rhetoricals became more and more the duty of the Demia Butler professors until, finally, under Noble, rhetorical lectures were discontinued.

Kitzhaber's narrative argues that faculty of nineteenth-century denominational colleges often consisted of untrained teachers who resisted change (6–7). Because in large schools, or those with inadequate funds, ill-trained tutors often filled in for regular composition teachers, Kitzhaber's assessment of teachers undoubtedly rings true for many institutions. During Merrill and Noble's tenure, however, the faculty of Butler University does not fit into Kitzhaber's picture. Although Merrill lacked formal schooling, both she and Noble were published writers and enthusiastic but demanding teachers, concerned with their students' intellectual and emotional growth (BC 3.5 [1888]: 93). Peers and students alike praised their excellence. A colleague described Merrill's presence on the faculty as one of the most "salutary influences" of his life (qtd. in Graydon 348), while the reminiscences of her students give proof of the exalted position she held in their minds.

Students remembered Merrill in particular for her ability to get them to talk and for her willingness to respect their opinions. "She seemed to learn from everyone," a student remembered, "because she had the tact to draw from everyone the thing he knew" (qtd. in introduction to Merrill 12–13). Noble, of sterner appearance and more demanding character, did not quite call forth the almost gushing quality of the praise heaped on Merrill, but everyone acknowledged her as a fine teacher and "helpful to her students" (BC 8, 1893: 402). In the classroom, in the literary society, and in their own homes, these woman professors motivated their students "to do their best" (qtd. in Merrill 36). Highly educated and gifted, Merrill and Noble infused their personal style into the teaching of rhetoric, literary criticism, and writing. Advocating growth, they presaged our current efforts to allow students to develop to their fullest potential. Dealing with their students in a nurturing way, Merrill and Noble were able to connect classroom teaching to the individual experiences of the men and women they taught, or in Gail Griffin's words, "relating [their subjects] to the minds and hearts of their students" (40).

The Demia Butler Chair was held by women professors until the end of the nineteenth century. Then the board of directors, coveting the prestige of a Harvard PhD, hired Will D. Howe, a Butler graduate and a newly minted doctorate, and in the new century made him and his successors Demia Butler Professor of English Literature. Only after the descendants of Ovid Butler threatened to withhold the money for the professorship did the university reinstate the original conditions of the endowment. In 1914, with the incumbency of Evelyn Butler, granddaughter of Ovid Butler and student of Harriet Noble, Butler University restored the tradition of the Demia Butler Chair.

Notes

I owe a great debt to Butler's archivist, Gisela Schlueter-Terrell, whose enthusiastic encouragement, knowledge about sources, patience with my innumerable questions, and reading of the Butler manuscript I found invaluable.

1. Nineteenth-century students received a "literary" or "liberal" education, "an education containing all knowledge—in the sense of the German *Wissenschaft*" (McLachlan "Choice," 487). Its product was the man of letters who had gone through the classical curriculum, acquired a knowledge of Latin and Greek, of higher mathematics, of rhetoric, and of the sciences and other subjects included under moral, mental, and natural philosophy. Since "liberal education was a matter of style more than it was a matter of subjects," the humanist tradition could also exist within the new courses entering colleges in the late nineteenth century: modern languages, English literature, and the fine arts (Rudolph 188).

2. Lydia Short's diary, which tells a great deal about writing instruction and women's literary societies at early Butler University, is the basis of a chapter—"Silks, Congress Gaiters, and Rhetoric: a Butler University Graduate of 1860 Tells Her Story" —in *Nineteenth-Century Women Learn to Write*, ed. Catherine Hobbs, UP Virginia, 1995.

3. Heath summarizes the canons as she found them in a September 1836 *Knickerbocker* article by an unknown author:

- adapt one's manner to the manner of the topic for conversation;
- pay close attention to evidence of the state of pleasure and satisfaction of others within the conversation;
- be sincere and show respect for those with whom one converses. (195)

Archival Sources

I use the following abbreviations for in-text citations to materials listed here:

BAQ	*Butler Alumnal Quarterly*
BC	*Butler Collegian*
BM	Minutes of the Meetings of the Board of Directors, 1855–1900
FM	Faculty, Assembly, and Committee Minutes, 1872–1900
UC	University Catalogues
UCIU	University Catalogues, Indiana University, 1874–1875.

The following items are in the Rare Books and Special Collections, Irwin Library, Butler University, Indianapolis, IN, and in the archives of Indiana University, Bloomington, IN:
Alumnal Biography B987d. 1900.
Board of Directors of the Northwestern Christian University. Ledgers, ms. 1852+.

Board of Directors of Butler University. Ledgers, ms. 1875+.

Brown, Hilton U. "In the Heyday of the Literary Society." *Butler Alumnal Quarterly* 16 (1927): 70–73.

Butler Alumnal Quarterly, 1912–1936. Ed. Katherine Merrill Graydon.

Butler Collegian. Vols. 1–15. 1886–1900.

Catalogues of Butler University. 1876–1900.

Catalogues of the Officers and Students of the North-Western Christian University, Indianapolis. 1856–1876.

Faculty, Assembly, and Committee Minutes. Ledgers, ms. 1872–1900.

Graydon, Katherine Merrill, ed. *Catherine Merrill: Life and Letters*. Greenfield, Indiana: The Mitchell Company, 1934.

King, Colin E. Diary. Ledgers, ms. 1879–1883.

Merrill Catherine. *The Man Shakespeare and Other Essays*. Indianapolis: Bowen-Merrill Company, 1900.

Minutes of the meetings of the board of directors. Ledgers, ms. 1855–1900.

Records of the boards of commissioners and letter-book. Ledgers, ms. 1850+.

Short Braden, Lydia. "Pages from a Diary." *Butler Alumnal Quarterly* 6.3 (Oct. 1917): 145–61.

University catalogues, Indiana University. 1874–1875.

Updegraff, Belle Hopkins. "Science and Poetry." Master's thesis. Butler University, 1891.

Waller, George M. "Colin Edward King." Unpublished ts. 1988.

⁓ 5 ⁓

Vida Scudder in the Classroom and in the Archives

Julie Garbus

WRITING AT WELLESLEY, 1887–1927

"A RICH GIFT of the gods was the indomitable, inspiring, never-to-be-forgotten Vida Scudder. . . . [She] made life more real and a sense of responsibility greater," one Progressive-era student rhapsodized about her favorite English professor, Wellesley College's Vida Dutton Scudder (Gilson 12–13). Another called Scudder's courses "the beginning of a new life" (Sampson 336). Yet another devotee told a friend: "When you touch [Scudder], sparks fly" (Bernard 5). Vida Scudder infuriated conservatives as consistently as she charmed students. One father fumed that he would send no more daughters to Wellesley to be inflamed by her, and Calvin Coolidge said Scudder and her ilk "turned women's colleges into hotbeds of Radicalism" (Bernard 5–6). Scudder's pedagogy stemmed in part from her activism. She wanted college

Archival materials used in this text come from the Wellesley College Archives and the Sophia Smith Collection at Smith College.

women to become agents of social change, and felt that they needed both teachable skills and increased self-confidence to do so. "Direct thinking is desperately needed among young women," she wrote. "Our job is to discredit the habit and shatter the formula, whatever it may be" (*Privilege* 87–88). Students who volunteered in the settlement houses Scudder founded could practice direct thinking and sharpen their commitment to social change. Those who took her groundbreaking "Social Ideals in English Letters" course experienced the first course in the country connecting socialist thought and literature.

My study of Scudder and her department complicated my initial assumptions about turn of the century English pedagogy—and yielded new questions as well. The first of these assumptions involved the ways scholars have characterized the "Harvard model" of composition during 1887–1927, the period when Scudder taught. Historians of composition including Albert Kitzhaber, James Berlin, and Robert Connors write that rhetoric and composition training dwindled after the turn of the century from four years of rhetorical work to a single first-year course at Harvard and colleges following the Harvard model, such as Wellesley. So I initially expected that Wellesley composition courses during the period Scudder taught would be minimal. However, I discovered that Scudder's forty-year career spanned huge changes in the composition curriculum; in the late nineteenth century, upper-level writing courses played a major role both at Harvard and at Wellesley. In addition, since Kitzhaber, Berlin, Connors, and other scholars focus on first-year composition, I was surprised to realize how much Progressive-era Wellesley students wrote after their freshman year—in upper-level composition courses, in literature classes such as Scudder's, in other departments, and in their extracurricular lives. My research showed me that scholars studying an institution's writing curriculum should not only scrutinize its first-year composition course but also its composition curricula for the other three years, its literature courses that emphasize writing or rhetorical training, and the other writing opportunities students enjoyed.

Although Vida Scudder never saw herself as a rhetoric or composition teacher, she is an apt subject to spark compositionists' interest in the rhetorical training that occurred in Progressive-era literature classrooms. James Berlin writes that the distinguishing feature of rhetoric is its concern with symbolic action in the material world, with practical consequences as an end. Poetics, on the other hand, is concerned with symbolic action for itself, with contemplation of the text for its own sake (*Rhetoric and Reality* 26). Within Berlin's taxonomy, Scudder's pedagogy as she and her students described it falls firmly into the realm of rhetoric, not poetics. First, Scudder believed in literature for use. Her most innovative course focused explicitly on social concerns, and she claimed that she always introduced social themes into her teaching. Second, Scudder wanted to mold Wellesley women into rhetors in the early nineteenth-century sense of the term: educated, moral citizens who could think independently and carefully, discern intellectual and moral truths, and articulate these truths for the good of the community. She aimed to "shake American youth out of cocksure satisfaction with our country, but only to restore deeper faith, and to suggest new avenues of chivalric service" (*Privilege* 97).

I initially assumed that since Wellesley's composition department during Scudder's teaching career followed Harvard's model, its courses featured unimaginative rhetorical principles, taught dully. According to John C. Brereton, restricting composition to the freshman year made for an unpleasant course; for Harvard freshmen "the gap between student and professor was maintained rigidly, with strict rules of behavior. . . . All students were expected to listen, to be kept under control, and to be passive learners." Composition epitomized this restrictive approach. "The composition teacher was, willingly or not, the accomplice of the authorities, or in fact the enforcer" (18). Whether or not Brereton accurately characterizes Harvard's first-year composition course or its treatment of freshmen, the atmosphere he describes bears no resemblance to the friendly ambiance at turn-of-the-century Wellesley. In a related criticism of Harvard's writing curriculum, James Berlin claims that Harvard composition professors Adams Sherman Hill and Barrett Wendell personified "a politics designed to preserve the interests of corporate capitalism and the university-trained experts who serve it" (*Writing* 189). Wellesley English professors in Scudder's day may have unwittingly aided capitalist interests, but the idea that they did so would have horrified most. Scudder would have been especially insulted by Berlin's charge.

Scudder falls into the camp of professors that Gerald Graff, in *Professing Literature*, termed generalists (as opposed to researchers). Generalists shared the belief that "great works of art and thought have a decisive part in shaping the life of a polity" (85) and an impatience with what they saw as pedantic research. Spokespeople for a missionary view of literary culture they inherited from Arnold, Ruskin, and other Victorian apostles of culture, they channeled into literature emotions that earlier in the century would have been expressed in Christianity, "investing the experience of literature with the redemptive influence their ministerial ancestors had attributed to the conversion experience" (85). Yet rather than actively striving to redeem society, Graff notes, most generalists ignored the world outside the university, hoping their ideas would trickle down to the hoi polloi.

The daughter of a Congregational missionary and niece of *Atlantic Monthly* editor Horace Scudder, Scudder lacked what she called "that dreadful PhD" (Letter to Mary Gilson) and claimed to shun research. Like other generalists, Arnold and Ruskin were her touchstones, but she read them as requiring active engagement with the world. As she wrote: "Beyond the institution, beyond the college, lies a community hungering for life. For the sake of that community the college exists" (*Privilege* 118). Although Scudder was the most socially active professor within her department, she was by no means the only one. Department chair Katherine Lee Bates cofounded the College Settlements Association with Scudder. Sophie Hart, the chair of composition during Scudder's career, was a "recognized social activist who inspired students to do something with their lives" (Palmieri 166).

The Wellesley English and composition departments during the Progressive era have received intermittent scholarly attention. John Brereton's documentary history *The Origins of Composition Studies in the American College, 1875–1925* reprints a description of the Wellesley program that Bates published in 1895 in the *Dial* magazine. Historian Patricia Palmieri, in her book-length study of Progressive-era Wellesley, *In Adamless Eden*, organizes descriptions of Wellesley's academic departments around specific teachers, not curricula. Palmieri calls composition the literature department's "handmaiden" (165) and spends two paragraphs describing its teachers, as opposed to eleven on literature (five of them about Scudder's electrifying teaching style). Graff mentions Scudder and describes the Wellesley literature curriculum in the 1890s as an example of the "coverage" model of departmental

organization: non-majors took an introductory survey course and a few elec-
tives in major periods or authors, while English majors moved chronologi-
cally from Anglo-Saxon through Victorian prose. JoAnn Campbell analyzed
one Wellesley student's freshman composition themes from 1901. She characterizes the school's composition curriculum as "not innovative" because it
was closely modeled on Harvard's English A curriculum ("Freshman [*sic*]"
115) and notes that the composition teacher's comments focused on usage.
An article I published in 2002 argues that a Wellesley student who took Scudder's courses and worked in a settlement house would have had an experience
much like contemporary service-learning ("Service-Learning, 1902").

Because Wellesley was an all-women's college with no male full-time
faculty, its institutional style and educational mission differed greatly from
men's or coeducational universities. The school was small: 146 students graduated in 1898 and 131 in 1899, for example (Palmieri 33). Closeness between
faculty and students made for an intellectually exciting, intimate atmosphere
during the first half of Scudder's career. Many professors shared dormitory
space, ate, and socialized with students. These students, the second generation
of college women, looked up to their first-generation women professors as
mentors, friends, and idols. "I was a Wellesley girl in the days of 'personal influence'" reminisced one student years later (Palmieri 169). In 1901 Scudder
wrote that a professor at a women's college has "the opportunity to influence
students and appreciates the opportunity that her position gives her" (Letter
to Jeanette Marks).

Unlike men's colleges, Wellesley did not explicitly prepare students for
careers, since women were barred from most established professions. Instead,
according to a Progressive-era alumna who became a settlement worker, it
trained women "for some kind of service" (Hurwitz 221). Most turn-of-the-
century Wellesley students expected that their service would take the form
of elementary or secondary school teaching. Some would marry and stay
home with the children. Others would be pressed into service taking care
of aging relatives: "the family claim." A few would become college professors or doctors.

Literature and composition had different chairs, but composition was a
subdiscipline within the English department, with Bates ultimately supervis-

ing Hart. Literature was more prestigious than composition from Wellesley's 1875 opening. As the English department's 1900 course catalogue put it: "The founders of Wellesley College . . . laid special emphasis upon the work in English. The subjects of Rhetoric and Elocution were relegated to distinct Departments." Katherine Lee Bates's report for the *Dial* called composition and rhetoric a "candidate" for a separate department and lamented entering freshmen's low level of writing ability, mentioning the "grievously inadequate" writing training in secondary schools (qtd. in Brereton 184). Wellesley's freshmen, she wrote, spent their first year of composition learning to write "clear, correct, well-constructed English sentences." In fact, she dryly noted, "[t]o have mastered the paragraph is to become, so far as the Rhetoric department is concerned, a Sophomore" (184).

Although the composition division lacked literature's prestige, its pre-1900 curriculum gave students practice in writing in different genres and for different audiences, and encouraged their development as independent thinkers and public citizens. In her study of upper-division writing in women's colleges, Katherine Adams writes that Hart asked students to probe their own experiences and critically evaluate their own experiences and values (46). Teachers held face-to-face conferences with students; first-year composition teachers "held regular appointments with the students for closer review of papers presented, and this contact between the instructor and the individual has been a highly valuable accessory to the work of the year" (Wellesley, *President's Report*, 1893). In 1909, the composition department reported, "A large part of the effectiveness of the work in English depends upon individual criticism from the instructor." Literature professors held office hours too, but their departmental reports never mention the importance of face-to-face conferences and individual criticism.

Until the first decade of the twentieth century, Wellesley's composition sequence spanned all four years. Sophie Hart, composition chair, had trained at Radcliffe with Barrett Wendell and George Pierce Baker. Hart's 1894–1895 curriculum began with a full-year course, "The Elements and Qualities of Style," based on Wendell's sophomore half-year course at Harvard and using his English composition textbook. The course included lectures on "certain English authors" and weekly themes first semester, and "critical work in literature" and biweekly themes in the second semester. It stressed description, narration, and criticism (*President's Report*, 1895). As in Wendell's program, personal themes, corrected by the instructor, were a vital part of the Wellesley course. Unlike Harvard students, though, Wellesley freshmen could select topics relating to their present circumstances (J. Campbell, "Freshman [*sic*]" 115). Ruth Bradford, the student whose themes Campbell studied, sometimes wrote about her high school years, but most of her themes anatomized her own experiences as a freshman: "Some Reasons why I am glad I came to College," "A Few things college girls should avoid" (slang, bragging), "Some Reasons why it is good for a girl to go to a distant college," "The Difficulties of a Freshman in Concentrating her mind upon College Work, as told by a Student's Clock," and "The Thing That I Can Do Best" (dust).

The rest of the writing curriculum was more varied and innovative. Once a student became a sophomore, her writing opportunities multiplied. In sophomore rhetoric students analyzed and wrote essays, drawing subjects from fields of study of their own interest. They were given a "slight opportunity" for "experiments in storytelling." In the second semester, they could take journalism and write for the *Wellesley Magazine* or report on college life for "newspapers the Union over" (Bates, qtd. in Brereton 184).

Juniors took a mandatory full-year argumentation course, known as forensics, taught by George Pierce Baker and based on his half-year course for Harvard juniors and accompanying textbook. It included lectures on argument, three briefs and three arguments, weekly debates, and criticism of the speakers (*Course Catalogue*, 1893). Kitzhaber describes Baker's *Principles of Argumentation* as "a massive work, heavily logical, and extremely careful in making minute discriminations" and "heavy and formal, presenting to the student at the outset all the mechanisms of logic in systematic array" (133). Wellesley students hated the course enough to invent a ritual called "forensic burning." Student Arlene Cohen described how, at the end of the first year that the course was required, the class of 1894 "in wrath publicly burned their forensics in the west woods. '95 buried theirs . . . and '96 made doubly sure by doing both . . . After the deed was accomplished, juniors would don white hooded robes and, in a serpentine fashion, slowly march around campus, their candles flickering, as they chanted the Latin dirge."

The required senior year rhetoric course in 1892–1893 was a writing across the curriculum class, consisting of criticism of essays presented in other departments and individual conferences instead of class meetings. The rationale for this method was explained: "As senior courses are widely elective, it follows that the student's efforts in composition have been mainly in the fields which appeal most strongly to her taste and bring out her best powers. It is believed that in this way training in composition becomes peculiarly serious and effective. Moreover, this interrelation of departments is in every way salutary" (*President's Report*, 1893). For example, students of economics professor Emily Greene Balch produced case studies of the neighborhood around Denison House, a settlement house Balch and Scudder cofounded. Each student wrote a final paper describing the area from personal observation, together with a "social map" showing community social centers like schools, churches, bars, and settlement houses. Outside of class, extracurricular literary activities thrived. In the 1880s, literary groups included a Shakespeare Society and clubs devoted to the study of Browning and Dickens. Members of two other literary societies, Zeta Alpha and Phi Sigma, discussed themes like Transcendentalism, Evolution, Higher Education of Women, and Darwinism "for recreation" (Palmieri 183). In 1888, the student newspaper, the *Courant*, began publication, with English department chair Katharine Lee Bates as editor. It published alumnae reports and recorded the activities of the Shakespeare Society, Christian Association, Temperance Association, and women's rights and Indian rights organizations. Liberal faculty members like Scudder often contributed to the paper (38). Scudder also belonged to the Scribbler's Club, a faculty-student group organized by the composition department's Laura Lockwood, where students could "discuss practical writing problems with 'honest-to goodness' professionals" (Hurwitz 230).

Both Harvard and Wellesley's composition department requirements dwindled during the Progressive era. At Harvard, upper-level writing courses evaporated by 1910 (Brereton 12). In 1894, Wellesley dropped its required senior course. After that, seniors could elect an advanced argumentation course with Baker or a daily theme course to "quicken observation" and practice writing about personal experience—a more popular alternative (Brereton 185). The mandatory junior forensics course ended in 1905. In 1915, mandatory sophomore composition came to an end, making freshman composition the only required course.

Besides following Harvard's lead, Hart may have cut composition courses because her program faced problems akin to those of today. Composition teachers' course loads were higher than elsewhere on campus; in 1923–1924, freshman instructors carried a seventeen- or eighteen-hour course load, including nine hours of teaching and nine of conference (*President's Report*, 1924). (In contrast, Scudder generally taught nine hours a semester, without mandatory conference hours. The number of students she taught per semester varied from a low of 11 in 1905–1906 to a high of 174 in 1910. And, because she could afford to, she took semesters or whole years off when she faced burnout.) Hart consistently pled for more instructors, urging "an increase in the time given to the reading and discussion of themes in class . . . students should . . . be taught to rewrite from 60 to 75 percent of their themes. . . . The greatest need in college instruction . . . is a larger teaching staff" (qtd. in Brereton 289). In 1909 the department complained of crowded conditions: "This year there have been ten instructors in the department of English Composition holding office hours in ends of corridors and in corners of rooms where there was nothing like proper privacy, so that neither the instructor nor student could feel at ease" (*President's Report*, 1909). A composition department report from 1897 hints that composition courses bored students: "The experience of many colleges proves that it is peculiarly difficult to find a teacher who can make these subjects at once interesting and thoroughly advantageous to young minds." Meanwhile composition teachers were swamped by requests from other departments who wanted to turn all poor writers over "to the Rhetoric Department for reformation. Unfortunately," the chair of English reported dryly, the instructors "are themselves mortal, and have thus far been unable to accede" (Bates qtd. in Brereton 185). Composition department pay was low and turnover high. In 1911 Hart wrote: "I look forward to the day when our required courses can be taught by really competent, highly paid instructors, instead of cheap and new recruits" (Letter to Bertha Hazard).

At the same time as the composition department cut its requirements and struggled to interest students, literature courses were the most popular on campus. Students praised other literature professors with the same effusive language they lavished on Scudder. Bates's students willingly stayed four or five hours instead of the required three in her Elizabethan seminar (Palmieri 162–63). Jeannette Marks, a Scudder protégé who became a Mount Holyoke professor, recalled that studying with Wellesley literature professors showed her "what it is to be a student and to love learning somewhat as the ancient Greeks must have loved it." Another student called Wellesley literature courses "an experience of challenging value for life" (Palmieri 164–65). In Scudder's courses, literature students wrote copiously. Student course notes from Scudder's Victorian Prose course, for instance, mention one ten-to-fifteen page paper (handwritten) the first semester and two the second, due six weeks apart, as well as a short "special topic" and a midterm and final with essay questions. Scudder listed possible paper topics. Many involve comparisons between writers, studies of how they influenced each other, or discussions of one author's work in the light of ideas presented in another. Others concern how historical trends affected literature or focused on historical subjects such as Latin hymns, various saints, or medieval costume in literature. None require close reading of particular textual passages, though a few involve examining a writer's particular style. I found three paper assignments that required explicitly creative writing. Victorian Prose students could "Write a symposium —set different characters to discussing Arnold's works by characters in Eliot's different books." A student in the Arthurian Romance seminar wrote an adventure in the style of Malory. And Scudder often mentioned her students' "writing their own Utopias" at the end of her Social Ideals in English Letters course.

Scudder apparently preferred essay exams to short-answer ones. Early in her career, she asked her chair for permission to assign a paper as a final: "I think that a thesis on some moderately broad subject would enable one to gauge the penetrative and critical power of the writer far more accurately than would the off-hand answers to half a dozen questions" (Letter to Hodgkins). The chair denied her request. Though she never asked again, her exams often employed the same method: "What are the points of contact between prose and poetry? Deduce from your conclusions a definition of literature" (Midyear Examination: Literature Five, 1892) and "Do you prefer the Perceval or the Galahad type of Grail-Quester? Why?" (Midyear Examination: Literature Twenty-One, 1910). In 1899 the midterm consisted of one question: "What new elements have the English poets of the nineteenth century brought to the poetic interpretation of life?"

In Social Ideals in English Letters, which Graff calls the first socialism and literature course in the country (83), Scudder merged topics considered the province of the social scientists with her own humanist and socialist orientation. Firmly Progressive in its conviction that the world was improving, the course traced "the imaginative expression of . . . the long struggle by which democracy and freedom are slowly realizing themselves, and the earth is becoming . . . the heritage of all the children of men." Scudder explicitly linked textual study with social action, pointing to "the special responsibility borne by our generation towards [the long struggle's] solution" (*Social* 1). Students read "Piers Plowman," More's *Utopia*, Swift, poems by Blake and other Romantic poets, Carlyle's *Sartor Resartus*, some Dickens and Thackeray, Eliot's *Middlemarch*, Matthew Arnold's essays, Ruskin's *Unto This Last*, some Walt Whitman, and the Fabian Essays. They discussed: "the ever-changing conception of liberty . . . the rise of democracy . . . the recurrent question concerning the right to private property . . . luxury versus the simple life . . . the eternal puzzle as to what luxury is. The ethics of War; the status of Woman; the relation of Christianity to social progress; the rise of compassion as a motive force; incentives-profit or other- to industrial energy; ideals of a perfect state . . . and more" (Scudder, Alumnae Reading List). Scudder referred to the Social Ideals course as "the permanent link between my social concern and my love of letters; I think most people left my classroom both more alive to the future and more sensitively conscious of the past than when they went in" (*On Journey* 128). Students agreed. In 1970, one woman reminisced that after sixty-three years the "breathlessly exciting" Social Ideals course remained "one of the most important experiences in a long and eventful life. She made us aware that idealism would not excuse shoddiness of expression and literary facility would remain an unused tool without it" (qtd. in Corcoran 27–28).

After World War I, however, Scudder's job became less gratifying. By 1918 a large generation gap had developed between faculty at women's colleges and their students, whose styles, opportunities, and concerns differed greatly from those of earlier classes. Students no longer looked up to their professors in the same way, and faculty felt betrayed and anachronistic. Paradoxically, students' changes in attitude stemmed in part from women's emergence into the public sphere in response to the urgings of Scudder and other activist women. Careers began opening up for women that did not involve settlements or other forms of humanitarian work; women moved away from Victorian "service" ideals and developed more social-scientific ways of seeing the world. Scudder's worldview and style began to seem old-fashioned as realism and modernism displaced Victorian idealism and effusiveness. Furthermore, Wellesley's administration had turned less tolerant. Scudder was nearly fired for giving a fairly mild speech at the Lawrence Textile Strike in 1912. Department chair Bates, Scudder's old friend, blocked her from teaching Social Ideals for several years afterward. To Scudder's horror, her friend Emily Greene Balch lost her professorship because of her pacifist stance regarding World War I. Scudder called the period from the end of World War I to her 1927 retirement the "ten exhausted years," recalling: "It was not easy to watch the surging flood of disillusion which threatened to submerge the idealism and drown the hopes of the world" (*On Journey* 300).

The vast shift in worldview between the Victorian and modern eras contributed to the downsizing and devaluing of college composition. The era shift between Victorianism and modernism also led Scudder to censor her own past—making archival research about her more difficult.

"MY OWN SECRET METHODS"

In historical scholarship on composition, even scholars who candidly disclose "the location of the teller, the impetus of her investigation, and her vested interest in the tale" (qtd. in Sharer 2) tend not to discuss their own research processes. Our methodologies remain our secret. That is understandable. I want my conclusions to look solid, well-supported. Yet as I worked, I felt torn between wanting to craft a compelling argument for Scudder's importance and uniqueness and wanting to map the messy complexities of the existing record as accurately as possible. Lack of time and money—perennial problems for academics, I suspect—complicated matters, too. Perhaps we need to begin discussing the process and complexities of archival research more openly.

In developing my claims about Scudder's teaching, I did not solely rely on the post-retirement recollections of a woman adept at using words to craft her public image. Many students, too, said that Scudder was an extraordinary, life-changing teacher who sensitized them to social issues. Yet I was disappointed that surviving documents from Scudder's actual classes do not match her own description of her teaching. This mismatch is alluded to in Scudder's work. After her retirement, she coyly wrote: "I had my own secret methods . . . to set young minds free from convention and orthodoxy" (*Privilege* 87). She briefly mentioned several of her teaching techniques but provided little detail. And she made tracing her "secret methods" harder by destroying many of her papers, including records of her teaching career. Although Scudder taught at Wellesley for forty years, the archivists and I could only find syllabi for several courses, three students' course notes, and one student paper on which she had commented.

Scudder said she had one teaching maxim: "Never ask a question that can be answered by yes or no" (*On Journey* 121). She recalled that she often began each course by collecting written statements about what students wanted to discuss. A typical year's questions included: "How remove the stigma attached to the word 'Labor'?" "How meet the problems of racial antagonisms in America?" "Relation of the college girl to the working girl." "In the light of human nature, can we hope for the perfect state?" and other weighty matters (*Privilege* 104–5). The class discussed its chosen issues throughout the year while she herself often withheld her own views; at year's end the group "tried to ascertain what has happened in our thinking" (90). However, the three sets of available course notes contain few questions. The ones that appear encourage extended discussion, but do not concern social issues, and were generated by Scudder, not the students: "Would you rather live in London of Pickwick Papers or New York today?" (Perrin) "Is Malory fatalistic or romantic?" (Abbe).

Another disparity concerns whether Scudder lectured or conducted discussions. In contrast to the usual Progressive-era class emphasis on lecture or recitation from memory, Scudder wrote that she preferred discussion and tried to keep a ratio of two parts discussion to one part lecture. Yet the three sets of student notes in the archives suggest that she lectured almost nonstop in those courses. Perhaps the disparity relates to class size: Scudder wrote that in large classes, discussion "went perforce by the board" (*On Journey* 121). Two of these three were large courses: a fifty-five student Victorian Prose course and a forty-eight student Arthurian Romance course. The other course, Literature Ten, had only thirteen students, but its fast pace probably lent itself to lecture instead of discussion. Scudder said of this course: "We 'rode a wallop,' like Malory's knights through English civilization . . . I ran that course with a firm hand" (*On Journey* 124–25).

Unfortunately, these three sets of notes include none of the "deft digressions" one student (whose course notes have not been preserved) remembered jotting in the back of her notebook (Sampson 336). Nor do they record the "breathtaking transitions" another student recalled, when Scudder would "suddenly speed from Giotto's tower to the sufferings of the poor" (Gilson 12–13). Occasional references to personal opinions of "Miss S" appear, but they always refer to the authors studied. Most of the student notes record biographical information about the authors and generalizations about historical periods and the authors' texts and personalities. Did these particular students doggedly remain on topic and resist recording interesting digressions, or did Scudder teach these classes more linearly than she taught others? I do not have enough documents to tell.

Unlike most people, Scudder knew that scholars might scrutinize her leavings. By the time she was in her eighties, archivists from Wellesley and from Smith, her alma mater, had expressed interest in her papers. She replied politely but sent no documents. In 1945 she wrote the Smith archivist: "I've been planning to dedicate next winter to clearing out my Past! Boxes on boxes of College lectures and syllabi. (Luckily there's a hearth fire in my study)" (Letter to Miss Grierson, July 15, 1945). Three years later, she told the Wellesley archivist, using the same words as before, "I am dedicating this season to clearing out my Past" (Letter to Whiting); in 1951, the year she died, she reported to the Smith archivist: "I don't think I have much left which is worthwhile" (Letter to Miss Grierson, March 30, 1951).

Perhaps Scudder consigned her academic past to the fire because she herself had "little interest in Education in the abstract" (*Privilege* 80). Instead of viewing her academics and her activism as intertwined and inseparable, she saw them as in conflict. She wrote of her life: "I was perpetually drawn in three directions at once, and racked in consequence." Academia, "the calm college world," provided her salary. But she valued her second direction more, "the tumultuous world of social reform": founding and working in settlements, organizing progressive church and labor groups, and giving speeches and articles exhorting audiences to work for social justice (*On Journey* 175). Scudder believed that the multidirectional nature of her life would consign her to future obscurity. As she once wrote to Bates: "I will work for my own generation; I will help the immediate need; I will abandon dreams of work that shall endure. . . . There must be people for their decade, as well as people for all time" (qtd. in Corcoran 1). Since she did not highly value the academic portion of her life, did not see its connection to her social reform activities, and did not think she would achieve fame beyond her lifetime, she might have felt that no one else would—or should—be interested in her old lectures and syllabi. In addition, Scudder's difficulties after her Lawrence Textile Strike might have prompted self-censorship. Scudder had joined the Socialist Party in 1912 and remained a member. She destroyed her papers in 1951, during a wave of national anticommunism and intolerance that must have reminded her of what she and her colleagues faced after World War I.

Changing attitudes about sexuality during Scudder's lifetime probably led Scudder to destroy certain papers, too. Like other activists whose lives spanned the Victorian and modern eras, such as Jane Addams, M. Carey Thomas, and Miriam Van Waters, Scudder never married and maintained close, romantically-tinged friendships with other women. Such relationships were accepted in the late nineteenth century but excoriated as pathological by the mid-twentieth. It is little wonder that personal letters between these women and their intimate friends have often disappeared.

Eighteen- to twenty-two-year-old students can be inconsistent record keepers; most students eventually throw away what course notes they have taken, not valuing them and assuming no one else would be interested either. As scholars who are interested in such documents, we need to try to preserve existing records, make others aware that they might be important, and make use of existing archival materials at our own institutions. Yet no professor wants her office stuffed with student papers from days of yore—and university archivists may shun them as well.

Scholars researching other activist academics may discover similar issues. Activist academics, ambivalent about their "ivory tower" careers, might not value the material they see as "academic" as highly as that they see as contributing to social change. They also might destroy their most radical or controversial documents. Adept rhetors like Scudder might be particularly canny about shaping and controlling the written representations of themselves that future scholars will peruse. And because neither colleges nor students seem to give college composition high priority—in the Progressive era as now—overworked instructors and uninterested students may throw away reams of interesting documents.

The archival records that remain can be familiar and sad, as in Hart's pleas for more experienced instructors and more money for composition. Even Scudder, though she fought to eliminate class distinctions and to foster positive attitudes toward immigrants often sounded classist and racist. No constructivist, Scudder never realized how thoroughly her own habitus informed her convictions about "reality" and "truth." In her classroom she never taught close reading and never pointed to the text to support her vast generalizations.

Yet Scudder, a product of her time and place, exercised admirable rhetorical savvy in controlling future representations of herself. And the difficulties that historiographers of rhetoric and composition have in tracing our discipline's past both point to our field's unjustified recent obscurity and pose worthwhile and fascinating challenges.

Note

I thank Wilma Slaight and Jean Berry, Wellesley College archivists, for their helpfulness and their astounding knowledge of Wellesley's history.

Archival Sources

The following items are in the Wellesley College Archives, Wellesley, MA:
Abbe, Hannah Tilton. "The Adventure." English Literature 21 paper, ms.
———. Class notes, Literature 21. Notebook, ts.
Cohen, Arlene. "Wellesley College Rituals." Unpublished paper, ts.

Hart, Sophie. Letter to Bertha Hazard. n.d., 1911.

Perrin, Edith Midwood. Class notes for Literature Six. Notebook, ts. Spring 1910.

Sampson, Harriet. "Vida D. Scudder." *Wellesley Alumnae Magazine*. August 1927: 336–38.

Scudder, Vida Dutton. "Alumnae Reading List," ts.

———. Letter to Mary Gilson. January 14, 1926.

———. Letter to Louise Manning Hodgkins. n.d.

———. Letter to Jeanette Marks. February 4, 1901.

———. Letter to Miss Whiting. April 8, 1948.

Wellesley College Department of English Literature. *Course Catalog*, 1893.

———. Midyear Examination: Literature Five. 1892.

———. Midyear Examination: Literature Twenty-One. 1910.

———. *President's Report*. 1893.

———. *President's Report*. 1895.

———. *President's Report*. 1897.

———. *President's Report*. 1909.

———. *President's Report*. 1924.

The following items are in the Sophia Smith Collection, Smith College, Northampton, MA:

Scudder, Vida Dutton. Letter to Miss Grierson. July 15, 1945.

———. Letter to Miss Grierson. March 30, 1951.

_⁓ᖕ 6 ᖖ⁓_

Mid-Nineteenth-Century Writing Instruction at Illinois State Normal University

CREDENTIALS, CORRECTNESS, AND THE RISE
OF A TEACHING CLASS

Kenneth Lindblom, William Banks, and Risë Quay

IN JULY 1857, Charles Hovey, founding principal of Illinois State Normal University (ISNU) and editor of the *Illinois Teacher*, explained that the term "normal" derived "from the Latin word originally being a 'square' or rule used by carpenters; as applied to schools, it means a pattern, model or example" (qtd. in Marshall 19, note 47). This analogy illustrates that the idea of "normal" as conceived in "normal schools" is a prescriptive normal. A normal school seeks to norm knowledge, the teachers of that knowledge, and the methods by which those teachers will teach that knowledge.

This prescriptive mission poses an alternative to Kathryn Fitzgerald's suggestion that contemporary composition's democratic impulses may "have precedent in the normal schools" (225). In her groundbreaking study, "A Re-

The archival materials referred to in this chapter may be found in the Illinois State University Archives, located in Williams Hall. We also cite several histories of Illinois State University, many of which may now be found online.

discovered Tradition: European Pedagogy and Composition in Nineteenth-Century Midwestern Normal Schools," Fitzgerald claims that "normal schools were established in a completely different social and educational environment from the elite schools on which historians have primarily focused so far" (225–26). For example, "normal schools were intended to be inclusive, democratic institutions" that operated according to "a unique normal school ethos" (244). Fitzgerald uses materials from several nineteenth- and early twentieth-century midwestern normal schools to argue that the normal school context may have given rise to attitudes that are "more compatible with composition's contemporary ethic" than the attitudes prevalent at northeastern research universities (226). Of particular interest are Fitzgerald's claims about normal school professors' views of "the linguistic competence" of their students. At elite, northeastern institutions, "Students held in first-year composition became convinced that their linguistic roughness disqualified them from serious public participation" (225). In midwestern normals, Fitzgerald finds pedagogical theory that may have improved students' sense of linguistic competence, thus allowing them to develop a stronger sense of self and right to participate in public forums.

Our findings in the Illinois State Normal University archives tell a far less affirming tale. While the pedagogical theories written by one professor of composition, Albert Stetson, largely confirm Fitzgerald's findings in Wisconsin normal schools, we have also examined a series of about twenty letters written by one of his students, Abbie Ripley Reynolds, and several more letters from a second student, Abbie's brother John Reynolds. The siblings' epistolary reflections on their coursework and expressed attitudes about writing suggest that the results of ISNU normal school pedagogy largely reproduced the elitist attitudes about grammar and composition prominent at northeastern academies. While focusing on one collection of student letters presents myriad interpretive problems, nevertheless, we believe these letters make a significant contribution. Stetson's writing and his students' letters, when contextualized within officialized accounts and other historical examinations of ISNU pedagogy, are strong enough to suggest more than just that "a unique normal school ethos" operated at ISNU. We believe the "normal school ethos" operating at ISNU may have created an antidemocratic educational movement wherein teachers were produced from the working class and those teachers would go on to set themselves against the children of the working class. These findings do not place ISNU in the mold of midwestern normal schools that Fitzgerald describes, but rather evidence at ISNU suggests another disheartening institutional co-optation of democratic sentiments.

ILLINOIS STATE Normal University was founded in 1857 to provide teachers for the rural areas of central Illinois. As such, ISNU served a function—providing credentials—that became common in many professions in the nineteenth century as the middle class emerged and upward mobility became socially desirable (Halloran, Clark and Halloran). The qualifications produced by normals had to have meaning; therefore it was important for a recognizable distinction to be made between the "credentialed" and the "uncredentialed" teacher. However, the elite attitudes prominent at aristocratic, northeastern academies were unpopular in the Midwest, and so the "credentialed teacher" could not simply be an imported aristocrat, but must be "cultivated" from the untamed territory of the Midwest. At ISNU, this set of difficult circumstances led to a militaristic pedagogical approach, which justified the imposition of rules that could be easily taught, assessed, and demonstrated to the public. This approach, buoyed in popularity by the contemporaneous Civil War, which made patriotic militarism attractive to the nonaristocratic members of the ISNU community, was not apparently elitist, nor exclusive to elite, northeastern academies. It left upon the students such an apparent set of behaviors that it created a very visible distinction between the "credentialed" and the "uncredentialed" teacher and created an atmosphere of rigor, which could be made a point of pride for the school, and which could withstand scrutiny from all sides. Such an approach coincided very well with belletristic assumptions connecting morality and "correctness," which several ISNU professors would have been familiar with from their work in northeastern universities.

This militaristic, rule-bound atmosphere of ISNU was successful in the larger cultural context of U.S. education because it did not challenge social boundaries; in fact, it very effectively reified those boundaries. For all of the democratic potential of the pedagogical theories emerging from normal schools (including some very influential theories from ISNU), the militaristic attitudes and the corresponding over-valuation of "correctness" indirectly taught midwestern working-class students that they were not really worthy of the status of teacher until they were "recultivated" morally and intellectually. Once ISNU students were taught to hold themselves and their future students to rigorous—but largely artificial—standards of decorum, morality and behavior, only then were they ready to be credentialed as teachers for the untamed prairie. We call this recultivation, and the social control it engendered, the rise of a "teaching class." The teaching class, a cadre of credentialed professionals, was made up primarily of working-class students who learned to self-correct and self-censor. Because they were teachers, they also reproduced these behaviors among others of their class origin, increasing their influence exponentially.

Our interpretations of ISNU's pedagogical work provide an alternative to Fitzgerald's suggestion that nineteenth-century midwestern normal schools may have set precedent for contemporary composition's democratic inclinations. In fact, we might argue that the normal school ethos we found set a precedent for the *problems* raised in many writing classrooms today. Often couched in liberatory, democratic intentions, some contemporary writing teachers' overemphasis of surface correctness unwittingly reifies social boundaries ever more effectively as they rationalize their pedagogy as an attempt to do the opposite.[1] Similarly, normal school professors of writing in the mid-nineteenth century may have been trapped in a spiral of social, political, and intellectual forces that encouraged them to feel radical while they reified the very boundaries they appeared to be breaking down.

ARCHIVAL MATERIALS AND THEIR LIMITATIONS

Albert Stetson, instructor of language at ISNU, wrote two essays—entitled "Grammar" and "Spelling"—for a Teachers' Institute held at ISNU for the first time in 1867 and for many years thereafter. Both illustrate a theoretical consistency with documents Fitzgerald reports on from the Milwaukee Normal School in 1900. Such officialized school documents, however, do not tell the complete story; Fitzgerald claims, and we agree, that "[a]s historians, we need to search for more direct access to teachers' thinking and to classroom practices" (244). About twenty letters written home by Abbie Ripley Reynolds, who graduated from ISNU in 1863 (she attended for one year while Stetson was instructor of Language), and John Reynolds, who attended ISNU at about the same time but never graduated, serve as triangulating data that evidences the disturbing results of Stetson's pedagogy.[2]

Lucille Schultz has pointed out that letter-writing in nineteenth-century America can be viewed not only as a form of cultural capital (that is, as a marker of the educated classes), but also can reveal the expression of "resistance to culturally imposed codes" ("Letter-Writing" 123). The letters of Abbie and John Reynolds, obviously not written to be viewed by their teachers, reveal not only useful information about their context and background but also their views of the education they are undergoing. Of course, no teacher's pedagogical depth can be accurately characterized by the representations of one or two students. Moreover, Abbie and John Reynolds had their parents as an audience and may have had rhetorical purposes that would limit the letters' usefulness as accurate descriptions of the pedagogical practices they were experiencing. That is, it may not be entirely out of the realm of possibility that Abbie and John Reynolds might have exaggerated their experiences to gain sympathy from their parents. Still, the siblings' letters are sufficiently detailed and internally consistent, and they confirm the official accounts of ISNU with enough frequency, that we should not dismiss them.

We took on this history as writing teachers first and as archival historians second. Our primary agenda is to fuel productive discussion of the work of teaching writing and, more specifically, of producing effective writing teachers. We offer our findings with that primary agenda on the record. In order to contextualize the letters by Abbie and John Reynolds and Professor Stetson's pedagogical essays in the broader educational atmosphere of Illinois State Normal University, we rely heavily on histories of the institution written in 1892 (Cook and McHugh), 1907 (Manchester et. al), 1935 (C. Harper), 1956 (Marshall), and on an especially relevant history written in 1995 by Sandra Harmon. As these histories demonstrate, institutional support of professional credentialization, militaristic rigor, and a fixation on correctness dominated the educational experience at ISNU.[3]

LINGUISTIC COMPETENCE

Albert Stetson was the first teacher of rhetoric and composition at Illinois State Normal University to stay for more than a few years. Stetson was a graduate of the Normal School course at Bridgewater State Normal School (1852–53), a teacher at Antioch under President Horace Mann (1853–1858), and a recipient of a master's degree from Harvard (1862) (Manchester et. al. 101). Hired as Instructor of Language at ISNU in 1862, Stetson was the principal leader in composition for the next twenty-five years. He replaced Leander Potter, who with several other teachers and the university's principal, left to fight in the Civil War. The other writing teacher to precede Stetson was Margaret Osband, instructress of grammar and drawing, who taught at ISNU for only three years. She resigned in 1864 upon her marriage to Albert Stetson.

Stetson begins his treatise on grammar with a dictionary definition of the word, defining grammar as "the normal or right use of language" ("Grammar" 103), a construction that conflates the terms "normal" and "right"— echoing the similar conflation of taste and morality that occurs generally in nineteenth-century rhetoric. Nan Johnson and others have demonstrated how the imposition of proper norms (often characterized as "taste") operated according to belletristic rhetorical assumptions of the eighteenth century and connected with a sense of morality. One of the major assumptions of this form of rhetoric was "the assumption that the cultivation of taste through the study of rhetoric is synonymous with the development of intellectual virtue and moral character" (*Nineteenth-Century* 76).

The philosophical position implied in Stetson's opening is made much more clearly a little later in his essay:

> All must have observed that children bred in families where they are accustomed from infancy to hear their mother tongue used only with grammatical propriety, acquire instinctively, as it were, and without conscious effort, the power of correct expression. The use of language is a habit acquired like other habits, by imitation and the unconscious tuition of circumstances. The slang of the newsboy is the vernacular of his class. If a man be known by the company he keeps, the company he keeps is not less clearly shown by his language. Now, since the children of cultivated parents alone can enjoy the domestic training so valuable in fixing at the

start those matters which will not afterwards require to be *unlearned,*
what is the best thing for the teacher to do? (103–4)

It is possible to interpret Stetson's stance as positively as Fitzgerald reads
normal school pedagogy generally. He indicates that grammar is a habit resulting from class training. And, in describing the reasons for students' grammatical errors, he does not use words like "stupidity, laziness, or moral
turpitude," as Fitzgerald reminds us that professors at elite eastern institutions
often did (234). She claims that for normal school teachers, "students' errors
are the natural outcome of a combination of inadequate teaching and incomplete learning—an explanation worthy of Mina Shaughnessy" (235). But Stetson's ease with static notions of "grammatical propriety," "correct expression,"
"cultivated parents," and the need for "fixing" and "unlearn[ing]" reveal underlying assumptions that impede more democratic interpretation.

For Stetson, despite the fact that grammar is a set of habits, there are
some habits that are normal and right and then there are the inept habits of
the working-class vernacular. The effects of such an approach to language
teaching is revealed by the frustration expressed by Abbie Reynolds, who
writes to her brother after several terms at ISNU: "[M]y letters are always
such a source of rebuke, and mortification to me that I feel discouraged and
at the same time ashamed that I cannot write better. It seems as if I was *improving backwards,* all the time and as if I could never say what I wished to"
(letter undated, emphasis is ours).[4]

Reynolds's phrase "improving backwards" is so remarkably similar to
Stetson's pedagogical dictum that working-class "habits" must be "unlearned,"
that it indicates a theoretical consistency. Far from having her sense of linguistic competence affirmed, Reynolds's linguistic confidence is wounded. And
the wounds come remarkably quickly. In a letter she writes home during her
first month at ISNU, Reynolds says, ". . . I am sure I shall try to improve, for
I deeply feel any need for it. During the few days I have been here, I have entirely lost what little self conceit I had when I left home" (9/19/1860). A few
weeks later she writes, "I guess you think my writing lessons have not done
me much good, the fact is I always write in such a hurry, and seem to take so
little interest in it . . . , that I have not improved much I am afraid, but I must
try to be more particular" (10/26/1860).

Acknowledging that normals work most often with students from "uncultivated" parents, Stetson recommends that the students be encouraged to see the need for grammatical correctness in their own written language, which, "if kindly and persistently followed, will stimulate a curiosity which the scientific pursuit of Grammar will further gratify. Hence the beginner will study with relish and not with ill-concealed disgust" ("Grammar" 104). For example, Stetson suggests having students look out a window and describe all they see in their own words, and then asking them questions about their own writing, until they understand the need for precise grammar. The success of Stetson's "kindly" pedagogy is suspect if Reynolds's experience is at all representative.

Even if we were inclined to read Stetson's grammar pedagogy in a democratic and contemporary fashion, Stetson's unqualified contempt for poor spelling is startlingly clear: "It is safe to say that no subject of school study demands more attention in the schools of Illinois to-day than Spelling, and the true teacher, recognizing this fact, will leave no means untried to correct an almost universal evil ("Spelling" 113). This language is significant and foreboding. His easy connection of alternative spellings and evil is surprising if we are to understand his view of grammatical habit as balanced and democratic. There appears to be an important inconsistency here. Working-class children learn their grammatical habits from "uncultivated" parents; but their spelling seems to be more directly linked not to cultural impoverishment but moral failure.

Richard Edwards, the president of ISNU, had a perspective similar to Stetson's: "When we reflect that the English tongue furnishes in itself a 'liberal education,' and that an unskillful and slovenly use of it is disastrous to any accuracy of thought, we can not otherwise than deeply regret this state of facts. The Normal University considers it a worthy service to do all that is possible to remedy this evil" (qtd. in Harmon 89).

Stetson's leadership in spelling pedagogy is important, for during his twenty-five years at ISNU, he gave the daily spelling exams. "Twenty-five words were assigned each day, and President Edwards decreed that a miss of more than one word in a term meant failure for the term" (*Alumni Quarterly* qtd. in Harper 135). Generally students did not officially "carry" spelling until they took it for five terms (C. Harper 135).[5]

Abbie's letters provide a firsthand account supporting the officialized reports about spelling practices at ISNU, and she includes additional information about the constant spelling surveillance the students experienced: "We spelled today for the first time writing the words in a blank book kept for that purpose. Those who spell a whole term without missing a word, are then excused for the exercise, though if afterwards they make a mistake in any writing seen by the teachers, they are obliged to spell another term" (10/09/1860). If Abbie's letter is accurate, students were expected to write always with perfect spelling, or suffer another term of daily spelling exams. To make matters worse, Abbie points out in the same letter that even self-corrected spelling errors are not abided: "I think I shall have to learn to be a little more careful than I usually am [in my spelling], for if a wrong letter is accidentally written & then corrected it is just as bad as if we don't know any better." The notion that getting the word right the first time is the only "correct" practice reveals a mistrust of revision that is seen elsewhere at ISNU. In his treatise on spelling, Professor Stetson says students "should be permitted to *try a word but once*. The object is to gain positive knowledge, and not ingenuity in guessing" (112).

The pressure to spell right the first time was compounded by the fact that paper was prohibitively expensive—preventing students from being able to produce perfectly edited final copies of their compositions. Reynolds's letter illustrates the difficulty of affording paper: "You told me to send some of my composition home, what few I have written were taken to light fires with long ago" (undated). This was apparently not uncommon for Abbie, nor for other ISNU students. In another letter, Abbie writes, "[A]s a last resort, I had been obliged to tear the old envelopes from your letters, for in order to make a fire, we have to furnish our own kindlings here, much to our inconvenience sometimes. I felt quite sorry that the last sermon of Henry Ward Beechers was accidentally torn up, before I had time to read it" (undated). Contrast Abbie's need to use her finished compositions for heat with the significantly less substantial concerns of a composition student at Princeton in the late 1780s, who "worries his good coat may not be back from the tailor in time for his speech . . ." ([Smith] qtd. in Halloran, "From Rhetoric" 158).

Elsewhere in his essay, Halloran claims that by the mid-nineteenth century, paper became much cheaper, allowing students more composing space

(170), but this was not the case at ISNU, if Abbie's frugal use of paper is any indication. It may have been less the fault of her "uncultivated parents" and more her lack of access to paper that interfered with Abbie's growth as a writer. Further, this lack of resources also contributed to the lack of ISNU student writing available today as historical capital.

Abbie Reynolds was not the only student to complain about the costs of spelling. ISNU historian Charles Harper writes that in 1874, 109 ISNU students submitted a formal petition to the board requesting relaxation in spelling standards—specifically, they did not want their "deportment" grades marked down as a result of spelling mistakes. The board made no change, and according to Harper, "evidently agreed with the professors that laxness in such matters as spelling betrayed a weakness in character or a moral lapse" ("From Rhetoric" 109).[6]

CREDENTIALIZING AND CORRECTNESS

Several factors may explain why normal school pedagogies—at least at ISNU —manifested in far less egalitarian methods than we might hope. These factors include the need to produce a visible distinction between a credentialed teacher and an uncredentialed teacher in order to justify the cost of a normal-school education. The methods used toward this end, a militaristic fetishization of rules and correctness, was not only unquestionable by its very nature, it was given cultural acceptance and even popularity by the fact that it occurred during the Civil War, when the military was popular. The resulting focus on mechanical correctness at normal schools shares features of the more traditional "Harvard Narrative" of composition history, but the context and timing of this history is significantly different, as are the attitudes with which correctness was rationalized and enforced at ISNU.

Johnson, Crowley, Halloran, Kitzhaber, and others have described the overdetermined focus on correctness in the teaching of writing in the nineteenth century. As Michael Halloran has put it, during this time "the idea that everyone has a 'right' to rise socially and economically took root" ("From Rhetoric to Composition" 165). This new desire for upward mobility and professionalization imposed a "credentializing function schools have perhaps always had in theory, but had never had to take quite so seriously before" and resulted in "greater concentration on correctness in the teaching of writing" (165). Albert Kitzhaber says, "Between 1850 and 1880, roughly, the emphasis tended to be on rhetoric for its own sake, rhetoric as a body of principles worthy in themselves of being learned without any necessary regard for actual writing" and that when the Harvard Reports began to take effect in the 1880s, "the ideal of mechanical correctness gained a dominant position in rhetorical instruction" (166–67). Kitzhaber also points out that due to this focus on grammar and mechanics, "rhetorical instruction in the early years of the twentieth century came to be dominated by an ideal of superficial correctness, of conformity to rules chiefly for the sake of conformity" (188). While this may not be a particularly proud point for the normals, the morality of correctness took on an especially intense emphasis at normal schools well before the Harvard Report.

The need to make a visible distinction between the credentialed and un-credentialed teacher may be the logic underpinning much of the contradiction in Stetson's pedagogy. It seems as though Stetson is rather unashamed at the need to make the kind of teaching he suggests "seem" valuable. One possible explanation of this aspect of Stetson's work is that much of his advice on teaching the abstractions of correctness has to do with the notion that students will learn better if they are made to believe what they are doing is fun or worthwhile. It is also possible, however, that he must justify how his teaching manifests in some notable distinction, especially at a point in time when professional training was not a necessary precondition for teaching.[7] His tautological explanation of the need for students to spell correctly lends evidence to the latter. He says, "[Spelling] is one of the corner-stones of the educational structure, and there is no greater proof of an imperfect and superficial training than frequent failures to spell correctly" ("Spelling" 110). And several pages later he explains, "The carelessness and indifference of teachers are, after all, the prime causes of the bad spelling now sadly prevalent" (113).

In his 1935 history of ISNU, Charles Harper says that "accuracy in pronunciation, spelling, grammar, and enunciation became a fetish which at times threatened to dominate and stifle the broader aims and outlook of the school"

(89). Despite this criticism, even Harper approves of Stetson's spelling exams: "Narrow and mechanical as this work was, it was vitalized by the enthusiasm of the teachers into something which actually seemed worthwhile." Harper too was a normal school professor and so similarly invested in the rationalizing ethos of rules that create a visible distinction between the credentialed and uncredentialed teacher.

This rationalizing ethos may also explain another difference between the normal school tradition and traditional composition histories. In *Composition-Rhetoric*, Robert Connors claims, "College teachers [in the nineteenth century] were ashamed to be professing grammar, punctuation, and lower-level skills" and that we only know that "shameful secret" today (that composition courses were "error-obsessed") because of surviving student papers (130). Stetson and the other members of the educators of a "teaching class" could afford not only to be open in their advocacy, but proud of it. ISNU professors served a credentializing function from the beginning, producing moral and intellectual models according to Hovey's carpenter's normal (or carpenter's "rule") analogy. The normal school agenda was actually buoyed by the intense concentration on correctness.

The creation of a visible distinction between the credentialed and uncredentialed teacher also manifested in a severe, militaristic tone at ISNU. Several of ISNU's earliest and most influential teachers were from Bridgewater State Normal School in Massachusetts, where they studied under Nicholas Tillinghast, a graduate of West Point and an infamous disciplinarian. Moreover, almost as soon at ISNU opened its doors, over two thirds of the male teachers and students left the school to fight in the volunteer Normal Regiment of the Civil War (C. Harper 59).

Stetson was one of five of Tillinghast's protégés who took influential positions at ISNU in the 1860s. Two of those students later become presidents of the university, leading the institution until the 1890s. According to a Bridgewater historian, "The [logical] mind of Tillinghast . . . called for severe and continuous application" (Martin 12–13). His approach required "strong, severe, exact[ing] rigor" and complete avoidance of the "frivolous" (15). Tillinghast's insistence on exacting standards would pervade the entire atmosphere of ISNU.

Charles DeGarmo, a professor at ISNU in the late 1800s, described Thomas Metcalf, a colleague and another of Tillinghast's protégés: "He respected truth as a sacred thing. To him a false pronunciation, a slip in grammar, a mistake in spelling or calculation was a kind of sin; a departure from the truth and right" (qtd. in C. Harper 86). Elsewhere DeGarmo said that thanks to Metcalf's efforts and influence on other faculty members, "thousands of future teachers left [ISNU] equipped with both a fonetic [*sic*] consciousness and a fonetic conscience . . . What the state owes to him and his college in the matter of correct pronunciation, it would be hard to estimate" (qtd. in C. Harper 86).

The teaching styles recommended by ISNU professors, notably expressed in the pedagogical advice of E. C. Hewett, instructor of geography at ISNU from 1858 to 1876 (and then president from 1876 to 1890), evidenced Tillinghast's militant disciplinary style:

> For instance, all the class facing you, give the order "Make a horizontal line six inches long." No pupil is to move until he hears a further order. At the word "Turn" each pupil faces the blackboard ready to work; at the word "One," he placed his chalk on the board; at the word "Two" he draws; at the word "Three," he lays down his chalk. At the word "Examine," the work is tested to see if the lines are horizontal. Then followed the word "Measure," when the little rules are applied to test the lengths of the lines. The pupils next hear "Erase," when the work is removed; next follows the order "Face," when all faces are turned toward you. Exercises of this kind should be had for a few minutes every day during many weeks, and care, promptness, and simultaneousness in working must be strictly insisted upon. (*Journal of Proceedings of Illinois State Teachers' Association* [1869], qtd. in C. Harper 134–35)

Several years later, President Hewett, in a note to the State Superintendent of Schools in 1880–1882, wrote that "the severity of West Point is not practicable in our common schools, nor is it desirable perhaps, but something of the same rigidness in imposing tasks and insisting on their performance must always be found in every school where there is right training" (qtd. in C. Harper 108).

Despite his criticism, Harper appears sympathetic to the "need" for rationalizing methods when he claims, "This Bridgewater influence was just what was needed in order to make teaching a respectable and respected occupation. It tended to make teaching a discernible distinction between the trained and untrained teacher" (89).

Abbie Reynolds describes her experience in Mr. Hewett's geography class in a manner somewhat consistent with the officialized accounts: "Geography is recited to Mr. Hewett; a lesson consists in describing a contry [*sic*], telling its rivers, towns, mountains, lakes & every thing worthy of notice neither teacher nor pupils using a map in the class. Mr. H says when we finish our course here, we should understand the subject so well, that for important features we shall no more need an Atlas than we do crutches when our feet are sound" (9/27/1860). Hewett's attitude regarding the need for textbooks is likely reflective of the widely accepted assumption of that time that "an educated person should and could know everything being taught" (Clark and Halloran 18); but, there is also probably more to Hewett's reasoning than that. The reason for this teaching appears to be, at least in part, to render textbooks and reference books unnecessary. There was a general distrust and dislike for textbooks, but there was a more compelling reason for training students this way: most of them would go on to be teachers in rural towns with no library and little money for books. In those cases, it was likely that teachers might have to rely on their own memory for the material they would teach. And forcing students to memorize the details of such features also provided a visible distinction for "trained teachers," and kept ISNU students engaged in rigorous study and unavailable to more "frivolous" pursuits.

This discernible distinction also manifested in a rather severe work ethic among the teachers and students. Letters written by Abbie and John Reynolds reference students waking up at night worrying about lessons, and Abbie becoming sick over her essay writing:

> [Abbie Reynolds recommends to her mother that her younger sister, Nettie, be sent to the ISNU model school because:] The pupils are made to learn and are not allowed to play, and do as they please in school. (Abbie Reynolds 12/06/1860)

> Sunday I felt quite unwell, ate but little and lay abed most of the forenoon, and the next-day went to school without my lessons, feeling but little like study. I was obliged to get excused from two recitations, had no

essay, and when night came felt about discouraged, but after many attempts and some tears, made out to scratch off something . . . (Abbie Reynolds 10/16/1861)

Sometimes I feel less sleepy and can study better when I eat no supper. (Abbie Reynolds undated)

Mr. Pillsbury says he did not think anything of sitting up all night to write essays when in College. I don't possibly see how he lived through it. The Normalites sit up very late now from midnight to two or three. C. A. T. T. has not finished her essay yet, says she would willingly sit up if she could possibly keep awake—think it is a mercy to her she can't. (John Reynolds undated)

All things go on about the same with us as ever, lessons to learn from morn till night with only a little time to rest and exercise. We have two meals a day and lunch which I save until after school as I have to drill half or more of the morn and it doesn't pay to begin to eat dinner and be called in in about five minutes and I had rather study that short time for every minute helps. (John Reynolds 10/10/1862)

I am always glad to have Friday night come because it brings a short rest and I don't have tomorrow's lessons to think of. My lessons don't trouble me enough to wake me up nights as they Miss Hatch [another ISNU student], for she wakes up, and thinks over all that she knows of her lessons and then goes to sleep again. (John Reynolds 10/24/1862)

My essays put me back in all my studies and I have not caught up yet, when I shall do so I shall get along very well with the Rhetorical Exercise, but shall have plenty then. Abbie has the same trouble about essays or rather worse for they make her fairly sick; I have not quite come to that but had to stay out of school one day to finish it or put two days work into one. (John Reynolds undated)

Albert Stetson was noted for his self-discipline and high expectations of his students, though the accounts are far less detailed and infamous than of the other Bridgewater men. A 1907 biography says he was "one of the tidiest of men" and that "[h]e was a constant reproach to the careless and untidy." Also, "He demanded prompt and rigorous recitations and his assistance was never uncertain" (Manchester et al. 102).

ISNU also became somewhat infamous for its swift application of discipline in the absence of a rigorous work ethic. Harper reports on several public reactions against ISNU's disciplinary rigor. In 1875 the *Chicago Times* once faulted President Edwards for publicly calling students names such as "uncouth," "awkward," "green fellows from the country," and "boors" (qtd. in C. Harper 109). An editorial in the *Bloomington Leader* said, "It seems the faculty have used such words as 'Indians,' 'boors,' 'nuisances,' and 'idiots.' One young lady was called a nuisance and she left the school. Another student was reciting Latin and not getting the exact construction, and she was called insane. Another professor became irate one day and gave thirteen zeros because the class failed in a question that was not fairly stated. Another professor told a young man he would rather mark students down than eat beef" (qtd. in C. Harper 109).

Abbie Reynolds makes clear that penalties go hand-in-hand with writing assignments: "For instance: Mr. Bass announced that Sec B & C must be prepared to hand in their compositions on the 'Character of Iago' next Tuesday morning; all failing to do so marked zero" (undated).

This work ethic at ISNU lasted for decades. In 1915, ISNU president David Felmley said of prior students, "Theirs was the courage to undertake arduous things." He paraphrased a letter he had recently received from an early ISNU alumnus: "It was his rule, he said, if a word is spelled in two ways always choose the harder; because it afforded more mental discipline in the learning of it" (Felmley 22).

Though these episodes may be unique to ISNU, they provide one unfortunate alternative to Fitzgerald's findings that "When the [normal] school teachers talk about the linguistic competence of their normal school students, we see explanations for poor performance based on prior experience and learning with none of the ad hominum descriptors like 'vulgar,' 'illegitimate,' and 'slip-shod' that we heard from Harvard men (Briggs 305)" (234–35).

THE FETISHIZATION of rules at ISNU had the benefit of much public support as a result of the ongoing war between the states. The Civil War was followed carefully by the members of ISNU and the surrounding community, as a quotation from John Reynolds shows:

The good news, that Richmond was taken, came to Bloomington Saturday night, and there was great rejoicing for two or three hours, but I did not wake to hear the bells and cannons. There has been no more news of importance since that time and many think that it is not so, for they think there would have been dispatches before now; they expect to hear more tonight, which will say for certain. I hope it is so, but fear it is too good to be true. It produced great excitement in town and Dr. Sewall and some others sat up all night, rejoicing over the victory. (5/11/63)[8]

One of Abbie's letters (one of very few addressed to her father) also indicates how the atmosphere of the war infused ISNU:

There are in the Normal 86 ladies and 46 gentlemen. Gen. Hovey—for he is now Brigadier General—made us a short visit last week. He told the school he thought the teaching would now have to be done mostly by ladies, and they should prepare themselves well for it as the army needs most of the men. (10/18/1862)

Public support for the rigid rules of ISNU training was particularly necessary because it allowed the university a hallmark that was both distinctive and yet not elitist. The local community was invested in ISNU not being an "aristocratic institution," and problems might have arisen from faculty members'—including Stetson's—connections to Harvard and other northeastern institutions had there not been something in the atmosphere to counter those associations.

THE EFFECTS OF ISNU WRITING PEDAGOGY
ON ABBIE REYNOLDS

The most compelling evidence against a positive interpretation of normal school writing pedagogy is how Abbie Reynolds' general attitudes and confidence in her writing deteriorate over time at ISNU. In the early letters, Abbie exhibits excitement in her writing. She chastises her mother for "talk[ing] about [her] writing so seldom," and in a letter soon after that she says that "as to writing, I believe I could write all night & then not say half what I want to." In her letters, Abbie writes of the room she lives in with great detail, and she is persuasive. Consider, for example, her appeal for more mail: "I assure you I was glad enough to find a letter in our little tin P.O. this morning. I expected one yesterday as much as could be and felt quite disappointed when I saw the other girls reading theirs & had none myself" (9/27/1860). And while Abbie is not oblivious to her errors, she is far more casual and playful in her attention to them during her first weeks at ISNU. "Mother I will try to be a good girl & do as you would want if you were here. Please excuse all mistakes" (9/27/1860).[9]

But over time, Abbie's excitement about writing fades. At first she dreads only the writing of compositions. She frequently complains that her composition work interferes with her letter-writing time. "How can I write my composition this evening. I could easily fill another sheet [of this letter] if that did not haunt me" (undated). And she begins to complain that the noise of the piano in the parlor or some other minor distraction is preventing her from writing her compositions. Finally, after three terms at ISNU, Abbie confesses in a letter to her brother that even the joy she experienced in writing letters to friends and family has betrayed her:

> My dear Johnnie,
> For the last two or three days, my conscience has been telling me that I ought to write at least half a dozen letters but I may as well tell you the truth at once. Letter-writing is above all things else, what I most dislike to do, as a general thing, though occasionally, I feel in just the mood for it, but not so this morning. I am writing merely from a sense of duty. Now you must not think I am losing my interest in the friends at home, for certainly nothing would please me better, than to drop in and have a chat with you all. No indeed, that is not it, but my letters are always such a source of rebuke, and mortification to me that I feel discouraged and at the same time ashamed that I cannot write better. It seems as if I was improving backwards, all the time and as if I could never say what I wished to. But I will not bore you longer with my self-upbraidings. (undated)

At this point in her education, Abbie Reynolds has been made to believe herself intellectually and morally inadequate. A woman who was once a vibrant writer has become a paralyzingly self-conscious critic of her own capabilities. What makes it worse, we should remember, is that Albert Stetson probably would have been pleased with Abbie's development. For what Abbie calls "improving backwards," Stetson may well have assessed as the productively negative work of "unlearning" that must be undertaken by the children of "uncultivated parents" ("Grammar" 104). But what we see has been done for Abbie's writing is that it has been deadened, sterilized, and made distant from her. In a word, Abbie's writing has been "normalized."

A CAUTIONARY ALTERNATIVE HISTORY
OF NORMAL SCHOOL WRITING PEDAGOGY

In May 1863, Albert Stetson signed Abbie Reynolds's autograph book with this sentiment: "Be thine a useful and a happy life; happy because useful— useful in being happy" (ISU archives). This study serves as a cautionary tale on at least two levels. Our triangulations of Albert Stetson's grammar and spelling pedagogies counter a too-progressive interpretation of his educational theories. We offer these sobering triangulations as an alternative to a more ideal history of composition in nineteenth-century normal school pedagogy. More important and sobering, Professor Albert Stetson developed a potentially progressive, remarkably contemporary-seeming pedagogy. His theories take into account relationships between socioeconomic class and grammar as "habit." And he suggests teaching methods that begin with the students and their experience, and not abstract, overly scientific "textbook" theories. But for all of his good intentions and socially-responsive educational theorizing, his pedagogy ultimately reifies the very socioeconomic boundaries some contemporary compositionists might wish to claim his pedagogy subverts. Like rhetoricians at more prestigious, northeastern institutions, Stetson may have "prepared students to leap social hurdles, while at the same time elevating the hurdles" (Halloran, "From Rhetoric" 167). No wonder Abbie Reynolds felt as though she was "improving backwards." If she was striving to meet artificial and ever-elevating hurdles, she was moving in exactly that direction.

Because Stetson was a teacher of teachers, his influence increased exponentially over time. If anything, normal school pedagogy may have contributed to the creation of an antidemocratic educational movement—what we have called the emergence of a teaching class—in which teachers were produced from the working class and those teachers would go on to set themselves against the children of the working classes. Given this, perhaps we should be pleased to note that although she pursued a career as a teacher, and lived to the age of 83, Abbie Reynolds taught only for one and a half years.

We also wonder about contemporary writing teachers who continue the tradition of focusing heavily on surface correctness, holding their students to discriminating, socially unfair standards. Like Albert Stetson, such teachers may imagine themselves as breaking down the very barriers their practices uphold. It is remarkable to think of how similar the context of the mid-nineteenth century is to the context of contemporary writing pedagogy. In both cases, first-generation college students flock to the university, seeking the keys to upward mobility. In both cases, potentially progressive writing pedagogies are stymied by broader cultural influences: in the mid-nineteenth century, "credentialization" was the problem, whereas perhaps now the problem is better framed as "standardization." And, a military-inspired patriotism stemming from the events of September 11 and the ongoing "war on terror" may make socially progressive changes harder to discuss openly, as the Civil War did at ISNU in the 1860s.

The education of writing teachers in mid-nineteenth century normal schools remains an important area for further exploration. As Kathryn Fitzgerald has pointed out, "Current historical research into alternate sites of writing instruction will give compositionists multiple options for identifying with as well as against our past" (245). We hope what we have presented from Professor Albert Stetson and his students, Abbie and John Reynolds—though less positive than what we may have hoped to find—will fuel further contemporary discussion and, ultimately, work to support truly effective writing pedagogies.

Notes

Many of the histories of Illinois State University cited here may now be found on-line at http://tempest.lib.ilstu.edu/index_isuhistory.php. We gratefully acknowledge the substantial guidance and detective work of Dr. Jo Rayfield, Illinois State University Archivist, and the research assistance of Daniel Griffin. Research for this project was funded in part by an Illinois State University College of Arts and Sciences Small Grant for Research.

1. For further discussion of contemporary writing teachers' overemphasis of surface correctness, see Dunn and Lindblom (2003 and 2005).

2. The handwritten letters of Abbie Ripley Reynolds and John P. Reynolds were sold to the Illinois State Normal archives in 1932 by Abbie Reynolds's granddaughter. These letters are dated inconsistently: sometimes the day, month, and year are given, but other times only "Wednesday Evening" or some similar designation is given. Where available, we list the date of the letter along with each quote; otherwise, we list the letter as "undated."

3. See also Lindblom and Dunn.

4. Context clues indicate that Reynolds has been at ISNU for at least three terms when she writes this letter.

5. Each year at ISNU was made up of three terms.

6. Harper cites the *Proceedings of the Board of Education of the State of Illinois*, 1874, p. 13.

7. Teachers often left ISNU before graduating to take on paid teaching positions.

8. John was right in his fear. His next letter reports: "The news has come that Richmond is not taken, but Hooker defeated: the rebels are rejoicing over our illuminations throughout the northern cities."

9. This comment may refer to Abbie's overall behavior and not just her writing, but she often makes reference to her writing in her letters, so we believe such may be the case here.

Archival Sources

The following items are in the Illinois State University Archives, Williams Hall, Illinois State University, Normal, IL:

Felmley, David. "Bridgewater and the Normal Schools of the West." *Seventy-Fifth Anniversary of the State Normal School, Bridgewater Massachusetts, June 19, 1915*. Bridgewater: Arthur H. Willis, 1915. 19–24.

Martin, George. "The Bridgewater Spirit." *Seventy-Fifth Anniversary of the State Normal School, Bridgewater Massachusetts, June 19, 1915*. Bridgewater: Arthur H. Willis, 1915. 11–18.

Reynolds, Abbie Ripley. Unpublished letters. 1860–1863.

Reynolds, John. Unpublished letters. 1860–1863.

Stetson, A[lbert]. "Grammar." Report of the Illinois Teachers' Institute Held at the Normal University, August 1867. Nason: Illinois Teacher Office, Peoria, 1867. 103–9.

Stetson, A[lbert]. "Spelling." Report of the Illinois Teachers' Institute Held at the Normal University, August 1867. Nason: Illinois Teacher Office, Peoria, 1867. 110–13.

7

The Platteville Papers Revisited

GENDER AND GENRE IN A NORMAL SCHOOL WRITING ASSIGNMENT

Kathryn Fitzgerald

FROM THE PERSPECTIVE of cultural studies, the value of examining the writing of common people through the distanced lens of history is to recognize the effects of practices not visible in our interested, contemporary context. Teachers immersed in white, middle-class American culture (the vast majority of teachers and professors) tend not to question goals and methods that their mainstream ideologies support. The history of composition is full of examples of methods at odds with users' aims, due, in part, to the users' inability to view their work from an outsider's point of view. The recent process approach to writing instruction and the earlier "correctness" approach are both cases in point. Each nearly monopolized writing instruction,

This paper is based on archival materials located in the Wisconsin Room of the Karrmann Library at the University of Wisconsin-Platteville. Besides the student papers that are the immediate focus of this paper, I also examined college catalogues, college histories, personal papers of professors, personal papers of students, preserved copies of student tests, the student newspaper, the local newspaper, yearbooks, minutes of student organizations, reports of the Wisconsin Board of Regents of Normal Schools, and records of professors' professional meetings.

enduring for decades without serious critique, until perspectives from outside the place or time were brought to bear. While a nonmainstream observer, Lisa Delpit, finally critiqued the social effects of process methods, it was the historical lens, not objective but tinted by contemporary theoretical perspectives, that brought to light the shortcomings of the correctness project (S. Miller, *Textual*; Connors, "Rise and Fall"; Berlin, "Writing"). This function of historical research—to enable us to critique still current practices from an outsider's point of view—is what I believe is the most significant contribution historical research makes to the contemporary field. This chapter continues in that vein, by investigating the genres employed in a set of student papers written over a hundred years ago to question the possible social effects of generic expectations and limitations on student writing.

How did I come to this particular question? A brief summary of my experience reveals, not a goal-driven linear process from question to conclusion, but a serendipitous, layered, recursive process moving messily toward insights. For a variety of reasons, when I began my first tenure-track teaching position I shifted the site of my research about composition's construction as a discourse from elite eastern colleges and academies (high schools) to midwestern, non-elite normal schools. I began the research at the University of Wisconsin-Platteville, formerly Platteville Normal, serendipitously both the oldest of the Wisconsin normals and the hometown of my in-laws. Even more serendipitous was the discovery of a set of student papers written in 1898, possible only with the help of archivist Mary Freymiller, to whom I had given the vaguest of directions: "I'm looking for anything about student writing toward the end of the nineteenth century." Yet finding the set of papers came with no guarantee that I would find anything to say about them. Topics as diverse as "The Economic Impact of the Helena Shot-Tower" (the paper came complete with schematics of the tower) and "Potosi in the Rebellion" gave me no clue as to how to approach the papers. It was only after reading them several times and beginning to see them as a set with certain unities (rather than as discrete papers), written at and defined by a particular historical moment, that I began to recognize significant questions on which they might shed light.

This is the second article to come from this set of forty-four papers written by seniors at Platteville Normal School. The first brought a cultural studies approach to the examination and interpretation of student writing, investigating the cultural work accomplished by the student papers in hegemonizing American frontier ideology and constructing new communal boundaries (Fitzgerald). It was as I was reading and rereading the papers for that article that I began to recognize the significance of genre in their production. Here, I shift my focus to the writing assignment itself. If these papers are viewed as representations of school cultural practices experienced by common people (i.e., nonelite, nonaffluent), the implications of this writing assignment extend beyond Platteville Normal school to contemporary composition classrooms.

Preserved with the papers was a cover sheet identifying them as follows:

PAPERS WRITTEN BY THE CLASS OF 1898.

Note: these papers were found in Dr. McGregor's (or what used to be) desk in Rountree Hall

Typical of archival finds, gaps in these holdings open numerous questions. The papers have no marks on them and, obviously, were not returned to students, though the professor kept them in his drawer until retirement many years later. We will never know why. Marks might have given us further insight into the qualities the professor had wanted to see in the papers, but lack of evidence foreclosed that path.

No written record of the assignment itself remained, but the exigence for these papers is quite clear from the internal evidence. Several student writers mention that the papers' purpose is to commemorate the fiftieth anniversary of Wisconsin's statehood. The year in which they were written, 1898, is importantly situated at the end of the settlement period and beginning of modernity for the old Northwest Territory, the upper midwestern states opened for European settlement by the Northwest Ordinance of 1787. In fact, noted historian Frederick Jackson Turner (himself a Wisconsinite) had only recently (1893) made his famous pronouncement that the American frontier had closed in 1890.

Though the assignment's exigence is quite clear from the internal evidence, the assigned genre(s) is more difficult to detect. Examination of the writing characteristics does reveal notable topical, stylistic and rhetorical consistencies. I will describe these regularities to draw conclusions about the genres for which the assignment apparently called, examine what this set of student papers reveals about the complex interactions among genre, subject matter, and the subject positions available to student writers of both sexes, and, after investigating what appears on the students' pages, I will note the (gendered) absences from this historical record.

Ruth Mirtz has recently characterized student writing itself as a "metagenre," a kind of "experimental, knowledge-building writing which contains many other kinds of writing" (194). I would like to think of this "metagenre," student writing, as at once both a site of experiment and knowledge-construction and as something else: as a cultural product; that is, as a product of the intense efforts of the schools to socialize students according to certain cultural standards. Among them are standards for appropriate writing in particular circumstances, standards which are exemplified by the Platteville Papers with some important consequences, especially for female writers.

These schooled conceptions of genre (Mirtz's "other kinds of writing") are more in line with literature-based definitions of genre as a set of conventions telling us what writing of a certain kind should look like than with contemporary definitions from the discipline of rhetoric. Recent rhetorical theorists have described genre as fluid, malleable, and dynamic. Genre operates within discourse communities to provide a normalized means of transacting business in recurrent situations (Miller, *Textual*; Berkenkotter and Huckin). Important to Berkenkotter and Huckin's analysis is the observation that genres not only control discourse but are reciprocally shaped by the changing needs of the community in which they are used. It is questionable whether such a definition can be applied comfortably to school writing. On the contrary, the genres employed in school writing are generally transmitted even more conservatively than literary genres, evidenced by composition's history and still-current practice of teaching the modes. However, the effects of genre in school writing become more complex in light of the subject positions school genres offer and the subject matter they elicit or, perhaps, erase from the page.

The similarities among the Platteville papers allow us to hypothesize the missing expectations for the writing assignment and examine the constraints apparently imposed by the generic conventions. If school genres can function as do the genres Berkenkotter and Huckin describe in active discourse communities, and are malleable, they might be made to accommodate previously excluded groups by resituating the subject positions they offer. But if school genres are static, they will continue to silence traditionally silenced voices. Bakhtin calls the powerful pull of genre to conformity its centripetal effect. It is these socializing tensions in school discourse—tension between, on the one hand, rhetorical forces pulling students toward assimilation to the standard subject positions constructed by the genre and, on the other hand, forces reshaping the genre toward accommodating new subject positions allowing expanded participation in school discourse—that the Platteville papers help to illuminate.

The papers are clearly the result of a formal assignment—every paper has a cover page with the title and writer's name, and many, though not all, include lists of sources. There are few crossouts, few misspelled words, and few grammatical errors, indicating these are carefully edited final drafts. Many are sophisticated in their construction. The papers can be sorted into five general topics about Wisconsin: its geology, economics, education, history, and notable persons. A sixth category, not quite parallel to the others, I will call representative narratives, or papers written to the "everyman" theme: rather than retell the life of an individual as biographies do, the "everyman" papers create a typical figure—the miner or pioneer farmer, for instance—and describe his life conditions. The historical papers include several subgroups: histories of towns (Milwaukee, Prairie du Chien, and others), histories of events (the Black Hawk Indian Wars and the village of Potosi's role in the Civil War), histories of groups in southwestern Wisconsin (Jesuits, "Negroes," and others), and histories of political processes (legislation creating the state government and state system of normal schools, for instance). Three of these topics are shared proportionately by women and men (of the forty-four students, twenty-five were women and nineteen men) but three were not: men wrote eight papers on economic subjects, while women wrote only four; women wrote five biographies while men wrote only two; and women wrote three "everyman" papers, while just one man wrote on this topic.

Very few of these papers can be considered "pure" examples of any single genre; in fact, the range of generic features among and within papers complicates the task of detecting the original assignment. Internal evidence suggests the occasion of a speech for at least some of the papers, while others are such detailed factual reports that it is hard to imagine their being delivered aloud. Perhaps students were given a choice between a speech and a written report. Besides variation in the possible medium of delivery, there seem to be two possible genres, the epideictic and the expository. Not only were these students, both male and female, familiar with the conventional expectations of both genres, several showed themselves to be adept at manipulating and combining them. Nor did the medium of delivery determine which genre was employed—features of both genres appear in the papers apparently meant to be delivered orally as well as those intended for readers.

A few papers by both sexes follow expository conventions fairly strictly, supporting the hypothesis that this genre was explicitly assigned. They are based on factual scientific or historical sources, they are logically organized, and they are developed by detailed evidence. Typical of these, Emma D. Jones's paper on "driftless" areas, clearly intended to be read, not delivered orally, describes a geological feature of the last Ice Age. In a closely reasoned argument, she first maps the reaches of Wisconsin's last glacier using geological data to demonstrate why geologists believe that the glaciers never reached the lower quarter of the state, as in the following description of the eastern boundary of the glacier: "On the eastern boundary are often seen heavy morainic heaps that are deposits of such boulders and gravel as scientists have decided are carried under or attached to the sides of glaciers." After summarizing the reasons for drawing glacial boundaries in all three directions, Jones outlines two explanations of why the glaciers stopped where they did. She carefully refutes the theory that the altitude of the driftless area was higher than that of the covered areas, thus presenting a physical barrier to the glacier, and arrives at the climatic explanation—climatic warming stopped the glaciers at these points. She ends her paper with a sentence stating why this topic is of importance: "With the retreat of the glacier, vegetation covered the surface and by its aid and action of the elements our fertile driftless soils, among the last and best of Wisconsin's formations, were produced."

In a similar though longer paper, Charles E. Rector traces the geological history of the iron deposits of the Lake Superior region. Rector begins with an opening strategy shared by several of the writers, to place the topic in a much larger historical context, in Rector's case, tracing the story of iron's significance to civilization from the Stone Age to the railroads. Once he has thoroughly established its importance in panegyrical terms, he returns to a data-driven report on the origin and mining of iron ore. Like Jones but with greater elaboration, Rector argues the pros and cons of several scientific explanations of the formation of the deposits to finally arrive at "perhaps the most plausible." After tracing the origin of the iron deposits, he describes in some detail the process of mining and transporting the ore. He ends with factual statements, apparently having exhausted his supply of encomiastic terms in his introduction.

While the factual grounding of many papers suggests that exposition was a feature of the writing assignment, these two papers seem to constitute a subgenre directly related to geology in which theories are in turn constructed and refuted until the "most plausible" emerges. Every claim is carefully supported with the available empirical evidence. In the case of Rector's argument, chemical interactions are integrated with observable geological features to arrive at likely conclusions about the formation of iron deposits. Though we don't know for certain how students learned this particular genre, we can infer from Rector's list of sources, which include the Geology Club as well as "class work," that these social experiences are responsible. Clearly, the geological subgenre of the expository paper was equally accessible to both male and female students, as was the larger expository genre. In addition to Jones's paper, women wrote expository papers about the early exploration of Wisconsin, about the legislation upon which the territory of Wisconsin was founded, and on grape culture in southwestern Wisconsin. Predominantly expository papers by men include topics like the history of banking, the Black Hawk Wars, the location of the state capital, the operation of a shot tower, and the development of normal schools.

The lack of panegyric in Jones's paper suggests that this feature is not a necessary convention of the geological subgenre, but its presence in most other papers in this set, including Rector's, leads one to conclude that the celebratory occasion for the writing, the fiftieth anniversary of statehood, pressured most students to make a particular effort to embed their topics in the encomiastic discourse suggested by the writing occasion. While a few papers, like those about the shot tower, banking, and grape culture, manage to maintain fairly consistently the neutral, objective tone expected of expository papers, Jay C. Davis's paper about a practical topic, the improvement of farm implements, exemplifies the pressure of the assignment's epideictic exigence. Davis begins with the following laudatory sentiments: "Rapid progress is one of the peculiarities of the American people; every industry which has attracted their attention, has received an impetus along the line of invention and discovery which stands without a parallel in the World's history. Show me an undertaking in which the sturdy sons of America have been engaged, and I will point out to you some discoveries in that industry which have startled the age." After several more paragraphs expounding upon the conditions responsible for Americans', and especially Wisconsinites', inventiveness, including race, values, climate, geographical location (the "parallel of 42 degrees 30 minutes"), and natural resources, the writer begins an effectively constructed and highly detailed essay in which he follows the farmer's chores from spring to fall, comparing the implements used in each season in 1848, the year of statehood, with those available as of his writing in 1898. He describes the advances made by the horse-drawn riding plow, the horse-drawn grain drill for planting, haymakers, the reaper superseded by the twine binder, and, finally, the steam-driven threshing machine. Each advance is embedded in a paean to progress, like that introducing the reaper and twine binder: "This spirit of invention and discovery is probably best shown, however, by the miraculous improvements in harvesting implements during the last half century." To celebrate the reduction of hard labor and increased productivity made possible by farm machinery must have seemed a natural rhetorical move to these rural students; the more studied move possibly imposed by the epideictic genre is the attribution of this progress to the character of Wisconsinites and to the natural climatic and geological conditions of the state.

While some of the Platteville papers display the detailed, neutral prose of the strictest of expository standards and others quite facilely embed empirical details in effusive praise, thus combining the two genres, some papers tend to become laudatory to the point where the expository demand for accuracy is forgotten. Characteristics of ceremonial discourse are, predictably, found most prominently in biographies and "everyman" papers. Aristotle's special topics for ceremonial discourse included praise of virtues and personal talents or accomplishments; these writers clearly were familiar with such rhetorical expectations, if not with their source (a question yet to be investigated). They render Aristotle's recommendations for attention to courage, justice, liberality (as opposed to selfishness), prudence, gentleness, and loyalty (Corbett, *Classical Rhetoric* 128) in their own terms. In her biography of Nelson Dewey, the first governor of the state and a minor figure according to historians (Nesbit; Wyman), Bessie Spaulding praises the man for his "great ability and integrity," and inaccurately describes him, the son of a New York lawyer educated in the east who was admitted to the bar in Wisconsin shortly after arriving in the state, as "a poor boy, without influence," who had "risen by his own industry and worth to the most exalted position in the State." Other biographies, often of admittedly minor people with whom the writers had family connections, such as Charles Dunn, John H. Roundtree, and Moses M. Strong, contain remarkably similar language to commend character and industry.

On the "everyman" theme, the pioneer farmers are described by Margaret Sullivan, Wilma Spiegelberg, and Myrtle J. Whitham in interchangeable terms: "bold" and "fearless," "steadfast," "content," "happy," "faithful," and "hospitable" (Sullivan); "faithful," "diligent," "possessing those excellent qualities of love, faith, friendship, truth and loyalty" (Spiegelberg); and "economical," "patient" people who appreciate the natural beauty of their environment as "food for the Mind" (Whitham). Like Jay Davis, these writers link the strength of the (Wisconsin) pioneer character to the theme of progress. Whitham writes, "So long as the people continue their life of patience and industry we predict for them progress and triumph" and Sullivan contends, "When the historian of the future collects the facts upon which to generalize to show our progress as a state, let him not forget to note that firm, shaping, elevating agency which has made us what we are—the Pioneer Farmer." The similarity in language and tone describing pioneer character among these "everyman" papers and biographies is a striking example of the centripetal force of the epideictic genre—it pulls these writers to a center where language itself is flattened to a single vocabulary and theme. In the case of Spaulding's "biography" of Nelson Dewey, the genre pushes toward the creation of a mythology rather than accurate reporting, a negative characteristic for an expository paper, but an effective strategy in the epideictic genre.

The repetition of these expository and epideictic features in the Platteville papers indicates the students' understanding of the expectations for the genres they have been asked to produce. We can conclude from the papers' internal evidence that two genres are in play, the information-transmitting expository paper and the celebratory speech whose social purpose is to strengthen communal bonds. Male and female students are equally capable of producing these genres in their various permutations from the most objective, expository stance to the most epideictic, and are often quite facile in weaving the stances together. Besides praising such human virtues as the Protestant work ethic and Yankee ingenuity, the students laud the state itself—its climate, geography, and natural resources. All these contribute to the master theme of progress. While these epideictic features are predominant in many papers, the numerous source-based "research" papers are evidence that students were also given the option of producing a fact-based "report" about the history, economy, or physical features of the state.

Pervasive as these characteristics are, the papers themselves are more complex than the simple manifestation of a set of generic conventions, or even an admixture of generic conventions. The celebratory occasion eliciting the papers obviously suggests an uncritical look at the advances the state has made in the previous fifty years—the praise-of-progress stance taken by nearly all of the student writers—perhaps to the point of actively discouraging critical evaluation. For instance, Englebert Ketterer's paper about the lumber industry, while tracing the denuding of Wisconsin's six lumber districts, nevertheless depicts the industry's impact as nothing but positive: "[The lumber industry] gives employment of millions of capital and thousands of men, and has peopled the wilds of our state with energetic communities, built up great cities, and covered the state with a network of railways, which furnish an outlet for its productions and an inlet for people, who are ever seeking for homes." Admitting at the end of the paper that Wisconsin's lumber industry is playing out, Ketterer does not acknowledge loss, claiming instead that

"With the advance of time, changes will occur in reducing the timber supply. Wisconsin will become the home of manufactories, which convert trees into finished products, giving employment to thousands and bringing in millions of revenue." Likewise, Thomas Heigell traces the history of banking through panics and mass failures two to three times a decade over the preceding fifty years, only to depict the bankers themselves as responsible men repeatedly conferring to set up new regulations to put banking on a sounder footing. For the most part, criticism is muted if not silenced, and it is probable that, at least in part, it was muted by the generic expectations of the assignment itself— neither the epideictic occasion of the writing nor the objective expository stance promoted critique of the state's history.

Yet fissures in the façade of praise of progress are visible. Ideological ambivalence and resistance sometimes break through generic constraints. One example is the nostalgia that seeps through several papers for the lost (idealized) wilderness of a past generation. Nostalgia for a lost Edenic paradise is not an uncommon theme in nineteenth-century American prose. One paper ends by quoting in its entirety a nostalgic poem describing a local river, the Pecatonica, written, according to the student writer, by a white settler, one T. H. Sheldon, for an "old settlers' meeting" in 1877. A few lines of this multipage poem suffice to demonstrate its nostalgic tenor:

> In summer green or autumn brown, Where spangled meadows lay,
> The birds sang as I paddled down
> > The Pecatolika.
>
> . . . .
> The catfish, bass and pike swam on
> Their unobstructed way
> As free the duck plied up and down
> > The Pecatolika.
>
> . . . .
> Until the stranger came to dwell
> > On Pecatolika
> Until the meddling Yankee came
> As Yankees do always
> And dammed the stream and spoiled the name
> > Of Pecatolika

. . . .
That deer and bear are cow and horse
Those graves are cocks of hay
A muddy slough now makes the course
    Of Pecatolika
As Rachel mourned so now I mourn
Who shall by grief gainsay
While here I tread the banks forlorn
    Of Peca<u>ton</u>ica.

The nostalgic language and sentiment of the poem, while readily available in nineteenth-century discourse, is here localized in the settler/poet's clever play on the change in the river's name (underlined in the original). Just as the white man has destroyed everything else natural about the river, he has also managed to desecrate the original Indian name. Though the sentimental discourse is readily available, the local application suggests authentic feeling. Quoting the entire poem as the coda for her paper, Anna Chamberlin reveals a strong sense of loss that implicitly criticizes the effects of settlement and progress.

Another student writer, Wilma Spiegelberg, catalogues the advances that replaced the pioneers' "vine covered gardens": "Some of these pioneers have passed away, and little dreamed these light-hearted [folk] of the great change that was so soon to be wrought in their vine covered gardens and primitive cabin—and yet many of them are still living to see in the place of their rude hamlet a vast city whose streets are surging with the never resting throng of trade; gigantic steamers move in the place of the frail bark canoe; the lightning train now usurps the path of the patient mule. . . ." Ideologically conflicted, a few of the Platteville papers to some measure escape the constraints of the genre, covering loss not quite so seamlessly as, for instance, Rector's paper about the mechanization of the farm, where the stillness lost with the advent of the steam-driven thresher goes unremarked.

Just three of the forty-four papers are overtly critical of any aspect of Wisconsin's history, economy, or society. Two are historical accounts of the Black Hawk Wars, which ended with the massacre of Indian women and children as they tried to escape their pursuers by crossing the Mississippi River to safe haven. One writer embeds her account in the epideictic genre, while the other employs the expository to make his point. The first, Pearle M. Robinson, writes an introduction that positions her topic complexly in the epideictic genre and the historical moment of her own writing. She shifts that moment subtly from the celebration of statehood to the imminence of war:

> Back in the days of pre-territorial Wisconsin, there occurred an event which will ever occupy a conspicuous place in the annals of our beloved state. It marked the epoch which witnesses the removal forever, of the red man from all territory east of the Mississippi. But unhappily, it is a chapter in our history of which no true Wisconsin patriot can be proud, it must always remain a shadowy blot upon our otherwise fair and spotless record.

She then repositions the topic:

> Today the catastrophy [*sic*] of war overshadows our land [the Spanish-American War threatened], and our ever loyal Wisconsin is not backward in sending out her brave and patriotic sons to fight, and if need be, die, for our country.

Robinson borrows from the present some glory for the fighters of the past:

> At this time sixty-six years ago, our forefathers were also engaged in this dreaded business, but instead of the canon's roar, their ears were greeted with the hideous warhoop [*sic*] which paled the faces of even the bravest of the handfull [*sic*] of white settlers who inhabited South-central Wisconsin and northern Illinois.

In a precarious balancing act, Robinson manages to maintain the tension between her moral outrage over the Black Hawk massacre and the epideictic demand of the occasion to strengthen the bonds of community rather than undermine them through splintering criticism. She goes on to summarize the several battles of the Black Hawk War in terms quite sympathetic to the white settlers, but then describes the final massacre as follows: "Col. Dodge and Col. . . . Taylor, with their united forces rushed to the [scene] and for three hours the pitched battle raged, with credit to the noble braves who so gallantly fought for the lives of their women and children, but with lasting dishonor to the whites who so indiscriminately slaughtered men, women and children."

Robinson moves toward her conclusion with some commendation for the white fighters, who included Abraham Lincoln, but finally ends with more than a page of encomium for Chief Black Hawk. She draws upon the "noble savage" discourse to depict Black Hawk as a man whose "manner at all times was dignified and gracefull [*sic*], [who] had a high sense of honor and propriety," though latent racism is evident in naming Black Hawk's fatal flaw as being born to an "uncivilized race." Though the "noble savage" ideology was available to provide a discourse in which to praise the Indian, Robinson's rhetorical accomplishment is to use it to manage even in the inhospitable environment of the epideictic assignment and racist social currents to criticize the settlers and laud the populations they displaced.

W. W. Woolworth's paper traces in detail an even-handed history of the events of the Black Hawk War that coincides closely with late twentieth-century accounts. In unemotional language, Woolworth describes "the trouble . . . known to us as the Black Hawk War," which arose out of "a controversy in regard to land." With this neutral prose, Woolworth describes broken treaties and betrayals by both parties and follows the last days of the Indians' flight in far more detail than Robinson. Consistent with expository expectations, his last paragraph finishes the story with minimal editorial comment:

> When completely routed some the savages swam to a few islands, from whence the men and women with their children clinging to them tried to reach the opposite shore. But as the steamboat directed the fire of its cannon upon the islands and the swimmers, many were killed and drowned trying to escape. The battle lasted only a few hours, but it seems less a battle than a wholesale slaughter. Black Hawk escaped but was captured soon after and surrendered to the United States authorities at Prairie Du Chien. This ended a war that had been conducted by spasms for two years.

Avoiding Robinson's complex moral and rhetorical positioning, Woolworth exploits the expository genre by aggregating detail to effectively pillory the actions of the white forces in the final massacre. Again, given the prevalence of laudatory language in the other papers, it is noteworthy that a student would find a way to use the assigned genres to challenge the prevailing ideology.

These two papers are rare in this set. Only one other paper is overtly critical, a paper castigating the low state of journalism in Wisconsin, though it manages to praise the work of a few individual journalists. Though atypical, these papers demonstrate that it is possible in some cases for students to escape the ideological and generic constraints of even the most centripetal of writing pressures.

However, sometimes the force of ideological combined with generic constraints seems to have been insurmountable. As Thomas Helscher reminds us, the shaping influence of genre remains a potent political force. Echoing Bakhtin's concept of the centripetal force of genre, he admits, "it is part of the irresistible attraction of genres, and perhaps their primary effect, to normalize, regularize, unify, impose order and identity" (27). The women students in this group employed given genres with equal skill as men, but they have disappeared from the pages as women. One paper in particular, authored by Gertrude Hoadley, demonstrates the thoroughness of this disappearance. Titled "Brick Making as an Industrial Factor in the History of the State of Wisconsin," this expository paper includes the following table of contents:

Introduction	p. 4
How Clay is formed	4 & 5
Kinds of Clay	6
Kaolui	
Potters	
Fire-Brick Clay	
Common Brick Clay	
Different Brick Clays of Wisconsin	6
Madison	6 & 7
Milwaukee	7 & 8
Platteville	8
How Bricks are Manufactured at Platteville	pp. 8–16

Part 4, "How Bricks are Manufactured at Platteville," is of particular interest here. While the first half of this paper traces geological details much as do the two geological papers described above, the eight pages of this final section, fully half of the paper, are devoted to a detailed tour of the local brickyard, conducted, according to the writer's list of references, by "men working in Platteville Brick yards namely Mr. Allen Grundel and Mr. Kolb." In fact, the tour is so detailed that a reader cannot help but visualizing the young coed as she hitches her skirts above her ankles and follows the manager from one muddy location in the brick-making process to the next, the entire time (awkwardly?) taking notes. Yet, nothing of the feminine subject appears in the paper (Fitzgerald). Instead, the subject position available is that of the objective (male) researcher voiced in such sentences as these describing the pallet system used to dry bricks at the Platteville yard: "These pallets are then arranged like shelves in covered frames. The frames are arranged end to end in long lines. Each one of these long lines is known as a rack, which contains about five thousand and four hundred bricks. These racks are arranged with aisles for passage between them running east and west. There are on all the racks together about one hundred five thousand bricks." The details of place ("passage between them running east and west") must result from an eyewitness account, yet nowhere is there any acknowledgment of the unusual presence of the young woman in the brickyard.

Not all of the female writers erase themselves quite so completely. In several of the biographies, women claim a presence by such passive means as having the same surname as the person depicted or by crediting a father as a source (Fitzgerald). Yet in the brickyard piece, not even these subtle tactics are used to assert a woman's presence, either as writer or field observer. Helscher notes, "To do business within a specific [discourse] community, we occupy the subject position offered by the genre at hand" (29). For Gertrude Hoadley, who disappears entirely into the male-coded discourse of the expository school assignment and the exclusively male scene of the brickyard, the price of assimilation into the discourse within which she must do business is erasure.

Historically, the epideictic and expository genres have both been the province of men. Epideictic discourse, a type of public speech, with few exceptions assumed male rhetors from classical antiquity to the nineteenth century. Moreover, the epideictic occasion, calling for public praise of public events, forced attention to subject matter taken from the public sphere, which has been dominated by men throughout Western history. The term "expository," popularized in nineteenth-century rhetoric texts (e.g., Bain), was coined to name a kind of writing for explanatory purposes evolving from the British Royal Society's and John Locke's advocacy of a plain style to convey the "objective" truths discovered by means of the scientific method. Because enlightenment epistemology was a male enterprise, the "objective" voice of the expository writer was by default male. Moreover, as Cinthia Gannett notes, academic discourse has been the exclusive preserve of males for all but the last 150 years of its 1,000-year history, thus: "many of the traditional scholarly and pedagogical discourses of the university have clearly been constructed on . . . historically masculine model[s]" (194).

The Platteville papers confirm the hypothesis, based on the history of these genres, that the male domain dominates content. None of the major players in the historical or economic events recorded by the papers is a female. None of the biographies is of women. With one exception, the domains described by the six papers in which women are mentioned at all are the home and the school. Yet even here, where one might think females would dominate, they are barely visible. One such paper, written by Elon E. Oates, described the development of education in southwestern Wisconsin and names two women, a Mrs. Harker and a Beulah Lamb, who started private primary classes in their homes in the 1830s. This writer also mentions that some of the "most influential women of the Northwest" graduated from St. Clara's Academy, a private Jesuit school for women. Without this passing reference, a reader of the papers would have had no reason to think that the state had produced any "influential women." Yet the paper as a whole is devoted to the legal and economic circumstances surrounding the establishment of a state supported education system in Wisconsin. Mathilde A. Schwerdt, whose topic is St. Clara's Academy, spends one-third of her paper recounting the story of Father Mazuchelli, the priest who founded the school, and another third describing the unique geological features of the school's site. Finally, after summarizing the academy's apparently rigorous scholastic program in the last third of the paper, the writer mentions the beneficiaries of the courses, women, only to excuse their commitment to education on the basis that their best accomplishments would be devoted to improving the home (Fitzgerald).

In the three pioneer "everyman" papers, which are complex in their conflicted stance between nostalgia and progress, the writers barely notice the presence of women on the homestead. If public affairs are the domain of men and the private or domestic that of women, one might expect that women students would have chosen this topic as a space where women's experience could be foregrounded, but this is not what happens. Though the writers observe that pioneer life was harder on women than men, they view women as appendages to the exertions of the pioneer farmer (Fitzgerald). Helscher notes in his article on genre and subjectivity, "The denial of one's place is one of the most insidious effects of ideology or power" (32). In these cases the effect of the genre's power is to deny not only the voice of women as writers, but also the physical presence of women on the map of the territory being depicted. Adding up the topics and examining the content of the forty-four papers provides irrefutable evidence of the erasure of women, especially remarkable from students enrolled in an institution which was by law equally accessible to women, where the majority of students were indeed women, and where at least half of the faculty consisted of women (Board of Regents). In all forty-four papers, not a single woman was featured.

In the rare environment of a coeducational institution of higher education at the end of the nineteenth century, it is nearly inevitable that the genres available for school writing would be coded male, and that women, to write at all, would assimilate to them. One might ask why it matters whether women are visible in the school discourse, when clearly they were physically present at the school, had equal access to the genres of school writing, and were indeed present and even "influential" in the larger community. What is at stake is the power gained (or not) through access to the discourse. It is not enough to be assimilated into a discourse when the only subject position from which one can be heard is that of the already dominant group. It is not enough to gain the use of a discourse if the newly arrived group is unable to give voice to its lived experiences and the perspectives they engender. As Helscher points out, "What we get [from the assimilation of new voices to old genres] is a normalization of experience and a leveling of differences that preserves [*sic*] the identity of the academic or professional community at the expense of . . . the lived experiences of those who have recently been admitted to it" (34). The genres of the Platteville papers more than leveled the differences between men's and women's experience: Platteville women writers were unable to access their own experience in the context of this school writing assignment. Therefore, it could not be written into the communal identity being constructed by these papers, and the richness and complexity of women's experience and perspectives were lost to this discourse.

The question of the malleability of dominant genres is of great concern to feminists and social constructivists today. Social constructivists, according to James Slevin, "share in common such questions as the range of discursive forms available to a writer, the ideological dimensions of these forms, the nature of authorship, and even the availability of a readership" (589). At stake is the question of what conditions enable or disable the production of writing by specific gendered or classed groups. Feminists have shown that curricular canonization of some genres as opposed to others (exposition rather than diary, for instance) determines "which types of literacy practices . . . will accrue literary, academic or pedagogical value" (Gannett 11). When the validated genres are the products of masculine discourse, they represent, not all human experience, but "primarily the perspectives of white, elite, heterosexual, Western males" (Gannett 11). The Platteville papers provide a case study of this phenomenon. When we recognize these papers as instruction and practice in how to assimilate to canonical academic genres, we as classroom instructors are forced to turn our attention to the genres we assign and examine them in the light of the powerful consequences of the genres the Platteville students wrote. While these genres can empower common students in uncommon ways, and while the common students at Platteville Normal School could be remarkably sophisticated and inventive in subverting and turning school genres, the genres also discursively constrained access to diverse subject positions and silenced the perspectives they could have imparted. Feminist, constructivist, and cultural studies theorists are beginning to uncover the silences and exclusions imposed by dominant academic genres. The Platteville papers demonstrate that student writing genres—the many kinds of practice genres students are asked to adopt in the experimental and knowledge-building "metagenre" of student writing—can, perhaps even more forcefully than mature professional genres, exert a centripetal pull toward assimilation to dominant subject positions and interests. A century later, we can no longer claim the excuse of the naïve practitioner for the effects of our assignments, but instead must reflectively examine the consequences of our practices.

Archival Sources

The following items are in the University of Wisconsin-Platteville Archives, Platteville, WI:

Papers written by members of the class of 1898. Accession/Series No. A820002.

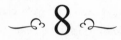

"Our Life's Work"

RHETORICAL PREPARATION AND TEACHER TRAINING AT
A MASSACHUSETTS STATE NORMAL SCHOOL, 1839–1929

Beth Ann Rothermel

IN 1923 THE all-women's senior class at the Westfield State Normal School staged a series of debates. Although these debates focused mainly on civic issues, they also included a reenactment of the Lincoln-Douglas debates, presented before the entire school in a general assembly. Westfield's 1923 yearbook celebrates the prime players of this drama, noting that "Helen Spelman looked the part of a politician in presiding. Helyne Mousley made a superb Lincoln, and Ruth Grady an inimical Douglas. One could almost imagine one's self as actually participating in the noted campaign for the senatorship of Illinois" (*Tekoa* 70). The women aimed to "reproduce the spirit and the main issues" of this famous historical event. The debate series in 1923 was not, however, the first time that female students at Westfield had imagined themselves into positions of rhetorical power. Westfield's newly enfranchised

Archival materials used in preparing this article are available in Westfield State College's Patterson Archive, located in Ely Library.

senior class was, in fact, drawing on rhetorical theories and practices critical to the school's academic programs since the mid-nineteenth century.

In the introduction to his documentary history *The Origins of Composition Studies in the American College*, John C. Brereton observes that we "still do not know enough about the connections between college course work and the public and private examples of female rhetoric" (20). Scholars of rhetoric and composition have been actively addressing this shortfall in a number of ways. The works of Karlyn Kohrs Campbell, Annette Kolodny, and Nicole Tonkovich on individual women rhetors and their educational backgrounds have revealed the "range of attitudes and instruction among women rhetoricians" (Brereton 21). Scholars such as Vickie Ricks, Kathryn Conway, JoAnn Campbell, and P. Joy Rouse have studied the rhetorical education offered to women at private women's colleges and seminaries. More recently, scholars like those writing for this collection have turned their attention to alternative sites of rhetorical instruction, focusing on institutions that educated women of more varied racial, ethnic, and economic backgrounds.

The road on which rhetorical education traveled at Westfield was a complicated one.[1] Over the course of the nineteenth century, the Westfield State Normal School developed a program of study that emphasized the value of future teachers studying rhetoric. Westfield's rhetorical curriculum introduced future teachers to rhetorical theory and guided them in applying that theory to a wide array of discourse practices, including oratory, debate, and written composition. It aimed not just to expand students' mental powers, as other institutions educating women argued it did; it prepared the future teacher to foster learning, win respect, and achieve meaningful moral influence among her pupils. However, archival research shows that in the late nineteenth and early twentieth centuries, these objectives, and the curriculum Westfield had built to achieve them, came into question. Shifting views on the purpose of rhetorical education for students training to be teachers, especially women, led the Massachusetts State Board of Education to pressure Westfield into adopting utilitarian approaches to rhetorical study. Normal schools were to train teachers to speak and write correctly and to pass those habits on to primary school students.

Some of Westfield's early twentieth century administrators responded favorably to such demands, yet Westfield's faculty asserted that along with "correct expression," "force" and "fluency" were essential attributes of the successful primary school teacher. Such attributes were best cultivated by presenting students with more complex rhetorical theories and practices than state officials advocated. Normal school faculty, thus, followed administrators' directives only in part, designing courses in written and oral expression, along with varied extracurricular activities, that aimed to help students understand the processes of communication and their pedagogical effects. Varied archival sources show, in fact, that within the context of late nineteenth and early twentieth century teacher training, Westfield's female students may have acquired a more complex rhetorical knowledge than many other students of their day.

The archive behind this hypothesis is a rich but fragmented one. As Carole Gerson points out, archival collections poorly document women's lives. While Westfield course catalogues, grade books, and student records suggest much about its official curriculum, they do not reveal much about women's day-to-day experiences. Thus, in trying to build a complex picture of Westfield, I have consulted a range of texts such as alumni letters, graduation programs, yearbooks, and student notebooks; I have also considered the extra-curriculum as well as the curriculum. These sources, lodged in what Karlyn Kohrs Campbell terms the "crevices" of the archive ("Consciousness" 59), have revealed more about the ways gender and educational ideologies influ-enced the rhetorical preparation of Westfield's female students. They have also provided keener glimpses of the ways teachers and students consciously and unconsciously resisted such ideologies.

THE NORMAL SCHOOL CONTEXT, 1839–1877

Memorial Hall Museum in Deerfield, Massachusetts, recently hosted an exhibit of photographs taken by Mary Allen (1858–1941) and Frances Allen (1854–1941), two sisters who graduated from the Westfield State Normal School in 1876. Innovators in the world of pictorial photography, the Allen sisters won a number of awards, published their work in national periodicals, and exhibited it around the country. They were also businesswomen, active members of their community, and published writers (Flynt). In 1901, critic

Frances Benjamin Johnson named them "the foremost women photographers of their time" (qtd. in Flynt 19). But the Allen sisters' "chosen career" was not actually photography (Flynt 21). They began their careers as teachers until hearing loss forced both to quit. It is interesting that Johnson also noted that "without any special training but that of well-read women of good taste they have put character, dignity and artistic feeling into their pictures" (qtd. in Flynt 19). During their two years at Westfield, the Allen sisters received considerable preparation for teaching, having been exposed to a rich array of sciences and to a number of theories on the child (a frequent subject of their photography). Westfield also honed their rhetorical powers, providing them with tools of expression useful to their writing and photography. The Allens' letters home during their time at the school "brimmed" with enthusiasm over "all aspects of school life" (Flynt 20).[2]

When the Allen sisters arrived at the Westfield State Normal School in the fall of 1874 to begin the two-year normal training program, they joined a student body consisting of 138 women and 18 men. The school was soon to celebrate its forty-fifth anniversary, having opened in 1839 as part of the Common School Movement, and had won a national reputation (Brown; Herbst, *And Sadly*). Public normal school founders Horace Mann and Henry Barnard, among others, had argued that the state's many new primary (common) schools needed well-trained teachers and that public normal schools could help to fill the demand, especially if they educated women along with men (Herbst, *And Sadly* 12–31). Building on the work of such educational reformers as Catharine Beecher and Emma Willard, Mann argued that teaching would provide women, who were already naturally inclined to working with children, a way "to expand the circumference of the home" (135). Facing public skepticism about the need for normal schools and about the appropriateness of educating women to become teachers, Mann assured the public that schools like Westfield would not duplicate the work of colleges and universities, but rather drill future teachers in the subjects they would teach, verify that they were of "good moral character," and teach them how to keep order in a school (Herbst 12–31).

Moreover, Westfield provided a financial alternative to universities. So long as students declared their intention to teach in the state of Massachusetts after graduation, Westfield required that they pay only for their room and board (*Catalogue*). Neighboring Mount Holyoke charged around $60.00 a semester in its early years (Woody 361). Most nineteenth-century students identified their parents as farmers or laborers. Frances Allen (but not Mary) received state financial aid during her stay at Westfield (Flynt 21).

By the time the Allen sisters arrived at Westfield, women had a more established place in primary school classrooms, and had even made some forays into secondary education and educational administration (see Matthews; Cogan). Yet the curriculum that the Allen sisters encountered at Westfield did more for female teachers than simply verify their character or "catch them up" on the subjects they would need to teach (i.e., arithmetic, geography, reading). Westfield catalogues suggest that women at Westfield in the 1870s encountered a rigorous program of academic study, one that required advanced work in subjects such as chemistry, botany, geometry, mental and moral philosophy, and the theory and art of teaching. More significantly, the Allen sisters' rhetorical training consisted not merely of orthography, reading, and spelling. They took courses called Grammar and Analysis of the English Language, Rhetoric, and British Literature, and completed general exercises in composition and extempore speaking (*Catalogue*, 1875).[3] With its "mix of oral and written composition throughout four years," and "a single rhetoric course to provide a theoretical grounding" (Brereton 9), Westfield's rhetorical curriculum resembled that of many a neighboring college.

Westfield's curriculum of 1876 was not new to the school. The school's early principals—including professor of rhetoric Samuel P. Newman, the Reverend Emerson Davis, and professor of rhetoric John W. Dickinson[4]—had subscribed less to Mann's emphasis upon basic drills and more to that of progressive educators like Caleb Atwater, who argued: "the main objects of educating females are precisely the same with those of educating the other sex—to develop all their powers and faculties, and to prepare them for happiness and usefulness. . . . In addition to the common branches of education . . . we wish to see superadded, geography, chemistry, botany, vocal music, astronomy, algebra, rhetoric, mineralogy, geology, mechanics, natural and moral philosophy" (118). Studies in subjects like rhetoric quickly became cornerstones of Westfield's curriculum.

Since views on women's education like Atwater's were not widely embraced by the public, early leaders had to justify their decision to require advanced study in such areas as rhetoric. Advanced study in rhetorical theory and practice would help teachers to "convey knowledge" (Atwater 118)—to use their discourse to foster learning, win respect, and achieve meaningful moral influence. Westfield's early leaders criticized conventional teaching methods that relied on rote memorization and conventional recitation. The teacher's goal was, as then-retired Emerson Davis remarked, to "infuse into young minds a thirst for improvement" and "call out [their pupils'] reasoning faculties" (qtd. in Graves).[5] In other words, with its special focus on the role of the mental faculties within the communication process and on the discourse practices commonly used within that process, rhetoric would help future teachers to better understand and reach the minds of primary school pupils.

In his eighteenth year as principal when the Allen sisters arrived at Westfield, John W. Dickinson played a particularly significant role in establishing the curricular link between effective teaching and rhetorical power, even as fewer and fewer male students were the recipients of that curriculum. A "dominant intellect in educational reform," Dickinson taught rhetoric courses at Westfield throughout his career (Brown 48).[6]

In a graduation address he gave in 1877, Dickinson represented the powerful teacher as one who would never "distort" or "dwarf" "the mind of the child." His teaching in rhetoric aimed to help future teachers avoid such disaster. The teacher who had investigated the minds of his or her pupils and employed varied and well-thought out rhetorical practices, such as inspired oratory and thoughtful discussion, would be best able to "take possession" of a classroom and to persuade pupils to adopt "lofty" ideals (qtd. in "Normal School").

As scholars Kathryn Fitzgerald and Lucille M. Schultz have both suggested, Pestalozzian learning theories strongly influenced nineteenth-century common and normal school instruction.[7] Along with other normal school educators, Dickinson repeated Pestalozzi's call for a "benevolent classroom environment and a pedagogy that moved from the simple and concrete to the complex and abstract" (qtd. in Schultz, *Young* 75). Observation and experience, "self-activity," and not textbooks, were central to the pupil's learning process (Dickinson *Limits* 24). Dickinson criticized teachers who depended heavily upon textbooks, arguing that the teacher should instead use "spoken words of his own as they are necessary to direct the pupil in thinking" (*Limits* 13).

In a lesson recorded by Westfield student Maria L. Tuttle in 1871, Dickinson illustrated this process of orally facilitating the thinking of their future pupils. He advised Tuttle and her peers that when teaching they should place pictures of vivid objects before the pupils and ask thoughtful questions that would promote discussion of their associations. This activity would help pupils to cultivate "taste" and "judgment," which would form the foundations of "effective expression." Since teachers would need to engage in constant "oral teaching," Dickinson also presented his students with the "requisites of a good orator" (qtd. in Arms), noting that both male and female teachers would be better conveyers of knowledge were they able to appeal directly to the particular passions of their audience of primary school pupils. Dickinson provided students with opportunities to connect theory to practice by requiring them to engage in mock teaching lessons and inviting them to give public addresses on educational issues at graduations.[8] He also encouraged both male and female students to take active roles in the school's literary society, members of which engaged in a variety of rhetorical activities, producing written and oral discourse of a persuasive and an informative nature (Rothermel).[9]

By the 1870s, Dickinson's view that teacher preparation required a theoretically rich program of study had gained currency. Mariolina Salvatori's work on historical conceptions of pedagogy suggests that a number of nineteenth-century educators "insisted on the necessity to provide teachers with the theoretical knowledge (science) necessary to guide and control their practice (art)" (*Pedagogy* 62). What sets his works apart from that of other reformers, however, is the central role he gave to the study of rhetoric within that complex process of investigation. Dickinson and his predecessors' practice of connecting teaching power to rhetorical power would remain a common one at Westfield, empowering women like the Allen sisters both in and out of the classroom throughout the late nineteenth and early twentieth centuries.

THE LATE NINETEENTH-CENTURY CURRICULUM

The Allen sisters were among the last students at Westfield to attend lectures and recitations given by Dickinson, as he left in 1877 to become Secretary of the Massachusetts Board of Education. Through the work of scholars such as Dickinson, who traveled to normal schools around the country, Westfield and its curriculum had gained prestige (Herbst, *And Sadly*; Brown). Yet anxiety over what was an appropriate education for teachers, especially female teachers, grew even more intense as more and more women entered the field; shifting perceptions about the role of women teachers resulted in a number of significant changes in the curriculum, particularly in the rhetorical curriculum.

As Brereton notes, through the latter part of the nineteenth century, colleges and universities replaced their traditional programs of rhetorical study with "new utilitarian writing courses" (7) emphasizing "error correction" and "the five modes of discourse" (17). Robert Connors's work *Composition-Rhetoric* provides a detailed account of this move away from studying the "actual process of communication" toward mastering the "lower level elements of mechanical correctness" (148). The Westfield catalogue and other school documents from the 1880s and 1890s suggest that this shift in emphasis occurred as part of a larger overhaul of the curriculum. In the early 1880s, for instance, state officials pressured the Massachusetts Board of Education to standardize the curriculum at the Massachusetts normal schools. According to public officials, normal schools were not adequately preparing future teachers to exert control over and teach basic skills to an increasingly diverse (and to them foreign and unruly) primary school population (Brown 116).[10] While the normal schools had won some public respect, legislators and their supporters also remained concerned that normal schools were duplicating the higher academic work of other more prestigious institutions (Brown; Herbst, *And Sadly*).

Westfield and its sister schools around the country responded to such charges by asserting, both orally and in writing, that its course of study was primarily "professional" in nature and thus different from the curriculum at liberal arts colleges (*Catalogue*, 1880). While Westfield continued to require advanced study in many of the same subjects, claiming these studies would increase their students' mental powers, the Massachusetts normal schools made the admissions requirements more rigorous and increased the amount of time spent covering educational theory and classroom methodology. These schools also adjusted the rhetorical curriculum to address concerns over normal school students' written and spoken English. In place of general school exercises in composition and extempore speaking, students entering Westfield in the 1880s were required to take two semesters of composition. The composition courses were to focus explicitly on technical matters such as "[c]apitals, punctuation, letter-writing, [and] business forms" as well as "paragraphing" and "spelling" (*Catalogue*, 1880–1897).

As Connors and others have noted, gender ideology probably played a role in this shift towards formalized composition instruction. At Westfield, 148 out of the 156 students enrolled in 1887 were women, largely from lower-middle class homes. The works of Michael Halloran, Elizabethada Wright, Nan Johnson, and others reveal the extent to which nineteenth-century norms defined women's rhetorical space. Women were deemed better suited to producing certain forms of written communication (works of moral uplift or family correspondence); engaging in oral or written argument would compromise feminine modesty. As already noted, few questioned the right of a woman (at least a middle-class white woman) to pursue a career in teaching, deeming it an "acceptable, noble alternative to immediate motherhood and wifely duties" (Cogan 239). In the public mind, however, women teachers were *not* training to become great orators (Wright and Halloran). Instead, they needed skill in aiding children to acquire correct spoken and written English.[11] Westfield's new composition courses would provide more suitable preparation.

Yet in the 1880s and 1890s Westfield's rhetorical curriculum required more than two semesters of composition instruction. Students continued to take a course in rhetoric much like the course Dickinson taught during his tenure, and Westfield's composition and rhetoric teachers continued to make connections between mastery of the art of oral and written expression and powerful teaching. Leaders of the 1880s and 1890s shared their predecessors' beliefs that exposure to a variety of discourse practices, including oral and written forms, and to the theories behind their use, would best prepare the teacher for her difficult work. These practices, furthermore, were introduced to Westfield students not by men, but by women, many of whom had graduated from Westfield Normal School themselves.

Several of Dickinson's former female students returned to Westfield to teach in the composition and rhetoric courses. From 1879 to 1890 Sarah Kneil, an 1867 graduate, returned to teach composition. She also covered the rhetoric course for a short time. Kneil may have introduced students to the practical forms and conventions of composition, but she also sought more from her students. A former student described Kneil as an "inspired teacher . . . one original thought meant more to her than quantities of parrotty reproduction," suggesting that like Dickinson, Kneil sought to produce teachers who might employ moving discourse in their classrooms (Sedgwick 7a).

Elvira Carver, an 1865 graduate, taught courses in algebra and geography as well as Westfield's rhetoric course from 1878 to 1883 and from 1885 to 1887. According to school catalogues, her course resembled Dickinson's, introducing students to "figurative language and qualities of style." It included "composition writing and criticism," but also "a study of the mind and its qualities." Since there is but little information available about Carver's teaching, it is difficult to determine how much attention her courses gave to such practices as oral and written argument. But like the midwestern instructors discussed in Kathryn Fitzgerald's work on European pedagogy and the normal school, Carver drew on a different intellectual tradition than her peers at neighboring colleges. Like most of her Westfield contemporaries, she had been well schooled in more interactive pedagogical theories like those of Pestalozzi, theories that emphasized "self-activity." Not surprisingly, she shared Dickinson's disdain for textbooks and his commitment to "oral teaching." In a preface to a geography text that she wrote in 1887, Carver noted that her text was to be only a guide for the teacher's "oral instruction"—to help teachers "train pupils to observe and think instead of memorizing" (9). Teaching the theories and practices of rhetoric was another way for her to enable future teachers to teach orally with success.[12]

There is additional evidence that "effective oral expression" remained a concern of the rhetorical curriculum. Westfield women of the 1880s and 1890s appear to have embraced the power of oral and written argument more readily than those of previous generations. Women in the 1880s exhibited a greater willingness to engage in extemporaneous debate as members of the school's literary society, and course outlines suggest that in their civics course, a course taught by Frances Gaylord from 1891 to 1897, Westfield students continued to learn about, and to try out, the procedures for oral debate.[13] These debates took up largely educational issues, such as the question of whether "high schools ought not be supported by the state," and whether "[w]omen should be educated to the same degree that man is." Women of the society also honed their oral abilities by giving dramatic readings, participating in informal discussions, and giving extemporaneous speeches when they became society officers (Normal Philologian Society, Nov. 4, 1883; June 18, 1884; June 11, 1885).

Furthermore, during the 1880s and 1890s students at Westfield were required to write extended themes or compositions, called "theses," often delivering these orally before an audience during graduation. Fifteen students, thirteen of whom were women, delivered addresses in June 1887, speaking on such issues as "Professional Meetings," "Dangers of the Common School," "The Teacher as a Citizen," and "The Province of the Public Schools." These addresses were, admittedly, readings. And yet the presenters were praised for their oral performances. One editor described the 1887 addresses as: "short because the thought is rigidly condensed, each replete with valuable suggestions. The reading was such that every essay was distinctly heard in the extreme rear of the church. Some were rendered with that grace and charm of tone and modulation which gave pleasure to the listener even if he was careless of the thought. The exercises gave abundant proof both of the excellence of the professional training of the school, and of the value of the course of study as a means of literary training" ("Normal Commencement").

A graduation essay entitled "Our Life's Work," written sometime in the 1880s, provides additional evidence that those attending Westfield in the late nineteenth century felt empowered by their rhetorical education. The writer notes that among women's many new talents is the "skill of composition which thrills and animates the mind to noble action." As evidence of women's potential to inspire such action both inside and outside of the classroom, she provides her listeners with a list of famous women public figures of humble origins, some of whom were educators known for their public appearances and powerful discourse, including Mary Lyons, Anne Judson, Anna Dickinson, Jenny Lind, and Sarah Bernhardt.[14]

The participation of the women at Westfield in such events occurred in the context of a number of social factors. Women were pursuing more public professions, in fields such as school administration and social work that re-

quired them to speak publicly from podiums. The suffrage and temperance
movements had drawn area women into their folds.[15] In a number of states
women could vote in school board elections. Westfield's women graduates
from the 1860s, 1870s, and 1880s went on to positions that required skilled
oratory outside of the classroom as well as within including school board
officials, normal school instructors, college professors, founders of schools,
and leaders in social service organizations like the YWCA (*General Catalogue*).[16] These graduates returned to Westfield to give addresses and share
their experiences during graduations and school anniversaries, offering inspiration to students of the late nineteenth century.[17] Their visits reinforced
Westfield's commitment to a more complex rhetorical education, which familiarized students with the communication process and the discourse practices
that have traditionally characterized it, and thus transform them into influential teachers.

THE TWENTIETH CENTURY

Westfield State Normal School historians have tended to choose the nineteenth century as opposed to the early twentieth as the focus of their studies,
perhaps because archival materials documenting the coeducational nineteenth
century are more plentiful than those available for the all-women's institution
of the early twentieth. Yet historians also generally represent the nineteenth
century as a period of greater innovation, one that trained both women and
men to become intellectually engaged primary school teachers, as well as normal school teachers, administrators, social reformers, and artists (like the
Allen sisters).

For instance, according to Robert Brown, by the early twentieth century,
Westfield had become "but a shadow" of its former self (120). Brown high-
lights the ways in which state and local authorities, influenced by the cult of
efficiency as well as other social and economic forces, pressured the Massachusetts normal schools into simplifying their curricula—normal schools were
expected to reject nineteenth-century ideals and theories and to become vo-
cationally minded institutions drilling future elementary school teachers in
practical methodologies.

Course catalogues, student records, and other official documents reveal that the early twentieth century was indeed marked by losses, particularly in the area of rhetorical instruction. Westfield's early twentieth-century students and their teachers were subject to more limiting conceptions of the role of primary school teacher, women's education, and the normal school itself. Yet other archival materials show that Westfield's teachers of rhetoric and composition, along with the student body, resisted those limiting conceptions. Course descriptions, student notebooks, and yearbooks suggest that teachers and students drew on the school's rich intellectual traditions and on new and more progressive educational theories to create a teacher training program offering more complex rhetorical knowledge.

Mariolina Salvatori's work reminds readers that a number of turn-of-the-century normal school leaders from across the country expressed complex ideals similar to those of progressive normal school founders (*Pedagogy* 169). For instance, in 1891, Thomas S. Gray, president of the St. Cloud Normal School and chair of the NEA's 1889 Committee on Normal Schools, asserted that the best normal school would be a "school of philosophy . . . making teachers out of scholars" (qtd. in Salvatori *Pedagogy* 206). Its prime purpose was to work out a "stupendous problem": "How does the mind work?" (201). His views were shared by members of the NEA's 1895 Committee on Normal Schools, who wrote that their institutions must train teachers for a "great field of labor"—that they must cultivate "a loftier conception of what the American teacher must become to fill the place of destiny conferred by democracy and Christianity" (National Education Association 29). For leaders like Thomas Gray and Albert Boyden, principal of the Bridgewater State Normal School and a member of the 1895 Committee on Normal Schools, a well-prepared teacher would have an education in which theory and practice were "conjoined" (Boyden 7).[18]

Yet other educators, such as Frank Hill and David Snedden, who ran the Massachusetts Board of Education for much of the late nineteenth and early twentieth centuries, argued that normal schools should adopt a more pragmatic mission, focusing strictly on "professional work" instead of pursuing the "advanced" study in the liberal arts that had come to guide places like Westfield during the nineteenth century (Brown; Herbst, *And Sadly*).[19] They shared the common belief that normal school students were "persons of indifferent intellectual acquirements" who needed training more suited to their academic deficiencies (Gordy 129).

Fed by the larger number of women choosing careers over marriage (Woody 204), continued cultural anxiety over whether women were biologically or intellectually outfitted for a complex academic education certainly lurked behind the labels assigned to normal school students.[20] Nineteenth-century theories on teaching, like those inspired by Pestalozzi, were also under attack. Educators worried that the interactive, child-centered approaches of women teachers were emasculating male pupils, particularly those at the middle or secondary levels (Woody 508). Granted, more progressive philosophies, like those of John Dewey, G. Stanley Hall, and William James were beginning to influence the work of some normal school leaders and teachers; but the leaders of the Massachusetts Board of Education did not share these pedagogical perspectives. The board's vision of the field of education was the one so well documented by Salvatori: members of departments of education at major public and private universities (mostly men) would take responsibility for developing and teaching scientifically proven educational theories to future scholars and administrators (also largely men), while the normal schools would provide primary school teachers (mostly women) with the formulas and methods needed to run a classroom full of children.

Pressure to modify the curriculum was felt intensely at Westfield, particularly by Clarence Brodeur, who became principal in 1904. In a letter to the board he expressed enthusiasm for "the vocational trend" in education, asserting that "the element of utilitarian instruction has increased the efficiency of our teaching at Westfield" and stripping down the curriculum to train teachers in the basics.[21] Brodeur assured the board that Westfield would place at the center of its rhetorical curriculum "correct speaking and writing" and the best means to communicate these "habits" to children.[22]

While Brodeur was indeed a force with which to be reckoned, those faculty members responsible for rhetorical instruction at Westfield did not entirely adopt his utilitarian perspective. The curriculum they developed calls into question Connors's argument that by the early twentieth century, classical principles and civic development were no longer clear goals of rhetorical instruction. The careers of Westfield faculty members also challenge the notion that responsibility for rhetorical instruction rested largely with graduate students of literature, usually women.

Westfield's early twentieth-century English teachers shared their principal's concern with "correct speaking and writing," yet their stories are more complicated. According to Connors, ill-prepared to teach writing, many college teachers of the day relied heavily on textbooks and made correction an "uppermost" goal of instruction. The demands of "theme correcting drove the more thoughtful scholars away" and turned teachers into "drudges" (*Composition* 151). But Westfield's instructors do not fit this profile. They received their training at nineteenth-century teacher institutes and normal schools, and not in university literature departments. Furthermore, they occupied positions of some importance, even power, at Westfield; and the curriculum they developed continued to stress the importance of future teachers studying rhetoric and composition as a means to develop powerful personae and voices.

Evaluations by Westfield instructors of teacher candidates are, indeed, critical of those who have "poor English." But instructors also praise teacher candidates when their discourse exhibits "force," "fluency," "presence," "earnestness," "sympathy," and "ingenuity" (Student Records). These traits enabled teachers to "win" the cooperation of classes, mold the characters of children, and foster their learning, particularly in the language-arts. These instructors also shared their predecessors' disdain for a dependence on textbooks. Furthermore, they saw themselves as preparing teachers to have an influence both in the classroom and in professional societies and civic organizations.

Adeline Knight's teaching career at Westfield serves as a case in point. A graduate of the Maplewood Institute and former high school teacher, Knight came to Westfield in the mid-1890s, helping to shape the rhetorical program that existed at the time of Brodeur's arrival. Under her, the course in rhetoric disappeared from the curriculum, replaced by a combined course in rhetoric and composition that focused on the modes of discourse: "Description, narration, exposition, and argument, with the qualities of style appropriate to each" (*Catalogue*, 1897). Students learned about the "correct order" in which to say things as well as "what not to say" (*Catalogue*, 1903).

Yet an essay Knight wrote for the journal *Education* earlier in her career suggests that she also shared her predecessors' belief that rhetorical instruction should prepare teachers to develop their pupils' processes of communication. She wrote, for instance, that a "real teacher" "set[s] thought and fancy flashing between soul and soul" (13). Knight also mistrusted textbooks, criticizing the primary school teacher who "makes no practical application of facts, and merely teaches textbooks thoroughly. Concerning political questions, foreign news, the work of the world, she knows nothing. . . . Neither teacher nor taught can be called literate. The teacher has absolutely no resources beyond 'the English branches'" (16). Descriptions of courses she taught show that she shared her predecessor John Dickinson's commitment to encouraging "self-activity." Her courses in rhetoric and composition, as well as those in literature and grammar, used the "laboratory method," where students received "daily practice in writing" and one-on-one critique from the teacher. By encouraging them to offer one another critique, she also "trained [them] to intelligent criticism of language work" (*Catalogue*, 1903). Knight was consciously modeling an approach she believed her students should take when engaged in "language work" with their own future pupils.

A contemporary of Knight's, Laura Knotts of the Lowell State Normal School, argued that normal school instruction in English enhanced students' teaching power by "broaden[ing] the mental horizon" and "quicken[ing] the thought" (4). For Knight, self-activity did precisely that—it not only improved future teachers' ability to use correct written and spoken forms, it also increased their thinking powers, which led to increased confidence, or force, and an ability to guide children spontaneously in their own language development. Knight's pedagogical perspective is consistent with that of the rising educational theorists of her day, such as John Dewey, who saw "the language instinct" as the "greatest of all educational resources," and who argued that to foster learning, primary school teachers had to be able to use their own discourse to create an atmosphere friendly to "the full and free use of language" (43).

The pedagogical context in which she worked may be one reason that Knight's conception of the composing process is actually more organic than mechanistic, placing her in a camp alongside more progressive composition theorists like Fred Scott and Gertrude Buck. Her course descriptions emphasize, for example, that the composition is "a living product of an active mind; therefore, there is constant and careful study of the way in which paragraphs grow" (*Catalogue*, 1903). Notes by Elizabeth Rowell, who took Knight's course in 1906, provide further evidence that Knight linked the composing process to the development of thought. Knight emphasized the importance of "original composition" and conceived of the invention process as not necessarily linear or formulaic. For instance, Knight suggested that as students reflected on their subject, they "jot down" their thoughts, "even though they seem unimportant, for one thought suggests another." She reminded students that in coming up with material to write about, reading widely was of value. As they read, she remarked, students should take careful notes on what the material says. But those notes, she asserted, should also include "conclusions and impressions of your own made as you read. These will be very valuable when you expand [your] outline into a theme."

Like her predecessor Dickinson, Knight also frequently linked her lessons in composition to instruction in writing. Rowell's notes show Knight discussing how future teachers might facilitate their pupils' language and, hence, thinking abilities. She suggested that future teachers encourage primary school pupils to use writing to "retell, condense, and expand" the stories they hear and read about in varied sources. Expanding, for Knight, was the most profitable activity: "a long step toward original composition . . . the writer has an opportunity to develop an idea in an original way. It is as if an artist should take another's pencil sketch and fill in the lights and shadows according to his own ideas." Knight's emphasis was not on producing teachers obsessed with mechanical correctness, but suggested instead the view of another contemporary, Laura Dunbar Hagarty, that an "overanxious pruning knife" applied to a child's written or oral expression interfered with "naturalness and vividness," and thus interfered with the child's intellectual development (17).[23]

The theses Knight's students wrote differed from those often decontextualized essays produced in many college composition courses of the day. Her students wrote essays for composition class, for other courses, and, at least for a time, for a school periodical, the *Normal Exponent*. As in the nineteenth-century normal school, students used their writing to advance their professional knowledge—to explore or argue for the effectiveness of a particular teaching approach (e.g., the Sloyd Method), or to understand the evolution of theories of education; they continued to write theses, at least until the time of Brodeur's arrival.

After Brodeur arrived, students engaged less frequently in oral public address, no longer presenting their essays at graduations, which Brodeur transformed into short church services (Graduation Programs). While Knight apparently did not emphasize oratory as her predecessors had, she did believe that effective oral expression, marked in her words by "exactness, force, and fluency," was essential to teaching power (*Catalogue*, 1914). Additionally, she frequently required her students to present orally before one another. Students also channeled their rhetorical energies into theatrical productions, some of which were written by the students themselves (Graduation Programs). During Knight's tenure, Westfield continued to provide normal school students with meaningful rhetorical models, inviting several prominent female reformers and suffragettes to give addresses at the school.

The profile of Westfield instructor Raymond G. Patterson, who came to Westfield in 1919, and the curriculum he developed, also differed markedly from that of the exploited instructor teaching freshman composition at the elite college down the road.[24] The training he received at a nineteenth-century normal school likely shaped his greater commitment to training teachers, in the words of the 1899 Committee on Normal Schools, not just to "write and speak," but to feel "at home . . . on the platform" (30). Patterson was probably even more under the influence of progressive educational theorists like John Dewey, whose belief that language learning must be "close to the life of most students" had taken hold in the primary schools of the 1920s (Applebee 48).

At Westfield, Patterson taught history, civics, and composition. Like Knight's, his composition course was student-centered, providing "useful" instruction in both oral and written discourse. He set out to train students "to use and to teach the forms of composition most essential to the active men or women of the modern world" (*Catalogue*, 1920–1921). For students, this meant "the development and organization of material into such forms as are certain to be demanded of a teacher in the life of any community: club papers, talks, book reviews, reports, stories, debates, descriptions, expository themes. Abundant opportunity for practice in spoken and written English in correlation with history, civics, current events, and in daily student activities" will be provided (*Catalogue*, 1925).

These varied activities might explain why Patterson's students exhibited a "zest for rhetorical encounters" not unlike that of Westfield women of the 1880s (Halloran 254). For example, in conjunction with his courses, 1923 students organized "The Seven Joint Debates" described at the opening of this chapter. The reenactment of the Lincoln and Douglas debates, with participants enthusiastically donning the language, demeanor, and clothing of these famous politicians, arguably provides us with a glimpse of female students and their instructors resisting limitations imposed on their rhetorical education by the institution and the state. In physically cloaking themselves in the characters of two famous male politicians of the previous century, these players strained creatively against the hidden and overt expectations that had restricted the education of teachers, and women, at various times in the school's history—claiming the public platform (and also perhaps mocking it) for their own use. In the words of Karlyn Kohrs Campbell, these women embodied an "innovative assertion of authority" over their own identities as women and teachers ("Consciousness" 57). Furthermore, their reenactment was one in a series of debates that generated original oral disputation on subjects such as immigration, education, and temperance.

Inspired by these performances and encouraged by their faculty, Westfield's female students went on to form a joint debate and drama society in the mid-1920s. They named this society Delta Omicron Alpha, or the Daughters of Athena. As in the nineteenth-century literary society, members of the 1920s and 1930s organized formal oral debates, facilitated school-wide discussions called "forums," and wrote and produced dramas on social and educational issues. Debaters also served as representatives for the Massachusetts Normal School Debating Council and competed against other Massachusetts normal schools in two "triangular debates."[25]

Institutional forces, gender ideology, and certain educational philosophies at Westfield in the early twentieth century led faculty to place more emphasis on the normal school student's future role as an "efficient, methodical, and professional educator."[26] Such a teacher needed to be capable of correct written and spoken English, as well as able to pass those habits on to children. However, Westfield's instructors also continued to represent the study of oral and written expression in more complex terms, as an exploration of the processes of communication. They exposed students to a wider array of discourse practices, including oral and written argument, than state and school officials demanded. They justified their curriculum, as their predecessors had in the century before, by emphasizing the role rhetorical education played in producing "teaching power."

I would argue that Westfield's continued faith in the connection between teaching and rhetorical power led it to develop a more rigorous rhetorical curriculum than other schools of its day—a curriculum that more effectively represented written and oral expression as complicated acts of communication with larger social implications. The extent to which graduates of Westfield applied what they learned to their own teaching invites, of course, further exploration. Also worthy of examination are the varied ways in which programs of rhetorical study at other normal schools evolved in the twentieth century. Comparative studies of normal schools may provide further evidence that more complex understandings of rhetoric and composition instruction were kept alive in the early twentieth-century not just by the primary and secondary schools, as James Berlin notes (*Writing*, 84), but also by normal schools.

In *Gender and Rhetorical Space in American Life, 1866–1910*, Nan Johnson discusses the various cultural and social forces that wiped women orators off the "rhetorical/oratorical" map. She asserts that in disregarding women orators, scholars have

> forgotten . . . the insight into the range of nineteenth-century rhetorical practices . . . : the vitality and cultural influence of oratory over nineteenth-century American life was found as often in the church meeting room, the convention hall, the town square, the community gathering, and the dining hall as it was in the Senate chambers, the law court, and the political-debating platform. When early canon authors chose to privilege only the rhetorical spaces controlled by statesmen, they erased not only the voices of women who helped to shape American political culture, but also the significance of the rhetorical spaces in which most Americans heard words that changed their views and lives. (171)

To that list of erased rhetorical spaces I would add the primary school classroom, along with the classroom of institutions, like the Westfield State Normal School, that prepared primary school teachers. Such an erasure fails to allow for the fact that teaching, in the words of Geraldine Joncich Clifford, "is a powerful molder of human beings" (176)—an act of suasion by which social as well as personal identities are constructed.

Westfield's rhetorical curriculum offered its female students access to rhetorical knowledge often denied to them at other institutions of higher education, which lends further support to Kathryn Fitzgerald's argument that nineteenth-century normal school faculty, and the rhetorical programs of study they developed, were shaped by their schools' unique institutional circumstances as professional training grounds for teachers, and by the progressive educational theories those grounds fostered. Furthermore, Westfield's particular institutional circumstances, along with a new generation of progressive educational theories, enabled the school's early twentieth-century faculty to resist institutional and disciplinary attempts to redefine rhetorical education in mechanistic terms.

My own position as a faculty member at the small teaching-focused institution that replaced the Westfield State Normal School has certainly inclined me to read the school's history in a more positive light. My institutional commitments also lead me to assert the importance of looking not just for those stories that our scholarly narratives erase, but also those that are consciously and unconsciously erased through the construction of an archive. Central to my work have been the varied scraps of paper—the letters, graduation programs, student writings—hidden in the backs of file cabinets.

Deep excavation shows that for almost one hundred years Westfield supported a curriculum offering female students access to a richer understanding of rhetorical theory and practice than more elite institutions of the nineteenth and early-twentieth centuries. While along the way Westfield may have produced "well-read women of good taste" who used their education to make inroads into a number of fields, it also armed teachers with a special rhetorical training aimed at empowering them to communicate meaningfully with those they taught.

Notes

I am indebted to the painstaking efforts of Robert Brown, a history professor from Westfield State College, who with limited institutional support created and sustained the college's archive for more than two decades.

1. What would become the Westfield State Normal School opened in Barre, Massachusetts, in 1839 under the direction of professor of rhetoric Samuel P. Newman. Led by Cyrus Peirce, the Lexington State Normal School had opened a few months earlier. In 1842 Newman died suddenly, and the Barre school closed for two years, reopening in 1844 in Westfield, Massachusetts (located in the western part of the state). Between 1839 and 1842 the school enrolled 165 students, 75 of whom were men (Brown, *Rise and Fall* 127). Forty-three women and twenty-eight men enrolled at Westfield in 1844 (*Catalogue*).

2. For a more detailed study of the nineteenth-century curriculum and extracurriculum at Westfield, see Rothermel, "A Sphere".

3. More specifically, the Allen sisters took one year of Grammar and Analysis of the English Language (4 hours per week), one half year of British Literature (4 hours per week), and one half year of Rhetoric (4 hours per week).

4. Emerson Davis (1798–1896), a Congregational minister and former principal of the Westfield Academy, where Emma Willard taught for a time, was principal of Westfield Normal School from 1844 to 1846. David Rowe, a former pupil of Newman's, followed him, serving from 1846 to 1854. William Wells, a philologist, served from 1854 to 1856 at which time John W. Dickinson became principal, serving until 1877.

5. These remarks come from a lecture given by former principal Emerson Davis on a return visit to Westfield in 1855, several years after he retired. The lecture was recorded by student Julia Graves.

6. John W. Dickinson (1825–1901) studied at Williams College with philosopher Mark Hopkins. In 1877 he became secretary of the Massachusetts Board of Education. After retiring from the board, he joined his daughter, Suzie Allen Dickinson, on the faculty at the Emerson College of Oratory. In addition to publishing *The Limits of Oral Training* and *Rhetoric and Principles of Written Composition*, Dickinson also wrote *Our Republic* (1888) and *Principles and Methods of Teaching, Derived from Knowledge of the Mind* (1899).

7. Johann Heinrich Pestalozzi (1746–1827) was a Swiss educational reformer whose work was especially influential in northern Europe.

8. No model school was available from 1855 to 1892, so students were required to practice teaching for one another. They had opportunities to observe real classes, however, and many students taught during their summer breaks.

9. Dickinson even encouraged female students to engage in the society's biweekly debates. They mostly refused to participate, although they did contribute to society discussions and applied what they were learning about argument to pieces they wrote for the society's literary magazine (Rothermel).

10. By 1900, over 50 percent of the children attending public schools in Massachusetts were immigrants or the children of immigrants (Brown 116).

11. Furthermore, the notion that women teachers achieved their rhetorical power in the classroom not through inspired oratory but rather through their ability to nurture their students led many to see the study of oratory and debate as impractical (Rothermel).

12. Also noteworthy is Laura C. Harding, who graduated from Westfield in 1869 and taught composition and other subjects on the faculty from 1872 to 1896. After Harding left Westfield, she completed a graduate degree at the University of Grenoble and then started her own school in Denver, Colorado.

13. In the 1860s and 1870s, female members of the school's literary society had largely confined their arguments to their written compositions and informal oral discussions. In their 1890s civics classes, students were expected to engage in mock town hall and school committee debates ("Civil Polity").

14. Mary Lyons founded Mount Holyoke; Anne Judson served as a missionary; Anna Dickinson was a suffragette and social reformer; Jenny Lind was an opera singer; and Sarah Bernhardt was an actress.

15. The *General Catalogue* of 1889, a record of what nineteenth-century graduates had done after leaving Westfield, lists a number of female graduates from the 1870s and 1880s who were members of temperance organizations.

16. Eldorah Eldridge (grad. 1871) became a normal school instructor in Whitewater, Wisconsin; and Helen Cleveland (grad. 1875) took a similar position at Platteville, Wisconsin, two schools Kathryn Fitzgerald has discussed. Ada Warner (grad. 1871) became a normal school instructor at St. Cloud. Clara Price (grad. 1878) and Caroline Knowles (grad. 1882) taught at the Hampton Institute, while Elizabeth Brewer (grad. 1863) taught at Vassar. A few, including Julia E. Smith (grad. 1875 from Westfield and 1889 from Howard University), became medical doctors. Charlotte Drinkwater (grad. 1862) served as General Superintendent for the Cambridge YWCA and then founded a school for economically underprivileged boys; Henrietta Smith (grad. 1871) wrote for publication; Fannie Rogers (grad. 1867) became a suffragette; and Minnie Russell (grad. 1878) became a missionary to India and Assam.

17. Kate Upson Clark, who graduated in 1872 and became a successful writer and editor, addressed the college during its fiftieth anniversary in 1889 (K. Clark; Rothermel 35).

18. Albert Boyden was principal of the Bridgewater State Normal School from 1860 to 1906.

19. Discouraged by the movement for more social efficiency characterizing educational debates at the end of the century, Dickinson resigned as secretary of the board in 1893. Ironically, he taught in California for a time, inspiring Snedden to become a teacher (Brown 93).

20. See Elizabeth Marbury's 1887 article "Education of Women" for such an indictment. Woody also cites a number of educators from the 1880s and 1890s who were debating the need for more utility in women's education (194–97).

21. Brodeur (1865–1923) was a graduate of Harvard and Boston Law School. He served as superintendent of schools in Chicopee, Massachusetts, before being hired at Westfield. Brodeur remained principal until 1923.

22. Harvard's 1897 "Report of the Committee on Composition" faulted normal schools for having an "unduly low . . . standard" in matters of correct English. The writers of the report demanded that normal school graduates "give evidence of severe mechanical and elementary drill received in the normal school" (Adams et al. 106).

23. Hagarty was a teacher of language and the history of education at the Buffalo Training School for Teachers.

24. Patterson was educated at a Pennsylvania Normal School and at Syracuse University. The Westfield Archives were named for him, as his initial donation helped establish them. Other English instructors of the late teens and twenties were Mary Grace Fickett, Alice M. Winslow, Emma Ramsey, Edith Dobie, and Alice Prescott Fay. Less information is available on these teachers, but course descriptions and other archival materials suggest they had similar philosophies to Knight and Patterson.

25. In 1929, Fitchburg, Bridgewater, and Westfield came up against each other in a triangular debate on the issue of "Equal Pay for Equal Work" (Westfield was the overall winner). In 1930 the three schools debated whether capital punishment should be abolished. Westfield's affirmative team was defeated in Bridgewater, but its negative team won in Fitchburg (*Tekoa*, 1931).

26. In the 1930s male students began attending Westfield again. The school also implemented a four-year degree program and became the Westfield State Teacher's College.

Archival Sources

The following items are part of the Raymond G. Patterson Alumni Archive, held by Ely Library, Westfield State College, Westfield, MA:

Arms, Charles. Notebook. 1858.
Biographical sketches of faculty and alumni. Three typescript notebooks.
Brodeur, Clarence. Letter to David Snedden. Clarence Brodeur Letter Books. 1911.
Catalogue of the State Normal School at Westfield Massachusetts. 1844–1931.
"Civil Polity." *Topics of the Course of Studies in the State Normal School, Westfield, MA.*
Class records, grades, attendance. 1854–1892.
Graduation programs. File folder. 1855–1920.
Graves, Julia R. Notebook. 1855–1856.
General Catalogue of the State Normal School, Westfield, Mass., 1839–1889. Boston: 1890.
Normal Exponent. Selected issues from 1897.
Normal Philologian Society. Records. 1872–1884.

"Our Life's Work." Student essay. Circa 1880s.

Rowell, Elizabeth. Notebook. 1906–1907.

Sedgwick, Herbert. Record of the class of 1886. Typescript prepared for the class semi-centennial. 1926.

Student records. 1904–1919.

The Tekoa. Westfield State Normal School Yearbook. 1919–1929.

Tuttle, Maria L. Notebook. 1871.

Life in the Margins

STUDENT WRITING AND CURRICULAR CHANGE
AT FITCHBURG NORMAL, 1895–1910

Patrice K. Gray

EMBLAZONED ON A large, bronzed wall plaque in the alumni room of Fitchburg State College is the institution's official origin myth: "In the beginning, even before there was that single building, there was the enthusiasm of one man, Joseph G. Edgerly, a former farmhand and bobbin boy from New Hampshire who struggled to get an education, studying by candlelight." The story continues: "He went on to graduate from Dartmouth College, but carried with him always a commitment to public education. As superintendent of the schools of Fitchburg, . . . [he] was a tireless education advocate, and pressed for better teachers with more formal training. He led the fight for a normal school in Fitchburg . . . [and] got his wish on June 6, 1894."

Archival materials for this article, located in the Amelia V. Galucci-Cirio Library at Fitchburg State College, include course catalogues; annual reports and transcripts of oral testimony to the Massachusetts Board of Education; the papers of John G. Thompson, principal; bound student theses; alumni records; local newspaper articles; and books and texts from the school's original library collection.

According to this narrative, Fitchburg State College continued to pursue a course forward toward an obtained ideal: it became a people's college, a place where "leaders" were, and continue to be, created. Somewhere in this narrative, though, its historic mission, the training of young people to teach in the public domain, has been lost.

Also lost in this simple rags-to-riches story are the rich complexities of the normal school itself, filled in its early years with mostly young female "pupils" and the faculty who sought to "train" them. As John Brereton reminds us, the more usual and available sources from which to construct institutional history in composition studies—textbooks and administrative documents—while valuable as "necessary props," cannot reveal the "everyday fabric of history as lived by the student, the teacher, and the general public" (xiv). The writing at Fitchburg reveals details of person and place which are often left out and constructs a curricular history closer to the lives of the first decades of the predominantly female students. This story, different in nearly all respects from the Harvard narrative which, until recently, has defined composition's history, is no less compelling.

IN THE BEGINNING

The history of Fitchburg Normal School officially began in 1893, when Joseph Edgerly, superintendent of schools in Fitchburg, testified before the Massachusetts Board of Education, which was convening to determine the locations of additional normal schools. Competition for the sites of these new normal schools was fierce. Superintendents spoke forcefully about their great need for trained elementary school teachers within their areas. After much deliberation, the board of education determined that new normal schools would be located in Fitchburg, Lowell, North Adams, and Barnstable, joining established normals at Framingham, Westfield, Bridgewater, Salem, Boston, and Worcester.

A genuine "literacy crisis" fueled Fitchburg's creation. Unlike the widely known and frequently commented upon literacy crisis surrounding the dismal entrance examinations of Harvard-bound youth of the 1870s, which became a "national scandal" (Connors, *Composition* 129), the literacy crisis in Fitchburg was more obvious and concrete. For example, examinations of young boys employed in the factories revealed that many were functionally illiterate (Kirkpatrick 377). School buildings, too, were inadequate: Fitchburg's South Street School was "more than a century old, crowded, and inadequately heated with woodstoves" (375). Of added concern were the large numbers of recent non-English-speaking immigrants to the area, who by 1900, composed one third of the city's population (Ringel 105). These issues, plus the concern of state educators that less than one-third of Massachusetts teachers had training of any kind (*Annual Report*, 1896, 15), led to the awareness that a normal school in Fitchburg was necessary to help solve a number of growing social and educational problems.

More can be said about the origins of Fitchburg, and its people and dates are traced in the college's official history, Francis X. Guindon's *Fitchburg State College: A Record of Leadership*. However, the original testimony before the Board of Education places Fitchburg's origin within a larger context; embedded in that testimony are perceptions about women's fitness to become professionals that may have influenced their education in the normal school. A Rev. Mr. Finch, for example, commented to the board that "there is [a] class who have just got to be teachers by hook or crook, the Lord knows how they get in, they get around school committees and everybody. Half of them ought to be over the wash tub or in the kitchen cooking." And Flora Kendall, who was then the only female superintendent in the Massachusetts public school system and who five years later became an influential teacher at Fitchburg, also derided what she called "untrained and incompetent teachers" in her testimony: "We are obliged to take young ladies from the high schools or academies . . . and some from the normal schools . . . who have fitted themselves to teach simply because they consider it a little more respectable than working in the shops" (Testimonials). Unlike the men at Harvard whose "literacy crisis" was thought to have been caused by poor teaching and not from a lack of their own abilities, the young women, this discourse suggests, had only themselves to blame for their inadequacies. As Geraldine Clifford has noted, such attitudes about female teachers were pervasive. Often thought to be immature and incompetent, young female teachers became part of a new "peril": "an invasion of the female product of the normal schools," which was frequently commented on in professional journals and national magazines (298). For people like the Rev. Mr. Fitch and even Flora Kendall, young women's presence in the normal schools and the elementary classroom was, at best, a mixed blessing.[1]

When Fitchburg opened in 1895, the normal school experience itself was already nationally contested and devalued. Writing several years earlier, in 1888, S. S. Parr, the president of the National Education Association, complained that normal schools had become "hopelessly confused" in their mission by moving away from vocational training to providing a more liberal arts education (qtd. in Borrowman 27). This controversy over the role of the normal school had local contours: as early as the late 1870s, Westfield Normal School had been singled out as an institution that was abandoning "unsolved problems" and "turning its back" on elementary and rural school teacher training (Herbst, *And Sadly* 90). While considered treasonous to the normal school's mission to "train," not "educate," teachers, this desired shift toward a liberal arts general education was understandable: many normal school educators believed that such a shift would elevate the curriculum of the normal school, raise the quality of students, and improve the morale of faculty who were "discouraged" by their institutions' vocational purpose (90). Despite these legitimate desires of many normal school teachers to educate their students more broadly, their efforts failed. As Herbst notes, these educators did not see that the widening "gulf" between normal school–trained elementary teachers and university-educated secondary school teachers was "deliberate and unbridgeable" ("Teacher Preparation" 217) and that their efforts would be devalued, if not condemned, by college faculty with whom they sought common intellectual status.

Also constraining the mission of Fitchburg Normal School were issues of eastern elitism articulated by many Massachusetts college and university educators. Unlike normal schools in the rural Midwest that evolved, by necessity, into institutions that more readily adapted to the changing needs of rural populations, normal schools in the East had become embroiled in a turf battle over who was better equipped to educate the rising professional classes. As Illinois Normal School historian Charles A. Harper noted, eastern normal schools were considered "a plebian thing, an upper-class gesture of philanthropy to the poor and ignorant" (qtd. in Herbst, "Teacher Preparation" 225). By the 1890s, particularly in Massachusetts, the educational hierarchy had already been determined. For example, Oliver Wendell Holmes, the first dean of the Graduate School of Education at Harvard, observed that at his institution there would be "no narrow peddling of methods for the schools as they now exist. . . . To train for school work as a mere craft is one thing; to teach education is another" (qtd. in Powell 4). The message for educators at the newly created Fitchburg Normal School was clear: as long as they knew their "proper" role to train students for elementary school, not high school, and as long as they did not attempt to provide their students a general education thought to be the province of the more prestigious colleges, they would be allowed to function in their narrowed capacity.

Within these constraints, then, Fitchburg Normal School opened its doors to forty-six young women, the daughters of largely middle-class families.[2] Officially, from the start, Principal John G. Thompson declared his school a success. Reporting to the Board of Education in 1896 that he had admitted "a number greater than was anticipated," Thompson observed, "certainly enough data have already been obtained to make it plain that there was a field for a normal school in this important and growing center of population." He continued: "Teachers have already exhibited such a knowledge of their duties and such an enthusiasm for their work that we have every assurance of a successful undertaking" (*Annual Report* 43). Of the pupils, he observed in the following year, "[They] are full of energy, zeal, and enthusiasm; they are willing workers and ready to second the efforts of the teachers. With a knowledge of method and principles, we believe that these pupils are also acquiring the professional spirit, that is, it must be admitted, of the greatest importance" (*Annual Report*, 1897, 46). Such zeal exhibited by Thompson is reflected in the emerging professional literature, which proclaimed teaching both an art and a science. Normal school educators, who had been discredited and devalued as mere vocational pedagogues, could now benefit from a new ideology, a new "science of instruction" (Tyack 413), in which students would be trained in modern teaching techniques. With this new, clear purpose, it was thought that any talk of a liberal education that had plagued places such as Westfield would now be unnecessary, even frivolous, given the normal schools' reinvigorated seriousness of purpose. At Fitchburg Normal School, there would be no mission creep.

The clearest of intentions are soon undermined, however, and even nobility of purpose and justifiable need could not immunize Fitchburg from the perception that normal schools were old-fashioned, quaint, and in the eyes of many eastern educators, even obsolete. Even the *Cottager*, a local newspaper that most often was a reliable cheerleader, made visible this divide between the normal school and the college experience. A feature story written about the school in 1900 concedes that while "progressive" in its reliance upon a "practice school" in which pupils could observe actual classroom teaching, for those young women who are "not ready to teach," Fitchburg could seem "a very indefinite, not to say, a plebian thing," with "none of the romance of a college, or even a female seminary" (xvii). A member of Fitchburg's first graduating class, Helen Bradford, writing in her 1897 essay entitled "Higher Education of Women," provides a hint of how Fitchburg students regarded their education. Wistfully, she writes: "We, as women here at the Fitchburg Normal School, have caught glimpses of that high table, the land of superior education. Do we need to ask what good it is to us? Would any one give up the joy and pleasure they have received even here and be satisfied with the learning they have had before? This school is not a seminary or an institution where women can receive the higher education, but it is here that they can imagine what higher training would be and the joy it would bring them" (Theses of First Class, 1897).

From the outset, students such as Helen Bradford may have been poised between what David Cohen calls "faith and doubt" (394) in the mission of normal schools. While Bradford might have agreed with her fellow classmate, Sarah Bacon, who writes with pride that "we will find the normal schools of today constantly graduating teachers who will aid in the great work of making the United States the most highly educated and therefore the most powerful nation on earth" ("Growth of the Normal Schools," Theses of First Class, 1897), she and others may have perceived their efforts as residing in the margins of higher education.

GATES AND THEIR KEEPERS

As a newly created institution for learning regarded by many in the community as a symbol of its coming of age, Fitchburg Normal School set forth its official policies and procedures in language that is clear and unequivocal. In the *Catalogue and Circular* guide, prospective students and their parents could read the orderly descriptions of the school's programs of study and entrance requirements. As stated in the first catalogue, "pupils" (only around the turn of the century were they referred to as "students") could choose from a two-year program geared toward "those who aim to teach in the public schools below the high school" or a one-year advanced course for those with prior teaching experience and "who give evidence of maturity" (*Catalogue*, 1896, 23). Pupils would receive training in methods of teaching English, which included reading, language, rhetoric, composition, and literature, as well as history, mathematics, and science. The curriculum was orderly. Pupils were divided into "groups of twelve to twenty" according to their "fitness to work together," receive "four to six weeks" of "general classroom work," then begin their observations in the kindergarten through grade eight school. In the morning, they would conduct their observations, then in the afternoon meet with the principal or "superior teachers" in "recitation of the methods of teaching." The object of this first two-year program was basic: graduates must have demonstrated "an ability to control and to teach," not necessarily demonstrate academic competence (23).

Entrance requirements were also specified clearly in the first years of the school. "Candidates must have attained the age of seventeen, if young men, and sixteen, if young women," "be free from any diseases or infirmity that would unfit them from the office of teacher," and "present a certificate of good moral standing." Most importantly, though, candidates "must give evidence of good intellectual capacity (marks of their scholarship and standing in their high school are desired) and be graduates of the high school under whose study has been approved by the Board of Education" (*Catalogue*, 1896, 17).

This last requirement was thought vital to the success of the Massachusetts normal schools. An 1894 decision by the Board of Education to require a high school diploma of all normal school candidates across the Commonwealth was believed to be necessary in allowing the normals to educate in pedagogy, not academics. As Frank Hill, the secretary of the Board of Education, stated in his 1896–1897 official report, the normal school "is not an academy" whose purpose is to "educate" (*Annual Report*, 1897, 122). In delineating the narrow focus of the normal school, he added, "As high school training is now required for admission to normal schools, the time in these schools should be devoted to professional study. At least there should be a division, and only professional work should be attempted in such subjects as are taught in the common schools." Hill continued to assert the specialized mission on the normal school in his report the following year: "It must be remembered that the people have, when admitted, much general knowledge of the subjects taught in the common schools. This plan shows what they lack, and enables the teachers to reach the difficulties with the least amount of time and effort" (*Annual Report*, 1898, 196). According to Hill, the better the candidates' high school preparation, "the closer the normal school can get to the ideals of a dominating professional spirit" (122). Clearly, what was at stake here was the normal school's need and desire to admit no pupils who would require remediation. Not only would remedial instruction tax instructional resources, it would undermine the central mission of the school to teach pedagogy, not content.

From the first, all candidates were screened for their fitness to enter. In the first year, prospective students were required to pass written and oral examinations, which became more complicated, at least in their catalogue description, over the next decade. In 1896, the details of the written and oral examinations were specific and straightforward. In the written portion of the exam, held over two days, students were required to write a "paragraph or two on several topics to be chosen by the candidate from a considerable number —perhaps twelve to fifteen—set before him in the examination. The treatment of these topics is designed to test the candidate's power of clear and accurate expression" (*Catalogue*, 1896, 19). Oral examinations followed and were used "to gain some impression on the candidates' personal characteristics and their use of language" (18). While prospective students were admonished to "avail themselves of the best high school faculties obtainable in a four years' course" in order to be successful in their entrance examinations, great length was taken to reassure candidates that "if the ordinary work of a good statutory high school . . . is well done, candidates should have no difficulty in meeting any of the academic tests to which they may be subjected" (21). Although these entrance specifications were clearly articulated, strict implementation was difficult. Trying to balance his need to supply the community with trained teachers, his prospective students' actual academic abilities, and the "fierce" competition for students among Massachusetts normal schools (Labaree 163), Thompson had to negotiate the complex demands of academic preparation and the marketplace in admitting students.[3]

Over the next five years, the rhetoric surrounding admissions standards and testing grew more heated and focused primarily on the writing skills of students. Catalogues from those years include language that is more specific, and, at times, more restrictive. In addition to the written examination standard in which candidates were to demonstrate "clear and accurate expression," students were to have demonstrated a background in "the principals of rhetoric" (*Catalogue*, 1899, 24). In 1900, candidates could read in the catalogue a warning that "the amount of work in this course [the two years' program] is so great that only those who can enter it most thoroughly prepared can hope to complete it, with the required practice, in the time assigned to it" (11). Additionally, prospective students could read this warning in the description of the oral examination: "The candidate may be required to answer questions involving the essentials of English grammar" (28). Throughout these later catalogues, statements about standards appear with greater frequency and urgency, suggesting that Thompson and others believed that many of their students lacked necessary literacy skills. One way to prevent the problem from occurring, it was thought, was to stiffen entrance requirements and even warn away the academically ill prepared. In 1899, prospective students were told: "No candidate will be accepted whose written work in English is notably deficient in clear and accurate expression, spelling, punctuation, idiom, or division of paragraphs, or whose spoken English exhibits faults so serious as to make it inexpedient for the normal school to attempt their correction. The candidate's English, therefore, in all oral and written examinations will be subject to the requirements implied in the foregoing statement and be marked accordingly" (19).

The early official documents gave a great deal of attention to gatekeeping. Frank Hill focused on the need for educators to be vigilant gatekeepers; his ruminations and admonitions reveal the school's attempts to maintain "clear" entrance standards: "The normal school experience," he wrote in his 1896 *Annual Report*, "should start from your intelligence, not your ignorance. It wants your energies for the science and art of presentation, not for the conquest of what is already known" (514). Writing a year later, this time with a

of the idea for normal school instruction" (Theses of First Class, 1897). About to enter an elementary classroom in her own community of Fitchburg where she would represent to her principal, other teachers, students, and parents a new breed of professional teacher, she figured the development of normal schools as a success story, one that was essential in furthering what she called "the noble cause of education."

The titles of the essays written in the first years of the school reveal the writers' broad scope: "The Teacher as a Character Builder," "The Value of Physical Education," "The True Meaning of the Expression, to Educate," "Educational Value of Play," "How to Develop Original Thought," and "Teacher's Influence." In their physical features these essays are similar: many begin, and end, with quotations from the classics. Lena Harrigan's 1897 essay entitled "Moral Education in the Public Schools" typifies a common prose struggle. In her introduction Harrigan writes, "Before discussing this topic of moral education, let us understand first the true meaning of the word 'education.' What is an educated man? Huxley answers the inquiry thus . . ." (Theses of First Class, 1897). Although many of the essays demonstrate the "unmistakable marks of student prose: self consciously formal style, specious generalities, and impossible broad topics" (Russell 82), these essays reflect more than just immature writing: such abstract prose was the kind of writing that "won prizes" in many nineteenth-century common schools (Schultz, *Young* 143). Thus, while the student writers may have adhered to rhetorical structures learned in high school, the essays also reveal them negotiating the complex intellectual demands of making sense of what they heard, what they read, and what they thought appropriate for their new professional audience.

In these essays it is also possible to see glimpses of the rhetorically rich environment of the normal school. Lecturers were often invited to the school to enrich the students' educational experiences. Of these lectures Thompson reported formally to the Board of Education, "It must be remembered that these are not popular lectures, the object of which is first to please, but lectures on important educational topics by men who have made a special study of the things which assume to speak and whose opinion is of great value to those who are preparing to teach" (*Annual Report*, 1898, 53). Despite the seriousness of purpose behind Thompson's words, the titles of the lectures themselves re-

veal a wider diversity of content and purpose.[5] Within the first decade of the
school, students heard lectures on "Training to Think," "Horace Mann,"
"Fatigue and Mental Hygiene," and "The Pedagogical Problem," as well as
those of broader interest such as "Literature and Its Relation to the School,"
"Ethical Interpretations of Social Progress," and "The Poetry and Symbolism
of Indian Basketry." Frequent references in the student essays to the lectures
in the form of "Mr. Edsen says" or "Miss Lawrence says" suggest a rich, tex-
tured environment in which oral discourse was valued.

Unfortunately, there are no lesson plans or assignments that reveal the actual writing instruction students received: who told students what about essay
writing; what kind of advice they got; or who edited the final drafts of the essays, which appear in the bound volumes error free (if one overlooks occasional strikeouts for typographical errors). However, we do know its basic
features. Unlike instruction at Harvard in which students took separate courses
in composition, at Fitchburg writing instruction was provided within the first
several weeks of general course work as part of a curriculum that resembled,
and perhaps even replicated, high school instruction, which at the time emphasized mechanical correctness above style (Connors, *Composition* 133). As
Levin notes, "virtually all the nineteenth century normal schools' programs
followed a . . . pattern of offering a remedial, elementary-grades curriculum
to their potential teachers, and then as standards were raised . . . a basic academic curriculum in high school-level subjects" (52). To meet its obligation
to provide the community with "trained" teachers, Fitchburg educators
adjusted the curriculum to meet the academic needs of their students. Thus,
despite Thompson's protestations that the work of the normal school was
strictly "professional," he and his faculty could not do otherwise than reteach
the content and skills they hoped their students already possessed.

Composition instruction in the normal school should not be dismissed as
simply inferior to instruction at the college level. Although normal school
students received basic instruction in their coursework, their experiences were
by no means simple: they were in transition, perhaps even experiencing a
"pedagogical culture shock" as they negotiated "what and how they learned"
in high school—mainly by memorization and recitation—and the "practical
demands" of the normal schools (W. Johnson 247). Further, as Kathryn

Fitzgerald demonstrates, the theoretical origins of the normal school need to be further examined. Markedly unlike the prestigious colleges whose intellectual origins derived from classical rhetoric, "the intellectual heritage of the normal schools, like the concept of the normal school itself, had different [and uniquely compelling] origins," those derived from "German systems of teacher training and European pedagogical theories" (Fitzgerald 231). Locating their pedagogies within the writings and practices of the nineteenth-century educational reformers Friedrich Froebel, Johann Heinrich Pestalozzi, and Johann Friedrich Hebart, all of whom the Fitchburg students referred to freely in their writing, normal school teachers embraced an ideology of a child-centered education that affirmed the need for children to experience the world from their own lives, not from teachers or textbooks, a perspective that had influenced much of the educational practices of nineteenth-century common schools. Normal schools, occupying that "middle margin" between the public schools and higher education, looked to the educational philosophy as practiced in the schools for their intellectual base, not to the traditions of classical rhetoric as did most colleges. Thus, the statement from the 1899 Fitchburg Normal School catalogue that "pupils are to be expected to get from books what they can, without too great an expense of time and effort" (15) is not anti-intellectual, but rather embedded in a rich pedagogical tradition of learning by doing.

Although we cannot know exactly what students' actual writing instruction looked like, we do know from the *Catalogue and Circular* what composition texts students were asked to refer to: Genung's *Practical Rhetoric*, Whitney and Lockwood's *English Grammar*, and Williams's *Composition and Rhetoric*, books which were standard fare in the academies and colleges. With the exception of Genung's text, which Robert Connors observes was the most rhetoric-focused of the commonly used, mass-market composition books of the time, the texts provide a "rules-driven" approach to writing. Williams's text, in particular, was "filled with grammatical mechanics and rules" (Connors, *Composition* 84). So, too, was Woolley's *Handbook of Composition: A Compendium of Rules*, published in 1907, preserved in the Fitchburg archives. As Connors notes, Woolley's book "provided in primitive form nearly all the elements that make up today's handbooks: it dealt with punctuation, spelling, legibility,

[and] sentence structure" and considered "no element of writing . . . beneath its scope" (146). While we must be careful not to assume too much about how these texts may have actually been used, we can see evidence in the essays that some of the rules had "taken." Evident in these early essays are the familiar principles of expository writing that had become newly codified in the handbooks, particularly patterns of classification that students used frequently to tame big ideas. For example, as Mary Lee writes in her essay "How to Develop the Power of Original Thought," "there are three steps in the process of thinking: conception, judgment, and reasoning" (Theses of First Class, 1897). And in her essay, "Childhood Influences," Harriet Bishop writes similarly, "The child's attention may be divided into three parts: within the home, within the school, and on the playground" (Theses of Ninth Class, 1905). Evident in many students' writing are the rudiments of the five-paragraph essay, which became fossilized in writing instruction largely because it was easy to teach. In an educational setting that focused on a science of pedagogy and "mental discipline," such modes and methods of organization seem suitable to its needs.

By 1900 the student essays, which for a few short years had been broad in topic and scope, began to be more "scientific," owing to the influence of Edwin Kirkpatrick, hired in 1898 as a teacher of psychology and child study. Not only does his name appear frequently in the student prose (as in "Mr. Kirkpatrick says . . .") and on students' reference pages, it was Kirkpatrick who wrote a new section in the *Catalogue and Circular* on the essay requirement. Under a section entitled "Courses of Study in Detail" appearing for the first time in 1903, he wrote: "In order to develop the power of self-direction and give a feeling of the mastery of some portion of a general subject, each pupil writes a thesis chosen by herself. In preparing to write she is expected to not only read but collect for herself a large number of facts bearing on the topic. In order that this may be done successfully and the thesis be a natural growth from observation, reading, and reflection, rather than the artificial product of hasty reading, the subject of the thesis is to be chosen the first year of study" (32).

During these years, student essays became almost formulaic: a statement about the importance of the subject; a description of the writer's study, which required that the students collect, in writing, answers to question prompts given to the elementary pupils in the practice school; the results of the study; and then implications for teaching, all followed by tables and charts.[6] Reference pages were required and include many of the sixty-two new "professional" publications in the library's holdings, including *Child Study Monthly*, *International Monthly*, and various professional articles from the *Journal of Pedagogy*.

Kirkpatrick was not the only influence on the students and their writing: G. Stanley Hall, a leader of the child study movement and then president of Clark University, was a frequent visitor to Fitchburg Normal School, lecturing on such subjects as "Literature and Its Relation in the School, "Fears of Children," and "Sex in Education." His most profound influence, however, was his insistence on a "scientific" approach to the study of children, believing that, as Arthur Powell notes, "education should be studied through the observation of facts or phenomenon rather than through a theory accepted beforehand" (43). From 1899 to roughly 1908, this methodology of observation-then-theory characterizes the majority of student prose. A sample of titles reveal the focus of many: "The Effects of Praise Upon Children," "Imitation in Children," "Spelling as a Phase of Learning," and "An Experimental Study of the Process of Teaching." A large number of essays were written on a small handful of topics: many students studied and wrote about "Fears of Children," for example, which suggests that they may have been steered early on in their two-year program to choose something already deemed suitable to their and their teachers' needs.

While many of these essays demonstrate considerable competence in clarity, synthesis of information, and application, their sameness is most striking. Unlike the earlier essays which reveal more experimentation with topic and form, these "scientific" theses display an agentless objectivity embedded in passive prose. Such formal writing, as David Russell tells us, began to be more and more typical of late nineteenth- and early twentieth-century student prose, which had "lost its celebratory, community-confirming role" (87). In these later, more "scientific" essays, only a few students become visible, and then only obliquely. For example, Mary Alice Davis, writing in her essay "Effects of Praise Upon Children," after dutifully noting that she observed "between thirty and forty children and found praise was eagerly desired by all and was usually beneficial," commented, "I only saw one girl from whom I thought it wise to withhold it altogether" (Theses of Fifth Class, 1901). Only occasionally do such writers allow their increasing professional expertise to emerge. What counted instead was that they display to their teachers and future superintendents their credentials in the "science" of child study.

From 1900 to 1910, however, along with the ever-present influence of Kirkpatrick and Hall were the growing influences of two other diametrically opposed curricular initiatives occurring at Fitchburg: the manual training program that began formally in 1908 and the more amorphous, but not less real, influence of literature and the arts. Both of these influences can be seen in the student prose, which by mid-decade reflects a curriculum that was being changed both within and without. The manual training program, for instance, the first in the country, had been formally designed as an alternative practice school for youth who were being designated for employment in local factories. With the strong support of local factory owners, as well as of Thompson and other faculty who regarded it as "emphasizing the physical development of the brain" (Ringel 49), the manual training program began to influence curriculum through the hiring of teachers and renewed conversations about the mission of the school. At Fitchburg, enthusiasm for the manual training program was high. James McNamara, writing in his essay, "The Moral Effects of Manual Training" expresses a common attitude about the "fitness" of manual training for the poor and black, positing that "developing a 'love' for industrial training in the hearts of young boys and negrows [*sic*]" would "guard against the mother of all the evil instincts, but especially idleness, the mother of vice" (Theses of Fourth Advanced Class, 1900). The manual training program was thought to be a direct response to local community needs, but it created a class-based view of education in which manual training was deemed appropriate for students of "lower-class backgrounds for whom academic study was not appropriate" (qtd. in Levin 54). Despite its national renown and the enthusiasm with which it was embraced by many at the school, the manual training program reinforced the public's perception that Fitchburg was growing even more plebian and removed from the educational mainstream.

This shift to the vocational, however, was balanced within the school by an even greater curricular shift to literature and the arts. Writing in the 1903 *Catalogue and Circular*, Flora Kendall, a teacher of English, noted that "the work on this department has been marked by a steady growth" and justified its place in the normal school: "The English department affords ample opportunity for the development of the mental and physical poise so essential in the teacher of today. . . . Selections from our best authors are strong factors in the development of the young mind in the present day. Recognizing this truth, and realizing the need for broader knowledge and greater love for the writers . . . the subject of literature is made to occupy a prominent place in the English department" (21–22).

What Kendall had in mind was the power of literature to elevate the senses and create an atmosphere of middle-class refinement. Beginning in the 1903 *Catalogue and Circular*, Kendall's influence is recognizable. She notes that the school has acquired "an appropriate collection of busts and pictures," and the *Catalogue*'s pages include photographs of these cultural artifacts: empty rooms with newly-acquired statues and busts prominently displayed. These artifacts of culture, she writes, "have created a literary atmosphere which has influenced students and teachers" (22). We see evidence of literary influence in much student writing, as well. Thesis titles such as "A Glance at the Novels of Thackeray," "The Value of Literature as a Means of Education," "Two Reasons for the Novel," and "The Cultural Side of Geography" appear in greater number. As Gerald Graff has noted, this embrace of literature had become a feature of more college curricula, with new departments of literature defending "appreciation over investigation and values over facts" (55). Even in the normal schools, which emphasized the practical, a shift to a liberal arts education had become more widespread and accepted.

Within all this curricular change, Thompson supported a move to a more college-oriented liberal education, particularly for the advanced students. Providing a retrospective about the first decade of the school in the 1905 *Catalogue and Circular*, Thompson notes Fitchburg's evolving curriculum. While stating that "the general aim [of the School] was then and has been through all the following years, to teach the history and theory of education, together with child study and a more or less hasty review of subjects to be taught in the grades below that high school," he admits, "another aim of the school, and one that was not clearly and fully perceived at first, has been to give those who seem particularly adapted to teaching an opportunity for broader culture and larger experience before they finally leave the care of the school" (10). Ironically, what captivated Thompson was the joy of college instruction: "No work done by the school has been more satisfactory in the doing or in the results than this of the advanced course" (10). Even for Thompson, the "professional purist" (Borrowman 26), the temptation to educate, not merely to train, was too powerful to resist.

LIFE IN THE MARGIN

Citing Anne Haley Oliphant's work on Wendell Berry, who wrote about "those places on earth that are on the edges, the edge of a field or the edge of a sea," Lucille Schultz invokes a metaphor of the margin, "places in the natural world which are often dismissed as unimportant or irrelevant" which "are less stable, less predictable environments . . . which can only be described in terms of something else" (*Young* 52–53).

However, as Schultz notes, in the margins there is freedom, for in them "new varieties of life are being created . . . through unanticipated, uncontrolled, and unplanned cross-pollination and intermingling; that the richness of activity, meaning, and responsiveness in the margins may not easily be detected; and that observers must get in deep . . . to sense the full value of these diverse places" (53). Such is the case for normal schools, which only recently have become the sites for historiography of rhetoric and composition and literacy studies. Always in the midst of the ebb and flow of changing educational theories and of shifting politics and priorities, schools such as Fitchburg were, and continue to be, places of change and possibility.

The curricular origins of institutions such as Fitchburg Normal School, located forty miles and light years away from Harvard, are located in its story and cast of characters. The story's leading men are Edgerly and Thompson, spokesmen for the school, and many played significant minor roles, such as Frank Hill, whose ruminations, cautions, and exhortations about the first classes of students underscore the importance of Fitchburg to the community. The students, who appear in the official documents only as "pupils," are people who would be trained in the service of the classroom. Although their essay writing did not allow easily for expression of personal voice and experience, they nonetheless reveal themselves and a sense of place. More than just "institutional voices," their writing suggests their lived experiences with the ongoing changes and debates about the curriculum and the mission of the school.

Storytelling often reveals more about the storytellers themselves than the subjects, for we can only interpret the past through the lens of who we are. Further, archives are never neutral spaces (Buss 27). Individually we determine what is of value and significance and then shape our own ways. In my study of the Fitchburg Normal School's early years, I am mindful of my role as historian and teacher, one who, at times, occupies some of the same physical spaces as my predecessors and who sees in the students' essays, both then and now, their efforts to write their ways into knowing. Telling the "alternative" story of Fitchburg Normal School or another institution from within, not from above or from without, allows us to see that life in the margin was rich.

Notes

1. We cannot discuss normal schools without discussing influences of gender. As James Fraser observes, "When one talks of urban elementary teachers in the years between 1880 and 1930, one is essentially discussing women's experience" (123). Further, as Altenbaugh and Underwood note, a study done in 1898–99 indicated that Fitchburg Normal School had the highest ratio of women to men, nationally, at 14:1 (163).

2. The first class admitted to Fitchburg included "46 young ladies, who represented 3 states and 17 towns" (*Catalogue and Circular*, 1896, 3). Fourteen of these women were admitted into the advanced class, which indicates they had prior teaching experience, "in some cases an experience of four to five years." Tuition was free for those who "declare their intent to teach in the public schools of Massachusetts" (25); for others, the tuition was $30.00. In 1896 the *Catalogue and Circular* also noted the availability of eight scholarships to Harvard in the "scientific departments" for graduates of the state normal schools (24). Later catalogues make no mention of these or any other scholarships.

3. Admissions data from 1898 to 1902, entered by hand in a ledger, indicate the following: In 1898–1899, Fitchburg examined forty-six students and admitted forty-four; in 1899–1900, fifty-five were examined and fifty were admitted; in 1900–1901, thirty-nine were examined and thirty-five were admitted; and in 1901–1902, forty-seven were examined and forty-five were admitted. Those few who were not admitted were listed as having "failed" the examination. Interestingly, in every recorded year after 1896

(1897–1903), several students were noted as having been admitted "on trial," suggesting that admissions criteria had become more arbitrary.

4. Judging from the holdings in the archives, student theses were required for graduation from 1897 (the first class graduating class) to 1912. I have found no mention of why the requirement was dropped. Also, each year, theses from the two-year and advanced programs were bound separately, although essay titles for both groups are nearly indistinguishable. I have given an approximation for the total number of essays, for a few are missing from the bound volumes, although the titles are listed in the tables of contents.

5. Thompson made many formal references to the lectures. They were scheduled on Saturday afternoons, "not for the benefit of students alone," but for "teachers of the community and all others interested" and had become so popular as "to tax to the utmost the capacity of the hall" (*Catalogue*, 1901, 18). As Altenbaugh and Underwood note, these lectures were designed by Thompson to expose students to a "general culture" (176), as well as, perhaps, to demonstrate to the community that his school was more than merely vocational.

6. In these observational, "scientific" essays, Kirkpatrick required that students create survey questions or prompts that they would, in turn, give to their pupils in the practice schools to answer. For example, one such essay, "Reading and Literature," included the following questions which the pupils responded to, in writing: "What were your favorite stories or books before you were eight years old? Between eight and twelve? Between twelve and fifteen?" (Grace Phillips, Thesis of Third Advanced Class, 1900). Although the methodology behind the essays was "scientific," we must be careful not to overlook the language-intensiveness of these essays, which required that Fitchburg students engage their own pupils in writing, then, through their own analysis and interpretation, draw conclusion within their own essays. For these student theses, though, Kirkpatrick gave strict guidelines: the normal school students were to divide their practice classes by sex, and then instruct each pupil to put on each paper his or her name, age (by year and month), grade, and nationality.

Archival Sources

The following items are in the Amelia V. Galucci-Cirio Library at Fitchburg State College, Fitchburg, MA:

Annual Report, Board of Education. Boston: Wright and Potter, 1896–1905.
Catalogue and Circular, Fitchburg Normal School. Boston: Wright and Potter, 1896–1910.
Cottager 9 (August 1900): xvi.

"A Faculty Meeting." Unpublished manuscript. 1909.

Goodfellow, Maud. *Historical Sketch and Lists of Former Faculty and Students.* Fitchburg Normal School Practical Arts Press, June 25, 1920.

Testimonials to [Massachusetts] Board of Higher Education. Transcript. December 31, 1893.

Theses of student classes. Fitchburg Normal School. 1897–1910.

Thompson, John G. Papers.

Woolley, E. C. *Handbook of Composition: A Compendium of Rules.* Boston: D. C. Heath. 1907.

─ɔ 10 ɕ─

William Rainey Harper
and the Ideology of Service
at Junior Colleges

William DeGenaro

WE IN COMPOSITION STUDIES have much to learn from the history of the two-year college movement in the United States. Our rhetorical roots suggest we attend to the ethical and political dimensions of public discourse, and few phenomena in the discourse of higher education present ethical and political problems as conflicted as do two-year colleges. We know that two-year colleges provide cheap, convenient, and open-admissions options for college students of various backgrounds. If mindful of Mina Shaughnessy's pioneering work on the logic of errors in New York City in the 1970s, we may even see the open-admissions institution as a site of cultural and linguistic differences, a prime locale for knowledge construction. Cynthia Lewiecki-Wilson and Jeff Sommers go so far as to suggest that we view open-admissions schools "not as a low-level site merely for the application of knowledge, but

Inventing the archive for two-year colleges presents a different kind of challenge from reading the archives of liberal arts colleges and universities or normal schools. This chapter examines that challenge and offers a way to address it.

as an intellectually productive and transformative site of disciplinary practice" (459). Even disciples of Shaughnessy who concur with these claims probably know little about the origins of two-year colleges, resulting in some erroneous mythology.

In fact, the prevailing myths about two-year colleges are dangerous. *Community colleges are democratic experiments in education. Community colleges provide ethnic and racial minorities and members of the working class access to higher learning, so they must be good.* These myths only tell half the story—the less useful half. Without a historical understanding of two-year colleges, these myths will persist. Historical inquiry facilitates the close reading of both human agency and the textual construction of ideology. Digging around in the archives allows us to piece together the dynamic interplay between human and text; we can watch ideas and values take shape. Defining what constitutes two-year college archives is problematic. Many two-year colleges that date back to the early twentieth century started offering classes before they had physical facilities. Courses were conducted in YMCAs, union halls, and other civic venues; and when the college obtained land, documents were lost in the move. Hence, two-year colleges are institutions with little historical memory. If they barely know themselves, how can our academic discipline know them?

As a field, our gaze rests firmly on the world of higher education. If we have an obligation to explore sites of ethical and political contention, we ought to care deeply about understanding two-year colleges. If historical perspective provides an avenue for transcending dominant mythology about the two-year college, then historical inquiry ought to be a priority. So how might we respond to the absence of archival materials?

Historical work is nothing if not creative. Robert Connors left our field the useful image of playing in the archive, noting that we need to take joy from the "directed ramble" of archival work ("Dreams" 23). Given the creative nature of the research process, I have concluded that we need to invent an archive for historical, two-year college research. In the absence of internal communication, student writing, and meeting minutes, I have utilized various "artifacts" or "primary sources" that have helped me come to productive conclusions about two-year colleges. I have defined this work as "archival" because I put the past and the present in dialectic by means of the critique of primary texts. In other projects, my archival materials included course catalogues (which helped me explore the textual construction of college mission) and published teacher narratives (which helped me critique first-year composition at early two-year colleges as a site of class conflict) (DeGenaro, "Social Utility"). Were these published texts technically archival materials? For me, the answer is yes because I looked to them not for information but rather as artifacts waiting for a critical gaze.

In this project, which centers on William Rainey Harper, a central figure in the development of the two-year college movement, my archival materials include several texts written by Harper himself. Two Harper essays, "The Associate Degree" and "The High School of the Future," come from obscure periodicals of the early twentieth century. Another essay, "Changes Affecting the Small College Which May Be Expected and Which Are to Be Desired," comes from a conference proceeding. Harper's *The Trend in Higher Education* is a book-length treatise published in house at the University of Chicago, where Harper was founding president. These are all "published" sources, albeit obscure. But more importantly, they are not sources of received knowledge. They constitute a historical record, and I employ them as artifacts. For me, this is the essence of archival work.

The two-year college as "democracy's college," as an institution committed to egalitarian values, is a myth. It is true that some five million students—many of them first-generation college students of working-class and racial or ethnic minority backgrounds—gain access to higher education by matriculating on two-year campuses. It is also true that the two-year college has a well-documented history of tracking students into remedial classes, vocational tracks, and eventually low-level sectors of the economy (Clark; Shor, *Critical Teaching*). This inherent contradiction in the nature of open-access learning cries out for critical narratives that give scholars, practitioners, and students at two-year colleges historical perspectives. Such narratives exist in fields such as higher education studies, history, and sociology, but are lacking in the field of rhetoric. Elsewhere I have argued that rhetoricians in particular should be interested in the material and discursive milieus that gave rise to open-access education in this country (DeGenaro, "Class Consciousness").

Here I take that argument a step further by critiquing the rhetoric of the "father of the junior college," William Rainey Harper, whose ideology helped to cement the duality of the junior college mission.

Historians of composition already understand dualities within the context of higher education. After all, historical narratives of the first-year writing requirement (most recently, Crowley's *Composition in the University*) have charted the uses and abuses of composition. On one hand, composition instruction prepares students for the rigors of both academic and civic life, where knowledge of the conventions of written communication impacts success in real and demonstrable ways. On the other hand, composition serves as a gatekeeper, separating students by so-called skill levels and instilling bureaucratic values. The history of the two-year college exists side-by-side with the history of first-year composition, sharing remarkably similar trajectories. While these similarities are interesting in and of themselves, paying attention to the connections between the histories of composition and the two-year college presents a further productive possibility. Specifically, this brand of exploration illustrates the imperative to critique the notion of "service."

The notion of "service" is broad and multivalent. All institutions and social movements take part in some form of service work. Organizations represent the interests of their members and, by extension, are self-serving. Anyone who subscribes to the cultural logics of supply and demand or social Darwinism believes that only groups that provide a desirable service will maintain any efficacy. Service is inescapable. However, junior colleges defined service in a particular fashion. By virtue of the phrase "junior college," institutions articulated precisely who they were serving: senior colleges. "Junior" is a term that immediately denotes "otherness." If an institution possesses a junior status, then that institution remains smaller or younger than its senior. "Junior college" denotes the intentions of the founders of the school; the two-year campus was a "junior" version of the four-year campus, a place of service. I see the phrase "community college," the preferred name for two-year campuses since the 1960s, as a euphemism, a politically correct marker that implies service to *the totality* of the geographic region surrounding a given two-year college. Two-year colleges were not necessarily focused on serving the community at large or all of the members of that community, choosing instead to be of service to the interests of capital (see DeGenaro, "Class Consciousness"). To call the schools "community colleges" when discussing the earliest years of the institutions is to ignore the aims and intentions of movement leaders. Problematic was the tendency among college founders to dismiss the interests and objectives of students. The leaders and founders made decisions about curriculum, mission, and organizational structure. Students may have wanted transferable courses of study, but leaders and founders pushed terminal and vocational programs. Decision making occurred in a top-down fashion. Junior colleges carried an ideology of service, but *not* necessarily service to the student body. And if the individual students' agency and choice-making potential were not being served, then by extension neither was the "community."

The work of William Rainey Harper provides a case study of the tendency to ignore students as autonomous learners capable of choice and agency. As an embodiment of the ideology of the junior college movement, Harper helped cement in the consciousness of higher education many of the hierarchical notions of "service" still operational in both two-year and four-year colleges. Those committed to fashioning higher education into a democratic locus of shared decision making will be interested in an analysis of Harper's rhetoric of college-as-service-provider. Under Harper's leadership, the two-year college movement set up an interesting dynamic in which lower-division teachers were constructed as *servers*. Those teaching foundational areas like math and writing as well as general education and sometimes even introductory classes—and anyone else doing work that the movement saw as "remedial" (better suited for secondary education)—was constructed as a service provider, a "junior" member of academe. Those doing research-oriented and specialized work (teaching graduate and upper-division courses, undertaking "useful" scholarship) became "senior" members of the academic professions.

The research into the history of the two-year college movement has implications for compositionists by addressing the question of why one area of academic work is more valuable than the other and historicizing the trends that have resulted in a problematic arrangement for academic professionals. The notion of "service work" has its antecedents in this movement. Access to higher learning certainly bodes well for a society interested in sharing decision-making capabilities among a wide cross-section of the population. What was problematic about the junior college movement was its emphasis on hierarchy, a dominant motif for higher education during the remainder of the twentieth century. As we notice the lip service paid to student-centeredness, the downsizing of academic departments, the increasing reliance on part-time teachers, the adoption of corporate models of management, and the introduction of for-profit higher learning, we see the results of a system of higher education that sometimes fails to respect students. We see an ideology of service in effect that has its origins in the rhetoric proliferated by William Rainey Harper.

Harper's achievements were many. He was the first president of the University of Chicago; the cofounder, in 1901, of Joliet Junior College (the first two-year college); one of the brightest scholars of Hebrew Studies of the late nineteenth century; and a leader in the transformation of higher education during his era. As founding president of the University of Chicago, William Rainey Harper stands out as an important figure in the birth of the American research university. As the "father of the junior college," Harper holds a place of equal importance in the development of open-access education. It is no coincidence that Harper involved himself on both ends of the spectrum of higher education, for he saw the two institutions as integral components of a larger plan for educational reform. Specifically, Harper envisioned the junior college and lower-division coursework as institutions of service. For Harper, the lower division, as a domain of liberal learning and general education, served the upper division, a domain of research. In kind, the junior college was an extension of the high school that served the senior college. The ideology espoused by Harper transformed lower-division courses from autonomous units of liberal learning into gatekeepers that maintained the selectivity of the "senior" level of higher education.

A debate in the literature of higher education surrounds Harper and his role within the history of the two-year college. Wattenbarger and Witt affirm Harper's dominant role in the beginning of Joliet Junior College, the first public junior college, and present documentary research that they claim proves that Harper single-handedly brought the junior college movement to California. This claim is significant because junior colleges enjoyed such prominence in California during the early years of the two-year college movement and re-mained a significant force in Californian education throughout the twentieth century. While most historians attribute the beginning of the two-year col-lege's presence in California to the 1907 law which allowed public funds to be used for the chartering of junior colleges, Wattenbarger and Witt uncover correspondence that suggests Harper's own "proselytizing" earlier in the cen-tury led to the founding of early two-year schools in the state. John Frye ("Expansion or Exclusion") and James L. Ratcliff ("Excitement of Discov-ery") have both questioned the validity of Wattenbarger and Witt's historical data (and have critiqued Wattenbarger and Witt for failing to corroborate their claims with other documentation).

Elsewhere Ratcliff, in his 1986 *Community College Review* article "Should We Forget William Rainey Harper?" argues that Harper played only an in-direct role in the founding of Joliet Junior College. Ratcliff points out that more Joliet graduates went on to the University of Illinois than Harper's own University of Chicago. Despite Harper's goal of starting a network of junior colleges, Ratcliff writes, only sixteen existed when Harper died. Ratcliff claims that from a historiographical standpoint, elevating Harper to patriarch status results from overreliance on the "great man theory," which dictates historians need only look to prominent individuals to craft valid historical narratives (16). In essence, Ratcliff writes, Harper was not so much a founder of the junior college as "an intellectual architect of a plan for curricular cohesion and efficiency" (17).

Ratcliff and Frye fail to account for ideology. They quibble with Watten-barger and Witt over the frequency of Harper's activity in interstate com-munication and the day-to-day operations at Joliet, but neglect his rhetorical influence. From a methodological standpoint, they remain too busy counting how many times Harper traveled to California and measuring how dirty his hands got outside the confines of his beloved campus at the University of Chicago. Harper's power resides in his ideology and his ability to articulate that ideology. Ratcliff draws an artificial line between the physical work of founding junior colleges and the ideological work of being an "intellectual ar-chitect." This is a false dichotomy. Spreading his beliefs about the future of higher education, specifically the subservient role of the lower division, remains Harper's legacy. The existence of the debate in the literature of higher education over Harper's role proves the power and ubiquity of Harper in the founding of the junior college movement. Even those who negate his dominant role quote Harper and ponder his life and work.

Those who labor in the lower division should be knowledgeable about the historical moments that gave rise to the current division of labor within higher education. Lower division work, which includes teaching first-year writing, the humanities, general education, and foundational courses, is too often looked down upon by the academy. At large institutions, graduate students do a great deal of the work of the lower division. Universities award tenure to faculty based primarily on research. Since Harper involved himself with various aspects of higher education's burgeoning pecking order at the turn of the century, a close examination of his ideology should be of interest to both two-year college practitioners and lower division laborers within four-year schools.

Harper invented the term "junior college" to denote the divisions of the University of Chicago in which first- and second-year courses were taught. Later, he used the word to denote a separate institution, autonomous from the university but in service to its interests. Industrialist John D. Rockefeller provided financial backing to a group of scholars, including Harper, then a faculty member at Yale, interested in starting a research university with a Baptist affiliation (Storr 41). The University of Chicago was incorporated in 1890 and opened in 1892 (86). At the University of Chicago, President Harper immediately went to work recruiting the finest faculty that Rockefeller's money could buy. He had to compete with Stanford and Johns Hopkins to attract cutting-edge scientists and scholars (69). Harper gave little consideration to the needs of undergraduates, caring more about the prestige of the senior faculty members he devoted endless resources to recruiting. He expected the university to attract students who were *already* well-versed in liberal education. According to historian Richard Storr, Harper looked at his university students as potential alumnae (109). After all, alumni represented individuals in powerful positions who could donate funds and do hard research as specialists in chosen fields.

Students in the first two years of study at the University of Chicago were particularly bothersome to Harper. By the time the University of Chicago opened its doors to students, Harper had decided he ultimately wanted fresh-men and sophomores removed from the intellectual space of the university campus. He divided academic units into an "Academic College" (freshmen and sophomores) and a "University College" (juniors, seniors, and graduate students) and in 1896 renamed the two levels "Junior College" and "Senior College," respectively (Eells, *Junior College* 47). By 1893, he was setting up articulation programs between secondary schools and the university wherein select high school classes could fulfill university requirements (Storr 120). Students who did not come from "strong" high school backgrounds were de-nied this benefit, a denial that at times hurt their progress toward a degree. For example, many students studying science during the 1890s at Chicago could not reach completion in a timely manner due to intense Latin requirements (121). There is an obvious class bias here. Students with "inferior" secondary careers faced an added obstacle at the university level.

Harper invented the two-year college to focus the University of Chicago on specialized research. As a separate institution, the junior college could pro-vide general education and training in the liberal arts so that the university could focus resources on disciplinary work among the brightest faculty mem-bers and advanced undergraduate and graduate students. The tuition-free Joliet Junior College, founded in 1901 as the first community college, was the brainchild of Harper and J. Stanley Brown, superintendent of Joliet Town-ship High School (Joliet). For Harper, Joliet Junior College was essentially a secondary school. Indeed, he hoped to spur a nationwide movement to extend high school to six years (Eells, *Junior College* 650). Joliet was the first institution to award the associate in arts, also an invention of Harper's, to re-ward two years of general education. The associate in arts, Harper main-tained, was not a "degree" but a "title." This was an important distinction for Harper, who thought a two-year degree would cheapen the very idea of a degree (Eells *Junior College* 361–62). Harper's junior college was founded as a locus of humanities and liberal learning.

Harper once called the humanities "those subjects which represent the culture of the past" (McGrath and Spear 97). Ever concerned with making public education in America more useful, Harper relegated the humanities to the status of an outmoded area of inquiry, quite literally a thing of days gone by. Curiously, Harper himself was a product of liberal education, graduating from Ohio's Muskingum College at age fourteen (he gave the commencement address in Hebrew) and completing a doctorate in Semitic Languages from Yale five years later (Diener 49). His dissertation, a comparative study of prepositions in Latin, Greek, Sanskrit, and Gothic, illustrates his affinity for scholarship (Storr 18). Harper got his first faculty job at the Theological Seminary at Morgan Park but, because he was only twenty-two, the institution would not give him the title of assistant professor (Goodspeed, *Story* 37). On faculty at Yale after leaving Morgan Park, his intense passion for research continued to grow as his area of inquiry shifted to Old Testament studies (Storr 19). Yale gave Harper several positions of honors, including the newly formed Woolsey Professorship of Biblical Literature (Goodspeed, *Story* 41). Increasingly he came to see his scholarship as the "salvation of souls" (Storr 45). While his own research prior to coming to Chicago took place within a humanities-based field, once he began to carry out his educational plan, the humanities became "foundational," something easily outsourced to a "junior" institution. He only accepted the presidency at the University of Chicago after much internal searching and only with assurance from Rockefeller that his academic freedom would never be compromised (51–52). Harper clearly had a passionate, almost religious purpose in his idolization of high research.

Although he valorized the research function of the university, he also held the ideals of a public intellectual. Thomas Wakefield Goodspeed, Harper's colleague on the University of Chicago's Board of Trustees and a prolific historian of the university, wrote of Harper: "The basic principle on which he would build a university was service—service not merely to the students within its walls, but also to the public, to mankind" (*Story* 55). Further, Harper saw himself as a rhetorician and gave speeches on biblical topics to women's clubs, churches, and civic groups (Goodspeed, *Story* 42). Harper's orations were a combination of scholarship and testimony. He had an inclusive conception of socially relevant education and saw specialized faculty working in broader domains than just labs and libraries. Perhaps Harper even valued "outreach" above lower-division teaching. Teaching introductory, culture-oriented courses required little specialization. Being an effective public intellectual required an ability to communicate with diverse audiences.

Harper took his scholarship off campus and expected his faculty to do the same. He insisted on setting up a press, a library accessible to the general public, and various extension initiatives, all of which would be overseen by faculty (Goodspeed, *Story* 53–54). Before assuming the presidency, Harper traveled in Europe, solidifying his vision for faculty. During this time he wrote: "The small number of hours required of professors (eight to ten hours a week) makes it possible for investigation to be carried on all the time, and in the climate of Chicago there is no season which, upon the whole, is more suitable for work than the summer" (qtd. in Goodspeed, *Story* 57). No faculty member would fail to be an active and productive member of the academic community. That meant a light teaching load and expectations for original research. Harper wrote: "It is only the man who has made investigation who may teach others to investigate. Without this spirit in the instructor and without his example students will never be led to under take the work. Moreover, if the instructor is loaded down with lectures he will have neither time nor strength to pursue his investigations" (qtd in Goodspeed, *Story* 60). Harper saw research as feeding effective teaching—at least at the upper and graduate levels. Many of the faculty he recruited were hired with the provisions that they would only teach graduate students. The lower the level, the less expertise was necessary.

Harper ultimately saw the new junior college in Joliet as a means to preserve the time and energies of his university faculty and also maintain high admissions standards at the University of Chicago. He hoped to start a network of two-year colleges in Illinois to serve as filters and funnels for university study (Eells, *Junior College* 48). He likely would have directly involved himself in the founding of more two-year colleges had he not died at only fifty years of age (Eells, *Junior College* 62). In 1900 in Charleston, South Carolina, Harper proclaimed: "It is not until the end of the sophomore year that university methods of instruction may be employed to advantage" (qtd. in Eells, *Junior College* 60). Since real university work, in Harper's conception, did not begin until the third year, he felt that only third-year students and higher ought to be studying at the senior college. Even before Joliet College started, Harper had attempted to eliminate calling students freshmen, sophomores, juniors, and seniors, limiting the markers to two: "Junior College Student" and "Senior College Student" (Goodspeed, *History* 138). For Harper, this was the meaningful distinction. The starker the separation between the two classes of students, the better. The lower institution would serve both the talented and the untalented and designate them as such. The junior college could thus be a place to locate the students worthy for higher study. He claimed that too many felt obliged to finish junior or senior years. Harper wrote: "It is evident that many students continue work in the Junior and Senior years of college life whose best interests would have been served by withdrawal from college. Many continue to the end, not from choice, but rather from compulsion, because of the disgrace which may attend an unfinished course. If it were regarded as respectable to stop at the close of the Sophomore year, many would avail themselves of the opportunity" ("Associate Degree" 50). Lower division coursework, for Harper, was a locus of discernment, a domain in which to study the past so the student could make decisions about the future—tasks fit for the junior college.

Harper argued with a religious fervor owing in no small part to his Old Testament training. In 1905, four years after starting Joliet Junior College, Harper wrote: "Democracy has been given a mission to the world, and it is of no uncertain character. I wish to show that the university is the prophet of this democracy and as well its priest and its philosopher; that, in other words, the university is the Messiah of the democracy, its to-be-expected deliverer" (*Trend* 12). Harper saw the university as a prophet that could articulate the values of democracy. He felt the university had the potential to put students in touch with themselves, a religious relationship that also could further American ideals. "During the last two years of college work the university spirit and the university method prevail," Harper said in his president's report from 1899 ("Associate Degree" 50). The religious rhetoric and evangelical tone come through in words like "spirit." Harper saw a moral distinction between those in the first two years of college and those pursuing a "higher" calling. This higher calling was not for everyone. Harper wrote in his 1905 text, "[T]he university men who occupy high places throughout the earth; the university spirit which, with every decade, dominates the world more fully, will be doing the work of the prophet, the priest, and the philosopher of democracy, and will continue to do that work until it shall be finished, until a purified and exalted democracy shall have become universal" (*Trend* 34). Again Harper uses religious imagery to exalt the potential of the university graduate. What becomes especially problematic is Harper's employment of this emotive rhetoric to justify the imperative to restrict enrollment. In his logic, university students are like religious leaders who will become the individuals protecting our democratic values, and because not just anyone can play that role, we need to be careful about who we allow into the university.

Part of the impetus behind Harper's leadership position in the junior college movement involved his feeling that in the first two years those who knew themselves well enough to confidently assert their potential for leadership might be inspired to continue their studies. Through testing, those *not* worthy for such positions would be inspired to cease pursuing higher education after two years. Just as scholarship took on religious overtones, so too did the notion of vocational discernment at the new two-year campus.

Harper wanted educational institutions to discourage supposedly less worthy students so as to soften the blow of exclusion. Not only did this ideology devalue the intellectual work done by those in the first two years of college study, it also devalued the professional work done by teachers. Harper stated that freshmen and sophomore courses were easier to teach and that secondary teachers could just as easily handle such grunt work ("Associate Degree" 51). Academics were wasting their time with introductory-level classes. After the transition to upper level, Harper wrote, "the student is given larger liberty of choice, and at the same time higher methods of instruction are employed" (50). Harper goes on to state, "The work of the freshman and sophomore years in most colleges differs little in content and in method from that of the last year of the academy or high school" (50). The lower division becomes an unworthy pursuit for his beloved, prestigious faculty and for students who Harper felt "by nature" were worthy to go on to the university (Eells, *Junior College* 61).

The only respectable four-year institution of higher education, in Harper's mind, was the university as a center of research and discovery. Smaller four-year colleges, where research was not the primary emphasis, were just "wasting money" (Cohen and Brawer 7). Small four-year schools "are not doing justice to the students in the higher classes. In reality they are defrauding the students who pay their fees in lower classes in order to obtain a meager sum of money with which to provide an entirely inadequate course of instruction for the higher class of men" ("Associate Degree" 51). It was natural for Harper, as an administrator, to be concerned with finances; but it is still unfortunate that Harper's emphasis on the bottom line obscures the genuine learning which goes on at teaching institutions. He called less elite four-year schools "so-called colleges" and suggested they have no business working with upper-level students. Harper wanted American universities to imitate the German research model (Cohen and Brawer 6; Ratcliff, "Seven Streams" 7–8; Frye, *Vision* 5). In short, Harper looked at lower-division courses as drains upon the energy and resources of educated scholars. This is a problematic conception of the scholar, particularly to those who see pedagogy as scholarship and the intellectual as a public figure involved in the everyday. Harper situated productive labor outside of the classroom and in the realm of science, the library stacks, and hard research. He praised the "large university in which library and laboratory facilities might be found which would make possible the doing of good work" ("Associate Degree" 51–52). Because of two-year colleges, elite four-year schools could raise their standards and keep out the less prepared.

Harper accused defenders of small, four-year colleges of nostalgia. Just as the subject matter taught at small, four-year schools was outdated, so too were their missions. It no longer made sense to spend four years providing a classical liberal education, in Harper's mind. Old-fashioned pundits supported liberal arts colleges out of a need to root for the underdog. He concluded that their logic was either "fancied or sentimental." Harper wrote: "The small college is loved and cherished, in most cases, just because it is small and weak" (*Trend* 353). Here Harper showed his dismissive side, insulting any mission rooted in inquiry and critical thinking as opposed to social efficiency and immediately demonstrable economic benefit.

Harper's discourse portrayed his idea as commonsensical. "Nature," Harper wrote in 1900, "has marked out the great divisions of educational work, and the laws of nature may not be violated without injury" ("Changes" 55). In the same document, Harper added: "The student who was not really fitted by nature to take the higher work could stop naturally and honorably at the end of the sophomore year" (57). He proposed a wholly new hierarchy for classifying college students, yet suggested his plan was natural and honorable. For rhetorical impact, Harper removed the possibility of opposition. He shut down discourse by stating a position and then glorifying it instead of justifying it.

The assumption on Harper's part, of course, was that as universities shift toward a research emphasis they should restrict enrollment. Centers of research would fuel the American economy by creating engineers and scientists. When Harper opined that "many students will find it convenient to give up college work at the end of the sophomore year," he begged the question of who precisely will find dropping out "convenient" ("Associate Degree" 52). Those who score lower on the increased number of assessments and batteries tend to come from minority and the lower and working classes, as Stephen Jay Gould brilliantly shows in *The Mismeasure of Man.* As learning institutions exclude non-dominant groups, they perpetuate the status quo. Not only does schooling fail to liberate, it facilitates and justifies oppression. Harper's gate-keeping conception of lower-division coursework did just this.

Harper advocated for a kind of social Darwinism for small four-year colleges. Since such institutions were less powerful than large research universities, Harper predicted they would die off. This process was natural and desirable since "the term 'college' has been misappropriated by these institutions" ("Changes" 54). Harper saw a natural evolution from small four-year college to community college. It seems that he did not want the unworthy unleashed on society with the same degree status as the product of a research institution. He tried to craft, with the invention of the two-year college, an extra level of difference. The harm in granting access to the same institution, or at least an institution that grants the same degree, to a larger cross section of the population, according to Harper, was that without the scientific focus of the burgeoning research school, small four-year institutions were counterfeit. He praised how things would be once these institutions were gone: "Our pretense of giving a college education would be given up, and the college could become an honest institution" (56–57). Harper described less worthy colleges in quantified terms, alluding to a "library of less than a thousand volumes, with scientific apparatus and equipment which has cost less than a thousand dollars, with a single building which has cost less than forty thousand dollars, and with an income less than six to eight thousand" (54). For Harper, once the small college reconfigured as a junior college, it would be more honest and it would be "stronger and heartier" (54).

The origins of first-year composition and the community college follow strikingly similar trajectories. Both composition and the two-year college boast mythologies of equality and assistance for those entering higher education who are perhaps less prepared for the academic rigors therein. Yet critics have pointed out that the community college has played a role in decreasing the aspirations of its students (Brint and Karabel; Clark; Shor, *Critical Teaching*). Critics of college composition, similarly, have argued that the writing course has been used as a tool for ideological and linguistic discipline and conformity (Crowley, *Composition*; Shor, "Our Apartheid"). Sketching the similarities between these two movements within higher education is a means for further understanding the disparaging of lower-division labor.

Although many of today's liberal-minded practitioners and scholars of college composition see the first-year writing course as training in critical, even oppositional, thinking, the dominant narrative about composition's beginning suggests that the course as we know it began as an offshoot of an elitist examination at Harvard. The contributors to this volume challenge many aspects of the Harvard narrative as composition's myth of origin, but the examination and English A's elitist aims are clear. Adams Sherman Hill, new to the English faculty at Harvard in the late nineteenth century, helped institute a "composition" test for entering students that assessed familiarity with high literature and formal knowledge of the grammatical features of the dominant dialect (Crowley, *Composition* 66). Half of Harvard's entering students failed the exam that asked them to write in flawless English about topics such as "Thackeray's account of the Pretender's visit to England" (67–69). According to historian and critic Sharon Crowley, who has advocated through much of her career that modern universities abolish the required composition class, Harvard began to test its entering students to assert its own institutional power and the power of English as a discipline (69).

Like Harper at the University of Chicago, leaders at Harvard such as Hill hoped to preserve selectivity among the student body. For Harper, the solution involved the manufacture of a two-year college proving ground. For Hill, the solution involved a biased writing assessment. Harvard created a course called English A, required for first-year Harvard men who failed the composition test. As Ira Shor wrote, the new Harvard course was intended to "exclude some and socialize others" ("Our Apartheid" 92). In other words, the less-prepared students were shut out of advanced study while they took a "service course" considered by the institution to be "remedial." Crowley writes, "The point of the required course is not to acquire some level of skill or knowledge that can be measured upon exit; it is instead to subject students to discipline, to force them to recognize the power of the institution to insist on conformity with its standards" (*Composition* 74). The same analysis could be made of the first two-year college at Joliet.

Both the new junior college and the new writing course at Harvard were born as gatekeepers. This occurred at the end of the nineteenth century when leaders of higher education in the United States increasingly came under the influence of the vision of the research university. At Harvard, leaders within the English department knew that English studies had to be a legitimate discipline in order to survive. At Chicago, Harper was convinced that junior divisions were little more than a drain on resources and energy. The new entrance examination told fifty percent of Harvard students they were not worthy of advanced study based on familiarity with both the dominant dialect and the liberal knowledge of high culture. The junior college sold the members of its student body that were not the best and brightest on the idea of a two-year title. Both new institutions operated under the assumption that the intellectual work was in service to something more important: the upper division. Just as the number of two-year colleges spread during the twentieth century (according to Cohen and Brawer, half of our nation's college students attend a community college), so too did the pervasiveness of the required first-year writing course.

Both the two-year college and first-year composition proved themselves resilient and overcame their identities as gatekeepers. Junior colleges are generally called "community colleges," a euphemistic term signifying service to a specific geographical region and the population therein, as opposed to service to a senior institution. College composition, likewise, is the site of a great deal of creative pedagogy, thanks in no small part to the growth of rhetoric and composition as a scholarly field. Both community colleges and first-year composition stand out as vibrant, though by no means perfect, bodies within higher education because their purposes are complicated and multilayered. Community colleges provide transfer courses, industrial and vocational training, affordable and flexible public-access courses for non-degree seekers, and basic skills courses for less prepared students who desire a college education. First-year composition courses provide foundational writing proficiency and introduce students to academic writing, teach research and computer skills, serve as an introduction to rhetoric, offer non-humanities majors exposure to the written word, and stress critical thinking and even cultural critique.

While some consider these competing purposes a weakness, they are actually an attribute. Both composition and community colleges resist static definitions. They are dynamic and evolving, which returns us to what was problematic about the ideology espoused by William Rainey Harper. Harper was sure he knew precisely what the (singular) purpose of his university was: to become a highly technical and specialized center of research and discovery. Harper's ideology put limitations on what higher education can be for its many constituents. His conception of the future of higher education ran counter to the ideals of liberal learning and the "lower division," to expand the possibilities and aid in the development of a well-rounded citizenry. Sadly, higher education still feels the effects of Harper. Community colleges lack the prestige of small four-year colleges, which generally lack the prestige of the large research university. Teaching lacks the institutional rewards of specialized research and publication. Academics still need to make a concerted effort to place value on the work of lower division, but for those committed to giving lower-division students agency and choice, it is an effort worth making.

The Progressive Faculty / Student Discourse of 1969–1970 and the Emergence of Lincoln University's Writing Program

Jeffrey L. Hoogeveen

LINCOLN UNIVERSITY (now Lincoln University of the Commonwealth of Pennsylvania) opened its doors in 1854 and was "the first institution found anywhere in the world to provide a higher education in the arts and sciences for male youth of African descent" (Bond chap. 1).[1] While Lincoln University is, and has always been, a school with an activist agenda, from the 1960s until the 1970s, it became a virtual activist beehive. That period of heightened so-

There are different views on what comprises the Lincoln University archive and, consequently, where it is located. Certainly, this 150-year-old university has a voluminously documented past, and much of this documentation exists in the lower level of the Langston Hughes Memorial Library, which has a dedicated university historian. I took stock of the university's and the Department of English's archives, all of which comprise several dozen boxes of official public documents. Reading these documents allows snapshot reconfigurations of official discussions, mainly department meetings that yielded minutes, which were kept from 1969 until the present. Documentation from before 1969 is spotty, and before 1965 is extremely difficult to find. Extensive Writing Across the Curriculum (WAC) records exist, from the inception of that particular program in the mid-1980s until its whimpering demise in 1999. Faculty meeting minutes are available in the archive, as are yearbooks, university bulletins, Horace Mann Bond's beautifully written history of Lincoln, and many other minor texts.

cial awareness, interestingly enough, would lead to a local discourse that would become the impetus for the establishment of the school's writing program. The national discourse of civil rights played a direct role in discussions regarding student writing at the end of the 1960s. Both impulses, the national and the local, played back and forth directly at Lincoln University, creating an intriguing and noteworthy local discourse, which I call the progressive faculty/student alliance of 1969–1970.

Berlin, Harris, and North tell us that composition, as a system of knowledge, was created roughly in late 1960s to early 1970s, emerging from the seeds of social science. However, the Lincoln University writing program tells a different story. In the late 1960s, the civil rights struggle was reacting both to escalating violence by civil authorities and to increasingly intense apathy by the larger dominant society, whose interests were shifting to other and newer discourses, such as feminism, the Vietnam conflict, Robert Kennedy's war on poverty, and middle-class consciousness raising. This escalating violence was spurred by Southern (and in some cases, Northern) hatred for and frustrations with the legislative and cultural changes enacted by the struggle. The violence was also a reaction by the authorities in the wake of the civil insurrection following the assassination of Reverend Dr. Martin Luther King Jr.

At about the same time, the civil rights struggle also faced a new internal pressure: the emergence of the Black Power discourse from the Student Non-Violent Coordinating Committee (SNCC), which grew out of a new radical involvement in direct action when in 1966 Stokely Carmichael became its chairman. Horace Mann Bond, who graduated from Lincoln at age nineteen and became the school's first African American president (1945–1957), raised his family in the Lincoln community. Horace Mann Bond also wrote the definitive history of Lincoln University, *Education for Freedom*, published in 1954. His son, Julian, who attended Morehouse College in the last year of his father's presidency, eventually found himself within the nucleus of SNCC, in 1960, as SNCC became the umbrella organization of several smaller, local direct action civil rights groups. Lincoln University might have been consigned to an unrelentingly rural location, but a vital connection between the important events in the civil rights struggle (as it was practiced from the period of abolitionism until today) and a local Lincoln practice is evident.

Using archival documents described above, I traced the official evolution of several department courses from discussion at the department level to the general faculty meetings where they were officially proposed. Similarly, proposals and ideas about writing curricula from faculty members, which became the germinal concepts for the future writing program, progress from the departmental to the general faculty level. Missing from the archive are records from the humanities division, a self-governing, unbudgeted entity that existed until 2001 (when a school with its own dean superseded it). It was through the humanities division that all departmental proposals were officially proposed to the faculty. Faculty meeting minutes often provide this analysis with a larger context for attitudes about writing throughout the campus community. Because of the documentation lacunae at the division level and the absence of documentation from many departmental subcommittees, which investigated and formed ideas about student writing problems, I have supplemented the archive with a second form of evidence: interviews with the key players from that period.[2]

Still another archival source used to reconstruct the modes of discursive production of what Pierre Bourdieu refers to as a habitus is my own observations as I interacted in this often contested academic environment. Relationships between the key players, intentions and motivations behind actions, and even, finally, access to archival records all involve different aspects of power in which I was implicated. Consequently, I have tried to minimize the personal hermeneutical nature of this investigation and have tried instead to focus on the rhetorical nature of the emergence of the writing program: not why things happened, but how things happened. (There seems to be no consensus regarding what happened when.) Hence, much of what I narrate here, even what happened well before my entry onto the scene, is tinged by my actions. In my reconstruction of the department's history, I became, in a sense, a part of its historical habitus.

Furthermore, my investigation also proved crucial in providing a link between the national discourse of civil rights and tensions regarding student writing on Lincoln's campus. To understand the progressive faculty/student alliance of 1969–1970, we need to grasp the connection between Lincoln University and the civil rights movement.

Ten months after meeting privately with candidate John F. Kennedy, Reverend Martin Luther King Jr. gave the commencement address at Lincoln University on the first Sunday in May (the traditional day of commencement at Lincoln) in 1961. King accepted a Doctor of Laws degree. King's commencement speech, "The American Dream," was a precursor in many ways to his famous "I Have a Dream" speech, which he delivered a little over two years later, on August 28, 1963, at the Lincoln Memorial in Washington, DC. It ends in a familiar way: "That will be the day when all God's children, black and white, Jews and Gentiles, Catholics and Protestants, will be able to join hands and sing the words of the old spiritual, 'Free at last, free at last, thank God Almighty, I'm free at last!'" (qtd. in Foner).

This pivotal year, 1961, marked increasing confrontation between the SCLC (Southern Christian Leadership Conference) and the SNCC, which questioned King's Gandhian policy of nonviolence as an effective method for advancing the causes of justice and civil rights. Commentators have remarked, "While [King] moved cautiously, southern black college students took the initiative, launching a wave of sit-in protests during the winter and spring of 1960" (Oliver). These tensions between King and the SCLC mounted: "The early 1960s saw conflicts between King and younger militants who organized mass protests during December of 1961 and the summer of 1962" (Oliver).

While King had become, for most Americans, the public face associated with the various discourses of justice, race, and civil rights, in the 1950s and early to mid-1960s, other civil rights leaders had risen to prominence, including NAACP chief Roy Wilkins, Urban League leader Whitney Young, and James Farmer, cofounder of the Congress of Racial Equality (CORE). "I lived in two worlds," Farmer said late in life, recalling his role in the movement: "One was the volatile and explosive one of the new black Jacobins and the other was the sophisticated and genteel one of the white and black liberal establishment. As a bridge, I was called on by each side for help in contacting the other" (Severo). In 1961, James Farmer helped to organize the second Freedom Ride (the first was in 1947), and he recalls: "Dr. King, on probation for his arrest during sit-ins in Atlanta, decided not to go and was criticized for his decision" (Severo).

It was into this context of divided political agendas that Dr. King came to Lincoln on that warm, sunny Sunday morning in May. In his commencement address at Lincoln, King warned that the "price America must pay for the continued exploitation of the Negro and other minority groups is the price of its own destruction." King also chided the critics of poor black communities who failed to understand that black criminality is "environmental and not racial" since "poverty, disease, and ignorance breed crime whatever the racial group may be." King railed against white supremacy and black inferiority, arguing that if "we are to implement the American dream we must get rid of the notion once and for all that there are superior and inferior races." Lincoln University, with its long tradition of religion and religiosity (via its association, since its founding, with both the white Presbyterian Church and the Union American Methodist Episcopal, or UAME, Church), also provided Reverend King with a rhetorical site from which to address directly the moral divisions created by racism. He declared:

> If you will allow the preacher to come out in me now, let me say to you that I never did intend to adjust to the evils of segregation and discrimination. I never did intend to adjust myself to religious bigotry. I never did intend to adjust to economic conditions that take necessities from the many to give luxuries to the few. I never did intend to adjust myself to the madness of militarism and the self-defeating effects of physical violence. I call upon all people of goodwill to be maladjusted, because it may well be that the salvation of the world lies in the hands of the maladjusted.
>
> So let us be maladjusted, just as the prophet Amos, who in the midst of the injustices of his day could cry out in words that echo across the centuries; "Let justice roll down like waters and righteousness like a mighty stream." Let us be maladjusted as Abraham Lincoln, who had the vision to see that this nation could not exist, half slave, half free. Let us be maladjusted as Jesus of Nazareth, who could look into the eyes of the men and women of his generation and cry out, "Love your enemies. Bless them that curse you. Pray for them that despitefully use you." (qtd. in Foner)

King's commencement message was aimed at a number of audiences, both local and national: political liberals, both sides of the African American constituency (i.e., the two sides, "Jacobin" and "genteel, educated," whom Farmer acted as a bridge between), and any progressive segment of America receptive to King's moral argument. Lincoln University, as a vibrant, local site with connections to the national discourse on race and civil rights, allowed Reverend King to meld together several arguments, and, perhaps more importantly at the time, to blunt some of the more activist criticism being leveled at him and the SCLC.

The year in which King spoke, 1961, became, in effect, the locus of the Lincoln University faculty/student alliance's genesis, eight years later, in 1969. Earlier in 1961, Lincoln University sophomore Calvin Morris met Jesse Jackson for the first time. He later recalled: "I met Jesse Jackson in 1961, at North Carolina College at Durham. The glee club for my undergraduate school, Lincoln University, was singing there. And there was a quartet in the glee club made up of Omegas, our fraternity. Jesse and I are [in the] same fraternity. And we sang all around and the brothers at the chapter at A&T where Jesse was heard that we were singing and they came over to hear us. And we met after the concert" ("Interview with Calvin Morris"). The connection between Lincoln University and Jesse Jackson would remain firm through the years. Morris graduated *cum laude* with his BA degree in History in May 1963.[3] In 1973, Morris would become the Director of the Martin Luther King, Jr. Center for Social Change in Atlanta.

While Lincoln alumni established connections to the larger national discourse of race and civil rights, prominent national leaders also gravitated to Lincoln: In 1967, famed civil rights leader James Farmer was a lecturer at Lincoln. In 1969, Reverend Jesse Jackson delivered the commencement address at Lincoln, hearkening back to King's commencement. In the same academic year, Floyd Flake, who in 1986 would go on to become a U.S. Representative for New York's Sixth District (Queens), began the first of his three years as the director of student affairs at Lincoln.

Between 1969 and 1976, the Lincoln University community became acutely aware of external politics. The violent police brutality directed at African Americans in the South (and especially at Morehouse, in Augusta, Georgia) led the Lincoln faculty and student body to initiate a new kind of dialogue, one concerned with both internal administrative politics and larger national issues. This alliance became a sort of Deleuzian predisposition, "the way that things were," and was, at its most concrete, a new knowledge dictating a new sense of reality. The unspoken "reality" that Lincoln students share intellectual and cultural parity with Lincoln faculty continues to this day, with each party considering itself equally responsible for educating the other. This intellectual assemblage enacted (and continues to enact) criticism, arising directly from the language instigated by the progressive faculty/student alliance discourse. This criticism also gave rise to a new kind of language concerning student writing abilities. While this criticism may approximate a reactionary backlash, a systematic analysis shows that it was formulated from within a language of liberation. It was not Hegelian, but was always productive, multiplying rather than negating, and ever creating new strands and threads of discourse.

INSTIGATING DISCOURSE

In the spring of 1970, undergraduate Gil Scott-Heron (who came to Lincoln after reading the poetry of Langston Hughes, a 1929 Lincoln alumnus) had already formed his first band with Lincoln classmates. Scott-Heron was finishing up his first book of critically acclaimed poetry, *Small Talk at 125th & Lennox*, from which the germinal song, "The Revolution Will Not Be Televised" (recorded by Scott-Heron and his band in 1970) would be taken (Bush). During the May faculty meeting at Lincoln University, Scott-Heron "informed the assemblage of his intention to meet shortly with the West Chester County Commissioner's Board, and to read a statement to it and to the press denouncing the atrocities in Augusta, Georgia" ("Minutes, Special Open Meeting"). He went on to urge the faculty and other students to protest these unjust actions.[4]

Scott-Heron's pronouncement was not a solitary action of an engaged student. It was emblematic of a form of activism that was being ushered into the rural Lincoln community by predominantly urban (Philadelphia, New York, and Baltimore) students versed in the realities of the civil rights movement that now lacked the charismatic leadership of Reverend Dr. Martin Luther King Jr. Scott-Heron's comments were just one of many student/faculty concerns that spring. During the same faculty meeting, Lincoln faculty member and famed Leftist historian Philip Foner, who had been fired from his position at CCNY in 1941 during one of the early, often anti-Semitic, Red witch hunts, helped mediate a week-long student strike of classes.

The student strike of 1969 had been called by a consensus among the Lincoln students with the goal of winning eleven points, which were discussed at the special open meeting of the college faculty. These points, formulated by the students with assistance from Foner, when adopted, placed students into active roles in university governance— roles that faculty normally assumed exclusively—and allowed students the right to partake in administrative hiring and firing decisions. As faculty members from that time recollect, students wanted more power on campus to help effect a greater involvement by the Lincoln community in the national political arena. Students were frustrated with the slow rate of progress in areas of racial justice.

The students also wanted (and Foner mediated) the successful creation of a "Student-Faculty Committee at Lincoln University to contact other Black Colleges and other colleges and universities interested in exploring modes of political activity that would effectively protest the killings in Augusta, Georgia." These ideas were presented in a public document, "Minutes of the Special Open Meeting," drafted by and circulated among the Lincoln community. Beyond contacting other schools, little was actually done to form a collective community among other historically black colleges and universities (HBCUs) and other small colleges.

As faculty and students became more involved in the debate over the role of political consciousness in the curriculum, both groups were also involved in external civil rights struggles. In the same academic year, 1969–1970, students and faculty heard rumors that the local Klavern from nearby Cecil County, Maryland, was going to attack Lincoln University. In the spring of 1970, faculty and students joined together and formed a protective perimeter around the campus, lit several bonfires, and, as rumor has it, armed themselves with a few rifles and handguns. The Klan never showed up, but the alliance was strengthened by the defensive actions of the faculty and students.[5]

With respect to the national political scene, the students and faculty were flexible but determined to accomplish something meaningful. Collectively, they discussed options: "The thinking of both students and teachers moved over a wide range: marching, whether on Washington or the United Nations, had outlived its usefulness; the moratorium (which Foner proposed so that students involved in a general classroom walkout strike would not be academically punished) can be most effectively used by studying the present struggle and its future direction; urgent telegrams to the White House are indicated; political analysis is perfectly compatible with a march on Washington, the effects of which can prove beneficial" ("Minutes of the Special Open Meeting"). This combination of events and factors brought the faculty and students together in an alliance, which was more than a group of active citizens. Persistent students had thrown light onto tactics that were more immediate and productive than those employed by faculty members. Conversely, faculty members were suddenly made aware that their students possessed more than just a canny awareness of social strategy. The faculty/student alliance was now an agent of personal and institutional, as well as political, change.

It may seem implausible that a contingent and unexpected change could have happened so quickly; however, archival documentation from before 1969 shows little resemblance in faculty/student cooperation to what occurred suddenly in 1969. There had been faculty/student projects before, many of them in fact; however, these projects had been essentially traditional and hierarchical.[6] Certainly, neither all the students nor the entire faculty bought into what had suddenly happened. But the change had happened, and it became institutionalized as students exerted hitherto unknown power in the new discourse of student/faculty solidarity. This was a time of growth and of vigor for Lincoln. Yet this was the time of open admissions, which, as has been documented, was a major factor in the discipline of composition. While many schools may have similarly recognized their students' knowledge of cultural improvement and social change, most practitioners of composition were grappling with the daily reality of writing errors. It is safe to say that few English writing professionals were dealing with the issue of open admissions to the extent that Mina Shaughnessy was at CUNY at the same time (Maher 141). In institutions like Lincoln and the CUNY system, "writing errors" and "underprepared students" were to become operative phrases.

In the early 1970s, Floyd Flake, then director of student affairs, recalls: "I saw that we were getting a number of students from the public schools who were not prepared properly for higher education" (Flake). The Lincoln

English department, like virtually every other department at the time, had no faculty member on its staff with a specialty in writing or composition. Flake also offers his insight into what was being done to help these students: "I realized that we were at a critical stage even then. Many of our public school students who came into Lincoln University . . . were not really at the competitive level to be in those environments. We provided remedial and other necessary services to try to bring them to that level, but in many instances they had been so crippled, so paralyzed by the school systems, that they were not able to overcome those historical barriers. Therefore, regardless of what we did, many of them wound up drifting out of those institutions" (Flake). Lincoln University, at that time, offered volunteer tutoring and some study/academic services, but no institutionalized "remedial" services specifically in English composition. Lincoln would later take several steps to work with these "underprepared" students. The faculty/student alliance created a means to help these students that would also allow others to assert their own authority in yet another distinctive and sudden way.

Lincoln's demographic changes in 1970 can be objectively measured. Graduating classes at Lincoln were small throughout the nineteenth century until the period of World War II. At the turn of the century, roughly 45 students graduated each spring, from a total matriculating enrollment roughly around 250. These numbers plummeted in 1945, when only 155 students attended Lincoln, and 15 graduated. But the numbers climbed well over the average in 1948, with 531 students and 63 graduates; in 1951, the total number of graduating students reached 110. In 1964, there were 488 students enrolled at Lincoln; the next year, there were 524. The number of students enrolled and graduating then rose rapidly: in 1970 there were 1,064 students and 198 graduates. After that the graduation rate climbed only slightly, with the student population remaining fairly steady at between 1,000 and 1,100 students (Bond xvii). In 1965 Lincoln opened its doors for females. Both the diversity in the gender population and the overall increase in the student population seem to be related to the new demands for institutional involvement.

Changes in student attitude are more difficult to measure. In the 1920s, an alumnus recalls that the white faculty largely ignored nonacademic student social activities, perhaps fostering a permissively progressive campus lifestyle with their paternalistic neglect: "'Did the faculty have faith in us . . . or did it not want to be bothered? Most of those who could answer that question are gone. The fact is that such faith, even if it were honest, was unwarranted by the facts . . . whiskey selling . . . women in dormitories. . . . This certainly would not have been condoned by the college authorities, had they known what was going on. They did not know. They made no effort to find out. Without the terminology, we were a 'progressive' school" (qtd. in Bond 445).

Although dress and fashion bear little conclusive relation to political activism, class yearbooks from the mid-1960s until the mid-1970s definitely show a marked increase in Afrocentric and Pan-African jewelry and clothing. This may signify more than the introduction of more colors from the palette, more dashikis and berets entering into the discourse of youth fashion. In a 1977 yearbook, for instance, there is a photo of an African American student angrily waving her finger at a white administrator. While no one can set a determinate moment, this behavior would never have been countenanced in the 1950s, when the hierarchy went largely unchallenged on campus. Lincoln community members from the 1970s recall a larger student population and an intensified political-social attitude.

A NEW WRITING PROGRAM

The originary impulse for the founding of Lincoln's ambitious English language instruction is now lost. Lincoln lore, that other rich archive, says that Lincoln was created to be "the black Princeton."[7] There is also a national context to consider, however: Lincoln's history is part of a larger narrative, not a local academic aberration. A "literacy crisis" had swept the nation in the two decades before 1894 (Connors, "Abolition Debate," 47–48), and coincided with a great stock market crash. As in other postsecondary institutions, this particular literacy crisis created at Lincoln recognizable writing courses. Societal concerns about the writing and reading skills of the bourgeois, white, male, dominant class entering the Ivies and the large land grants were amplified on Lincoln's African American campus. Concerns about the reception and hypercriticism of students' writing (and therefore an entire host of their skills within a much larger range than that within which white students would be judged) influenced the teaching of all disciplines.

Beginning in 1970, a new way of discussing student writing emerged, and emerged in conjunction with the progressive solidarity forged between faculty and students. The sense of disrupture one gets from reading both of the solidarity and of a new, almost shrill, tenor concerning English department teaching of writing makes it seem as if one were reading about two different universities. Before the 1960s, a sense of benign paternalism reigned over student writing: benevolent teachers, mostly white (although in its defense, the English department had the first African American professor, Professor Joseph Newton Hill, class of 1920—who taught at Lincoln prior to pursuing his graduate degree and then went on to serve as chair for twenty-three years), pointed out good writing and coaxed mainly African American students into modeling it. Although the paternalism can seem nauseating to the archivist, the tone that emerges, beginning in 1970, is shocking and bracing. Whereas students and faculty were working together to create social change, concurrently and almost suddenly, student writing became a sign of pathology, perhaps even to question larger abilities. Perhaps some faculty were uncomfortable working with students and wanted to regain a more traditional, hierarchical relationship. For whatever reason, the errors in student writing were now legion and had to be corrected. Benevolent paternalism, as faculty members worked with students on larger social issues, now focused on the language used, as opposed to the content of writing: a crusade to erase errors ensued. This shift helped determine a new understanding of how students would function in society: not only as leaders among their own race, but also as leaders in the world.[8]

Perhaps the collective political activity between the faculty and the students, however positive, had caused some members of the faculty to question (and become more vocal about their concerns with) the university's academic integrity. In a memo titled "Reparations Standards," dated September 12, 1970, and addressed to the entire English department, a department faculty member (who shall be referred to as Professor Literature) questioned what she called "reparations standards." By this, Professor Literature meant a two-tiered system of grading that she perceived as allowing African American students greater academic leeway than that given to the dominant (white) students she had seen at a larger state university, where she had taught before coming to Lincoln.

Several seasoned faculty members who taught during that time in the humanities departments, including English, have no recollection of this term surfacing before this September 1970 memo, which gave voice to those few faculty members opposed to the social equality of the alliance. Let me state this as clearly as possible: faculty attitudes toward the alliance never conformed to a racial delineation. A more conservative majority essentially slowed down the discussion of new courses, possible speakers, and projects to be undertaken. That majority was made up of International (African/Caribbean), African American, and white faculty members.

Earlier documents from 1970 discuss a new first-semester writing-intensive course, Freshman Humanities 102 (hereafter to be called by its more common appellation, "Language and Literature"), launched in the aftermath of the student strike and faculty/student solidarity of 1969. This course eventually replaced the belletristic freshman writing course, which the department had offered, essentially unchanged, since 1894. Language and Literature was taught by a member of the humanities division, which encompassed the departments of art, foreign languages, music, philosophy, religion, and English. Professor Literature wrote several memos problematizing "this new interdisciplinary course." In the late fall of 1970, in the next academic year, Professor Literature, who had earlier raised the issue of reparations standards, raised issues about Language and Literature that probed at the unspoken rationale for the concept of "interdisciplinary."

Faculty meeting minutes from that period state that the rationale for the "interdisciplinary" course was "to create an excitement among our students and for those faculty teaching the course that matches the tenor of our time." Apparently, insufficient discussion (about what was meant by "inter" disciplinary: specifically what would result from the convergence of two or more traditional humanities disciplines) had preceded the adoption of the course by the humanities division. Professor Literature thought English professionals should teach writing, especially when a crisis was present in student literacy skills. A later memo, by Professor Literature, argued for the return of this course and any other English text-based interdisciplinary course to the English department. She wrote: "This course, Language and Literature, should be under the exclusive jurisdiction of the English Department, and it would be taught exclusively by English Department faculty members who LIKE BEING ENGLISH TEACHERS AND WHO LIKE TEACHING COMPOSITION AND LITERATURE. (General noise signifying student approbation at this point)" (capitalization and parenthetical comment both from the original text). Jurisdiction was not awarded to the English department.

Professor Literature's syllabus for Language and Literature illustrates the highly divisional and highly standardized pedagogy common to the practice of writing: "Course materials will be largely literary, with student grades determined mostly by performance in impromptu writing exercises." At the time, Language and Literature was the main course for teaching first-year writing. At Lincoln, there was no first year Introduction to the University course. A faculty member who taught Language and Literature recalls assigning excerpts from texts like *Soul on Ice* (the first paperback edition of which was released in 1970) and *Invisible Man*. The same faculty member recalls discussing the readings in the context of writing assignments, which encouraged students to use narrative experiences to provide evidence for any of the strands of class discussion. Excitement about the rigorous social analysis that was raised during the course prevails in the memories of faculty members.

Yet documents authored by Professor Literature reproduce a vocabulary used by proponents of the new solidarity movement, growing at the same time as the progressive possibilities of the Lincoln experience. These documents reveal concerns not only with the possibilities of "reparations standards" grading and the lack of rigor with which other humanities faculty might teach writing and literature, but also the possibility that other humanities professors might not address and correct "Black English."

At Lincoln, the dispersal of writing, reading, and other literacy skills was being strongly resisted. As seen in the 1970 memo and the "Discussion Agenda Item" from the humanities division meeting of December 15, 1972, a case was being made for the consolidation of writing instruction under the aegis of English department professionals. Within a few years, this argument would dominate the local discourse. Eventually, Language and Literature would be considered ineffective as a writing course. Of course effective writing was never its primary aim or originating rationale. In some quarters, it was hoped that effective writing could be produced by engaged students (in an ever-increasing student population, in uncertain times) already versed in the realities of the world.

The larger discipline of English was, at the same time, disavowing its efficacy in the face of a new literacy crisis. Stephen North quotes Carl Klaus from his 1976 article, "Public Opinion and Professional Belief": "In other words, Klaus concludes, to be saved from 'the appalling state of our ignorance' (338), and to prevent writing teachers from being treated 'like second-class citizens, like dedicated amateurs, which we are, rather than genuine professionals, which we are not' (340), practitioners must steep themselves in knowledge and methods that are not their own" (North 328). The discipline at large was historicizing itself in a very different way from what was happening at a smaller institution, where literacy skills had become associated with external, national, political contexts. However, as our historians make clear, composition, as it was practiced in the larger schools, and as it is textualized in journal articles, had virtually no external context. There is also something to be said about the almost absurd self-renunciation of professional efficacy, especially when those skills were most needed, if indeed there was a literacy crisis.

At Lincoln University, Professor Literature had become embroiled in a dispute over writing instruction that required that she acknowledge her professional skills first and foremost, and then educate less skilled practitioners. Obviously, North and other historians seek to locate a kind of historical professional transformation, a transformation aimed at the overthrow of an established tradition of teaching and its scholarship, characterized simply as "lore." These terms and their usage in writing instruction, while particular to the history of Lincoln's English department, were similar to what Stephen North describes as the newly elevated social-scientific (as opposed to what he quotes as "erratic circles" lore-based) knowledge being disseminated and producing the positivistic growth of the emerging disciplines at that time (327). At times, it seemed she wanted to hold the line against any kind of change. Professor Literature's teaching and evaluating strategies, which she shared with the English department and the humanities division, certainly represent an attempt to control and disseminate knowledge within the ranks of the technicians.

Professor Literature was successful in textualizing and disseminating her research. As a result, writing in the English department at Lincoln University became dominated by a nuanced discourse of correctness. In 1972, Professor Literature shared with her writing instructor colleagues documents produced for students in writing courses. The first of these documents, a mimeographed department handout called "Vocabulary of Writing," delineates the strict definitional differences between prose, poetry, explication, plain sense, figurative sense, and a variety of literary genres. In this memo Professor Literature writes: "I have seen teachers of English mistakenly accept one kind of writing, when it is inappropriate at the University level." These terms and their usage in writing instruction, while specific to the history of Lincoln's English Department, were also similar to the new "scientific" and less "lore" driven research that, according to Stephen North, marked the same place in time (328–40).

The best local description of the writing process—a process of reproducing thought first into words and then into grammatically and mechanically correct sentences—is to be found in Professor Literature's 1974 student handout from Language and Literature, entitled: "Review of Introduction to Semantics, or, The Use and Abuse of Language." Providing a scale extending from left to right, with 100 identified as the highest ("mathematical precision") and zero the lowest ("subjective indeterminacy"), this handout states: "A clear prose style is a prose style falling on the left side of fifty." The handout defines the writer's responsibility as follows: "to make his ideas clear by expressing them in a prose style that represents his best effort to produce an accuracy of statement that approximates the precision of mathematical language." Placed below that statement is a definition of the "writer's technique," first in philosophical terms and then in political terms. Philosophically, the "truth" of language is said to reside in the world of Platonic ideals: "Allow the meaning to choose the word; i.e., let the physical images and sensations associated with the events being described dictate the choice of words and language structures." Politically, meaning is said to follow from a local, historical continuum of hyperawareness concerning what in 1974 at Lincoln and many other places, was called BED (Black English Diction): "Be sure that the words and language structures chosen are used according to the consistencies obtaining in educated usage." Yet, within this reactionary posture was something much more aligned with composition historiography: a movement to disseminate to instructors and students alike the "process" by which instructors understood how good writing came to be, and how writing was to be evaluated. This "double bind" (i.e., a scramble to hold the line pedagogically while simultaneously making knowledge available for criticism and dissent) helps us to understand that the local discourse, manifested by larger social events, is in touch with the larger historiography but in a much more nuanced way than we might expect. A paternal political approach to student language use had become part and parcel of the student/faculty alliance by this point in time. Concern by faculty over how students would be judged as humans in society based mainly on their grammar was becoming a dominant trend in the discourse.

The history of the so-called literacy crisis can be understood as the historian's textualization (and validation) of an unrelenting conservative elegy about language use in America. This elegy, of course, was brought about by the language problems supposedly shared by all youth; however, at Lincoln University, where the political perception of race and language had been under study for years, another level of concern over youth and language developed. Recognizing the pragmatics of the situation (i.e., that dominant society would police African American language use even more keenly than it did the pathologies of white youth language), the faculty at Lincoln began to reconceive the importance of writing instruction for its students. It may be that the so-called "process movement" (and many of the other disciplinary movements taken for granted in our discipline's epistemology) was not the major influence on disciplinary growth. Instead, our discipline's progress, at least as reflected in one small school's concern for its students, might have resulted from the pragmatic and realistic affirmation that the dominant society's problems with student writing had to be addressed on the dominant society's own terms. The implications of this possibility are that another kind of knowledge, not opposed to process but not recognizing the need for it, became buried in the widespread disciplinary practice of composition. This may be the point of disrupture where historians see disciplinary growth but ignore disciplinary bifurcation (i.e., that old saw about theory opposing practice).

Susan Miller correctly discerns that "composition was established long ago to be a low site where certain students, corrective teaching, and inevitable anxieties from nineteenth-century claims for vernacular textual research could be displaced" (*Textual* 143). However, she links her historical project too tightly to the official historiography when she writes, "the novelty of composition has no obvious sources in larger political changes in the 1960s and 1970s" (142). I believe that Miller is correct in categorizing process as a "return of the repressed" (143), in the shape of grammatical correctness and older instructional forms. However, her macro-disciplinary analysis ignores the political movements on smaller campuses (and like many other historians, she overlooks the HBCUs altogether), when she writes: "current composition has more to do with movements within its originating traditions" (142–43). At Lincoln University, the two seemingly irreconcilable political threads—the scrutiny of error-filled grammar under the warning cries of under-preparedness and the solidarity between faculty and students—were never mutually exclusive: they were always linked through formative utterances made during the academic year 1969–1970. These utterances were obviously tied to external events, and these utterances eventually birthed the writing program at Lincoln.

The new chair's decision to create an autonomous writing program in 1978 showed remarkable foresight. Whatever departmental problems the new chair was to solve, the decision to institutionalize the curriculum, standards, and pedagogy under the independent (with the chair's advice and consent) control of one person brought the "reparations standards" strand of dialogue into a controlled sphere under the aegis of "writing standards." The discourse of local composition "writing standards" apparently disallowed any further racialization of the discussion of grade inflation. Archive documents from the beginning of the writing program to the present moment show plenty of evidence of "standards" and "perfection in the final product," but say nothing about racial inequality in grading. Although the new director lacked institutional standing in terms of tenure, the chair's support and canny use of interpersonal skills put an end to nefarious discussion. The new writing program essentially employed the so-called "current traditional" model.

The progressive faculty/student alliance was still very much visible even in 1974. During the May 1974 commencement, Paul Robeson was awarded an honorary doctorate of law degree. Robeson was no stranger to Lincoln. His father was an alumnus, and Paul Robeson had been a sports coach at Lincoln, where he had also been inducted into the Alpha Phi Alpha fraternity (Bay Area Paul Robeson Centennial Committee). Robeson was still quite a controversial figure during the 1960s and 1970s. His Left politics had made him an unwelcome person at many institutions, but not at Lincoln. The honorary doctorate bestowed on him represented the culmination of the progressive political alliance of 1969.

THE IMPORTANCE OF DISRUPTURES IN THE LARGER HISTORIOGRAPHY

The opening (or disrupture) in the traditional faculty/student hierarchy—an opening that reinvigorated the entire university—led to a profound discussion about language use by African American students. Although the archive is silent on this matter, the specific concern with student language might have been connected to a larger examination of language in the post–Dr. King civil rights movement. With respect to students, however, the paternalism of the faculty hierarchy had shifted by 1974, almost invisibly, into a paternalistic concern with standards of absolute correctness. Faculty members publicly discussed how difficult it would be for African American students to challenge racism without "mastering" (a term that shows up again and again) standard English.

The role played by students in institutional and pedagogical transformation (a role which is almost totally absent in our discipline's historical imagination, except in the form of errors and blunders) becomes obvious when the emergence of a particular writing program is carefully scrutinized. Furthermore, the consideration of a particular writing program may also provide evidence of the role played by non-English faculty in the establishment of a writing curriculum. This was certainly the case at Lincoln University, where non-English faculty exerted considerable pressure on the department to create innovative courses that would address their concerns not only about student writing but about the need for literacy skills in the larger social-cultural context. In the future, I hope that more histories about smaller writing programs will be written, so that through a collective effort, a more inclusive form of historiography might emerge within the professional discourse.

Notes

1. Lincoln University was founded as the Ashmun Institute by John Miller Dickey to educate two former slaves whose applications to white universities had been turned down. Lincoln had an unofficial interracial admissions policy around the time of President Wachman, the last white university president, in the 1960s. Up until then, and since, LU has been a Historically Black College/University (HBCU).

2. During my first few years at Lincoln, as I tried to create a modern Writing Program, I interviewed and discussed the history and rationale of the nascent Writing Program and the composition courses with all the people still in Lincoln's employ. There has never been any consensus regarding the genesis of the writing program, except that a 1978 tenure-track hire was given responsibilities for the writing sequence a year or so after he began. These interviews were conducted informally and are not listed separately in the archival source list.

3. As a contextual note: in Oakland, Huey Newton and Bobby Seale formed the Black Panther Party for Self Defense on October 15, 1966.

4. Scott-Heron, it was rumored on campus, finally left Lincoln after being told not to bang the keys on a piano while auditioning for a major in music. Whatever the case may be, the wildly talented Scott-Heron, already an accomplished poet and soon to be a major force in music as one of the most significant influences in spoken word/rap, left Lincoln after his first year.

5. As an FBI investigation into the racist Right's threats against the Lincoln Community in academic year 2000 indicate, concerns about the local KKK were not baseless paranoia. Even today, this area of Chester County, northern Cecil County, Maryland, and parts of nearby Lancaster County, Pennsylvania, are considered havens of racist activity. In the summer of 2001, an undisclosed farm was the site of a weekend reunion of hate groups. I provide this information to illustrate the sense of isolation one feels upon arriving in this section of Chester County.

6. As a case in point, during the *Brown v. Board of Education* case preparation, Lincoln faculty assisted, and in some cases created, class assignments for their students by

gathering information for its alumnus (of 1930) then NAACP lead attorney Thurgood Marshall.

7. Princeton was founded as a seminary, with philanthropic missionary goals similar to those of Lincoln's founders, in 1746 (as the College of New Jersey).

8. As a matter of fact, Lincoln's shift in its sense of what one could do with a Lincoln degree may have begun about the time of the graduation of Nnamdi Azikiwe (1930), Nigeria's first president; Kwame Nkrumah (1939), Ghana's first president; and Rev. James Robinson (1935), founder of Crossroads Africa, which served as the model for the Peace Corps (in addition to other alumni already mentioned). A Lincoln education clearly prepared one for world prominence.

Archival Sources

The following items are in the English Department Archive of Lincoln University, in Lincoln University, PA:

"Discussion Agenda Item." Humanities Division Meeting Notes. December 15, 1972.

"Faculty Meeting Minutes." Fragment of entire document. November 1970.

"Matters for your Attention." Memo. October 22, 1970.

"Reparations Standards." Memo. September 12, 1970.

"Review of Introduction to Semantics, or, The Use and Abuse of Language." Student handout. 1974.

"Standard Syllabus for Language and Literature." 1972.

The following item is in the Langston Hughes Memorial Library at Lincoln University, in Lincoln University, PA.

"Minutes of the Special Open Meeting of the College Faculty." October 1970.

❧ 12 ❧

Disciplinary Histories

A MEDITATION ON BEGINNINGS

Patricia Donahue

BEGINNING AGAIN

THIS CHAPTER EXPLORES the idea of "beginning" not as an initiatory gesture but as an act of interpretive reframing. It asks you to reread the previous chapters in this volume from the dominant perspective that Harvard provided the history of writing instruction with its originary moment and served as a site of imitation—the same perspective that is suggested by the following comments:

> Modern composition teaching began, I presume, about 1884, when Barrett Wendell introduced the famed "daily theme" at Harvard. . . . It quickly spread throughout the colleges of the country. . . . How fast it spread I am unable to say, but probably not fast enough. At least it had not reached DePauw University in 1896. There we were still in a pre-theme era, or an era that owed much to Harvard also . . . when I reentered college, it was after 1900, I was in another institution, and I had a

professor of English who did something for my writing. This was Will Howe, with a fresh Ph.D. from Harvard. . . . Already by 1910 the books of specimens were in wide use. . . . The typical book was, I should say, another Harvard product. (Creek 5)

We have been told at previous conventions that Freshman English, like so much else, began at Harvard, when, in 1874, Harvard College . . . introduced a required course in freshman rhetoric. . . . Somewhere in those expansionist decades between the Civil War and the Spanish-American War, freshman English, by Harvard's example, by the spirit of westering, by spontaneous generation, erupted across the nation. (Greenbaum 175)

Since the freshman English course at Harvard was the progenitor of so many others, in fact, since its influence is still readily perceptible, its description warrants extended treatment. . . . This freshman English course at Harvard spread rapidly to many of the eastern colleges. While some installed it bodily, others incorporated its major features. The Harvard influence becomes even more apparent in the next decade and carries into the advanced elective courses as well. (Wozniak 125)

Harvard established the first modern composition program, and for two decades its faculty wrote extensively about the subject. (Brereton 26)

To prepare the ground for such rereading, this chapter will proceed in several ways: first, by examining the larger problematic of "beginnings," which is implied by the Harvard narrative; second, by examining the narrative itself, its production by that exemplary figure, Albert R. Kitzhaber, and its status (and his status) within composition studies; and third, by considering the pedagogical possibilities embodied within disciplinary history. Since you have already read these chapters, you know that many of them—especially those that situate their stories in the nineteenth-century context—allude to the Harvard narrative in some way, aligning itself with it, complicating it, often challenging it. This chapter—this "new" beginning placed, paradoxically, at the end of this collection—attempts to provide a rationale.

Before I begin, let me mention that from our earliest conversations about this project, Gretchen Moon and I talked about it as a potential event.[1] Offering more than a series of loosely connected institutional histories, it was to provide a diverse set of narratives, narratives that were thematically and historically connected, which would encourage a reexamination of prevailing ideas about disciplinary formation, development, and transmission. To make these connections apparent, we asked contributors to use a common format: the chapters were to explore the teaching of writing (or the administration of a writing program) at a specific point in its development; to bring to light new archival materials (and struggle with the challenge of constructing an archive); to attempt to look "behind" theory to the pedagogical practices embedded within them; to provide an archival note and salute their archival guardians. John Brereton, whose work has enriched the disciplinary archive in so many wonderful ways, tells us, "Theory is easier to get at" than is practice; "what often got left out was the detail, the everyday fabric of history as lived by the embodiments of courses" (xiv). The chapters in this collection attempt to "get at" that practice.

While the material conditions referred to above lend the collection its formal coherence, the chapters also share deeper conceptual ties. One of those ties is a theory about history: that history is not a scene of objective enactment, but a textual phenomenon, consisting of unstable signifiers to which numerous and equally unstable signifieds can be and have been assigned. When expressed so baldly, this idea may seem obvious. Yet it can be easy to forget that "history" represents a set of materials that have been afforded documentary value and that to read a text as a document is to construct it as evidence for a larger argument (no document announces itself as such, as argument). In his essay "The Discourse of History," Roland Barthes makes the point that "Historians are those who assemble not so much facts as signifiers" (67). Within these chapters, one often repeated "signifier" is "Harvard," or, more specifically, the "Harvard narrative." As the story goes, freshman writing began to assume shape as a separate academic program at Harvard in the nineteenth century, and the Harvard model was then widely reproduced elsewhere. Its reproduction was sometimes direct, with Harvard graduates and former Harvard faculty taking academic positions at other colleges and spreading the instructional gospel. But it was also indirect, as textbooks by Harvard were adopted by other schools to impose conceptual order upon a new subject matter and to legitimize it as a curricular effort. The Harvard narrative as a story of origin and imitation has become so deeply entrenched within our discipline as to function as an "always already" beyond which it can be difficult to go. It has acquired an iconic function as a moment of instantiation, origin, beginning.

Those chapters in this collection that refer to the Harvard narrative do so not to eradicate it, or to offer a replacement, but to situate it within an expanded analytical framework as one of many possible sites of pedagogical innovation. This is not to say that the Harvard narrative goes unchallenged in these pages. Some essays question its identification as an "origin," in order to draw attention to the difficulty of writing disciplinary histories. Other essays question the "obviousness" of pedagogical reproduction, making the point that strange things happen to teaching practices when they travel from one place to another, Finally, still others challenge the idea of pedagogical reproduction itself, saying that until more archives are explored, more local histories written, we should exercise caution in our claims about originals and copies.

As they confront the challenges of writing their histories, these contributors invite us to reflect on the larger problematic of beginning itself, whether it is the beginning of a particular course of instruction or the beginning of a particular writing program.

The writing of disciplinary history is a highly collaborative act; "new" work contains traces of numerous precedents. In the process of undertaking this project, the contributors and the editors felt a considerable sense of excitement and were well aware of the many exemplary scholars who already occupy a seat in the disciplinary parlor: James Berlin, Richard Reed Braddock, John Brereton, Jean Ferguson Carr, Stephen Carr, Robert J. Connors, William Covino, Sharon Crowley, Winifred Horner, Nan Johnson, Albert R. Kitzhaber, Susan Miller, Thomas P. Miller, James J. Murphy, David Russell, Mariolina Salvatori, Patrick Scott, John Schilb, Lucille M. Schultz, Donald Stewart, Victor Vitanza, Kathleen Welsch, and many more. Their work provided this project with an inspired beginning.

EDWARD SAID AND A THEORY OF BEGINNINGS

For a consideration of the larger problematic of beginnings, perhaps no better work is available (although it has received infrequent attention in composition studies) than Edward Said's book, *Beginnings: Intention and Method*, from which I have also borrowed this chapter's subtitle.[2] In its preface, Said poses what serves as his guiding questions: "What is a beginning? What must one do in order to begin? What is special about beginning as an activity or a moment or a place?" (xi). While the purpose of Said's entire book is to respond to these questions in considerable detail, using literary texts as his primary evidence, his introductory response is to say that a beginning is a "kind of action" and a "frame of mind, a kind of work, an attitude, a consciousness" (3). He goes on to explain that sometimes beginnings can assume various forms: some beginnings are material and can be identified through such graphic markers as the indentation of a new paragraph. Other beginnings are strictly conceptual, such as the beginning of an idea, the beginning of a historical era, the beginning of a literary movement. Whatever the status of a beginning, whether it is material or conceptual, Said explains, it acquires its "meaning," its significance, its value only within a system of relationships with other texts: "relationships of either continuity or antagonism or some mixture of both" (3). Said's final point in the introductory pages of his book is that a beginning cannot just exist: it has to do something, function in a particular way, produce a particular effect. One of these effects is to create a moment of differentiation by distinguishing itself from what preceded it. Another effect is to serve as a strategy of delimitation by imposing constraints on how what "comes after" is explained and interpreted.

To say that a beginning serves as a point of demarcation is not to say that it emerges *ex nihilo*, because a beginning can only exist (to the extent that it has any existence at all) as a response to what came before it. It may try to represent itself as the "new," and may try to efface evidence of its contingencies, but those traces can always be recovered by a reader willing to put in the effort. The major problem thus faced by any reader is deciding when to call a halt to the process of recovery, since one trace leads to another and to another and so on. Another effect of a beginning is to place restrictions on how what follows it is read and understood: it establishes a certain line of inquiry, encouraging the creation of particular patterns. Take this chapter, for example. By beginning with terms like "Harvard narrative" and "beginning," I have probably overdetermined my readers' response, setting them up to anticipate certain issues and to ignore, or at least deemphasize, possible digressions.

To think about beginnings along the lines suggested by Said is to think differently about the writing of disciplinary history. Such a history does not simply "begin," nor does it simply organize a series of "facts." While it must offer a beginning—for beginnings are necessary and inevitable—the boundary a beginning creates as a way to separate itself from what preceded it can only be temporary; its conceptual dependency on what comes "before" will be marked in numerous ways. Since a beginning is, indeed, ultimately arbitrary, we should not be surprised—and, in fact, Kitzhaber's work bears this out—that disciplinary histories may find it difficult to settle on a particular beginning: beginnings are constantly being displaced, progenitors are constantly being replaced, and the writing of history becomes an interminable process. Said's work also helps to remind us that whatever is identified as a "beginning" imposes constraints on how what follows it is read: histories produced "after" Kitzhaber's are required to acknowledge his work in some way, to build upon his insights, even to criticize them. As Said himself says, a critical purpose of a beginning is to produce difference where difference was not apparent before.

ALBERT R. KITZHABER AND A HISTORICAL BEGINNING

To even raise the specter of Kitzhaber and his book (the man and his work have become synonymous) in 2007 might seem peculiar: since the book was first made available in dissertation form in 1953, much has been written about it since, and many might even remark that composition history has moved far beyond it. Even if we have moved beyond it, it continues to exert a powerful effect in the disciplinary unconscious as a point of beginning which, like all other beginnings, serves to demarcate and to constrain—often in arbitrary ways. Entitled *Rhetoric in American Colleges: 1850–1900*, it circulated widely in manuscript (as a dissertation) for many years until finally being published in book form in 1990 by Southern Methodist University Press, with an introduction written by John T. Gage. It is consistently invoked within composition studies as the *beginning* of a new type of historiography, one written at a pivotal point in the formation of the discipline, when rhetoric/composition was just *beginning* to establish its autonomy. While this process of disciplinary formation and consolidation would take many years to complete (and many would argue that the project is ongoing), it is likely that it would have taken even longer if Kitzhaber's book had not been written. It provided a much needed story of origins and development, the kind of story a field of study needs in order to establish a separate identity (its bibliography also provides an extraordinarily rich archive). Kitzhaber's book, therefore, is not just as a story about a beginning: it is itself a beginning. Those disciplinary histories that have come after Kitzhaber's book have had to contend with it in some way, either through adaptation, resistance, amalgamation, or attribution.

Thus, it is possible to refer to Kitzhaber, as Foucault referred to Freud and Marx, as a "founder of discursivity." Like Freud and Marx, Kitzhaber created a discourse;[3] he generated not only a subject but the terms for its future discussion. As Foucault explains:

> . . . when I speak of Marx or Freud as founders of discursivity, I mean that they made possible not only a certain number of analogies, but also (and equally important) a certain number of differences. They have created a possibility for something other than their discourse, yet something belonging to what they founded. To say that Freud founded psychoanalysis does not (simply) mean that we find the concept of the libido or the technique of dream analysis in the works of Karl Abraham or Melanie Klein; it means that Freud made possible a certain number of divergences —with respect to his own texts, concepts, and hypotheses—that all arise from the psychoanalytic discourse itself. (115)

What Foucault's definition suggests—and this is an important point—is that the work that follows the foundational text announces its dependency not only through agreement but also through divergence. To express this idea somewhat differently, we can shift to a term provided by Samuel Weber: "conditions of imposability." By this Weber means, "the conditions under which arguments, categories, and values impose and maintain a certain authority, even where traditional authority is meant to be subverted" (19). From Weber's perspective, we can see that Kitzhaber's book continues to "maintain a certain authority," even if its authority is continuously questioned. At the very least, any "new" history that follows in his wake must acknowledge his contribution or risk being denigrated as incomplete.

As evidence for these ideas, we can turn to the work of recent and important disciplinary historians. In his introduction to Kitzhaber's published book, for example, John T. Gage says the following: "More than a necessary work for the student of contemporary composition to know if he or she wishes to understand the history of the discipline as it now exists, *Rhetoric in American Colleges, 1850–1900*, is in fact one of the important markers of the *beginning* of that discipline. It is the first book-length historical study of this subject, by a scholar who helped to *initiate* the reevaluation of rhetoric in American education that made the so-called 'paradigm shift' in composition during the 1960s possible" (vii, my emphases).

Sharon Crowley, in her 1991 review of the book, claims: "The stature of Kitzhaber's work is such that any historian who would disagree with his findings must acknowledge that disagreement in her text or a footnote." And Robert J. Connors, perhaps the most passionate advocate of Kitzhaber, goes so far as to refer to him as "the lion in the road" who cannot be circumvented without being directly confronted. About the book itself Connors says: "That work—its amazing assembly of sources without any previous bibliographic help, its informed analysis of destructive ideas and methods in composition teaching, its attractive division of our forebears into competing camps, and its narrative of the tragic victory of the mechanistic, form-obsessed 'bad guys' who created our own troubled period—*influenced in ways great and small everything that followed it in composition history*" ("Writing" 54, my emphasis).

Perhaps anticipating some resistance (although as Foucault reminds us, resistance is but another sign of dependency), Connors says that his claim that Kitzhaber's work is the "first really respectable work" in composition studies is "not hyperbolic" (54). Nor is it hyperbolic, he adds, for him to say that Kitzhaber's dissertation provided composition with a significant "methodological" legacy. For Connors, composition histories written after Kitzhaber's felt the pressure to display certain commonalities: for example, a preference for theoretical over cultural concerns, a belief in the past as a determinate of the present, and the analysis of writing textbooks as enactments of writing theory. Connors is constructing a *beginning* for the history of composition by constructing Kitzhaber as an *exemplar*.

The idea of "exemplarity," like the idea of "beginning," calls for some explication. To refer to Kitzhaber as an exemplar (Gage, Crowley, and Connors may not use this term, but they certainly imply it) is to make an important interpretive move. Alexander Gelley, in his introduction to his edited collection, *Unruly Examples: On the Rhetoric of Exemplarity*, explains that asking "what is an exemplar" can be understood as asking, "what is it that elevates the singular instance to the authoritative?" Furthermore, while an exemplar is to be understood as an authority, what kind of authority should we understand it to be? In considering these questions, Gelley returns to two foundational moments in the history of exemplarity (a term that is closely related to "paradigm"): Plato and Aristotle. From Plato, Gelley explains, can be derived a notion of exemplar as *paradeigma*, a model of multiple instantiations, in which each part can be substituted for the whole (1). From Aristotle, Gelley also explains, can be derived an idea of the exemplar/paradigm as resulting from a singular event being elevated to singular status through a process of induction, "whereby particulars are linked and traced" in terms of similitude. Plato's model, Gelley goes on to say, is primarily cognitive (at stake is its truth value), while Aristotle's is primarily rhetorical (at stake is it persuasive value). While these models may seem oppositional, they are actually complementary. Employing Gelley's perspective, we can explain Kitzhaber's "exemplarity" in terms of the validity of his arguments and the authenticity of the documentation he provides. Or we can explain it more in terms of its ability to "outward[ly] reach to the agency of reception" (3). The latter requires us to consider why it exerts the power that it does, how it speaks to the voiced or unvoiced desires of its readers. Gelley also insists that in matters of exemplarity, one must always consider what the example is *an example of* (5). The question can be answered in numerous ways, of course. What is perhaps most important is that it is indeed asked. But let me offer this possibility: Kitzhaber (and his text) exemplifies the construction of a disciplinary beginning, both the beginning of freshman writing, which is one of the many historical "facts" it conveys, and the beginning of a particular problematic, whereby certain questions about writing instruction—such as "where did it begin" and "where did it come from" and "what did it turn into"—became permissible to ask. The fact that we are still asking them demonstrates the extent to which we are all Kitzhaber's heirs. If there had not been a Kitzhaber, composition studies would have to have conjured him.

KITZHABER'S EXEMPLARY TALE

Structurally, Kitzhaber's book is organized in terms of twelve chapters, of which only a small part will be considered here. Chapter I, "Main Trends in Higher Education, 1850–1900," examines the decline of religious influence upon education and the concomitant rise of science and technology as powerful determinants, and the importation into America of a German model of disciplinary specialization. Chapter II, "The Field of English," in which the Harvard narrative first emerges, explores the teaching of English at Harvard between the years 1850–1875, the development of philological study, and the formative stages of literary instruction. Chapter III, "Rhetorics and Rhetoricians," discusses the early British rhetorics, early American rhetorics, and those Kitzhaber calls the "The Big Four" rhetoricians: Adams Sherman Hill, John Franklin Genung, Barrett Wendell, and Fred Newton Scott. It is in the section on Hill that Kitzhaber examines the origin of freshman English in considerable detail.

Until 1885, Kitzhaber narrates, Hill taught a course in rhetoric required by sophomore students; this was the only course freshmen were required to take after their first year. (By 1885, it should be noted, Harvard had made the transition from a generalist curriculum to a specialist curriculum.) For many years, however, Hill had been arguing that this course should be taught in the freshman year, the "threshold of college life" (Hill's phrase). In 1885, his efforts finally paid off. This new course, "English A," which eventually became known as "freshman English" was, in Kitzhaber's words, "the parent of all later courses in freshman composition." It was a course with a stalwart history. As Kitzhaber tells us, "Its demise at Harvard was not observed until 1951. For the remaining years of the nineteenth century it was regarded as a model course in rhetoric and widely imitated throughout the United States." These events form the core of the Harvard narrative.[4]

When Kitzhaber refers to the freshman English course at Harvard as the "parent of all later courses in freshman composition," the parent of this parent appears to be Adams Sherman Hill. But within Kitzhaber's text—and also implied by his argument—are various other (male) parents: "parentage" is as slippery a category as is "beginning." For example, another possible parent might have been Charles W. Eliot, who was inaugurated as president of Harvard in 1869, and who in his inaugural address called for systematic attention of the teaching of English. One of his first decisions was to replace the then Boylston Chair of Rhetoric, Francis James Child, with Adams Sherman Hill, who had been brought to Harvard as an assistant professor of rhetoric in 1872. Implied by Kitzhaber's argument, although not directly mentioned by him (and this omission is curious) are two additional potential parent figures: Paul Henry Hanus and William James. As Mariolina Salvatori tells us, Hanus was a professor of pedagogy of Colorado State Normal School. In 1891, Eliot invited him to join the Harvard faculty, where he remained until he was pressured to resign in 1921, at which time he established the Harvard Graduate School of Education (*Pedagogy* 215). William James was another major figure on the Harvard faculty at the time. As Salvatori also points out, James's lectures, compiled in his book, *Talks to Teacher on Psychology; And to Students on Some of Life's Ideals*, played a formative role in the development of a pedagogy of "inspiration" (218). The presence of Hanus and James at Harvard presents promising lines of inquiry. Hanus may have had considerable influence on figures like Hill and on the efforts within an emerging English department to graft pedagogy of rhetoric onto pedagogy of composition. Likewise, it seems likely that James also would have exerted a considerable influence (again, one trace leads to another and to another).

Kitzhaber attributes the exemplarity of "English A" as the model for first-year writing instruction in colleges and universities across the country well into the 1950s in part to Hill's publication of a textbook, *The Principles of Rhetoric, and Their Application in 1878*. Revised and enlarged in 1895, this textbook became, Kitzhaber claims, the "standard text at Harvard from the time it first appeared until some years after Hill's death" (62). "It was widely adopted in other colleges and universities," he explains, due to "the considerable prestige enjoyed by the Harvard English Department" (62). An interesting line of thought thus presents itself: a textbook that codified a particular institutional practice is published; the author of that textbook happens to be a faculty member at an institution possessing considerable cultural capital; thus, a course that had emerged under particular conditions at a particular institution at a particular historical moment for particular reasons acquires "exemplary" status. It may not, however, be reasonable to assume that such pedagogical innovation took place only at a school like Harvard (in fact, less prestigious colleges might have had more flexibility in their curriculum because less might have been at stake). Moreover, the idea that a textbook can simply import pedagogy without complicating or simplifying is seriously flawed: how a book is produced and used will always be shaped by institutional contexts and various reading conditions. A promising subject for study might very well be the "migration" of Hill's text, the nature of its incorporation, and the nature of its transformation. But again, such a study cannot take place until more archival materials become available.

Kitzhaber's text is saturated with the trope of "beginning" and his beginnings are very problematic: perhaps no better example of Said's idea of the arbitrariness of beginning is available to us in composition studies. As concerned as Kitzhaber is with establishing Harvard's freshman English as a stable point of origin, he finds himself continuously blurring distinctions and pushing back his timeline. Speaking of Hill requires him to speak of Hill's predecessors (speaking of some of them, while possibly effacing others): Boylston, Child, and Eliot. Speaking of "English A" requires him to refer to the curricular transition from a generalist model to a specialist model. Furthermore, speaking of English A also requires him to consider the administration of an admission exam at Harvard, the existence of which predates the creation of the "subject A" requirement by many years. This exam is first mentioned in Harvard's college catalogue in 1865–1866: "Candidates will also be examined in reading English aloud" (Kitzhaber 34). The 1869–1870 catalogue reveals that the exam was revised to include works that a candidate would be asked to recite Shakespeare's *Julius Caesar* and Milton's *Comus*. In the 1872–1873 catalogue appears the first mention of correctness and propriety, in addition to the first mention of writing (as opposed to speaking): "Correct spelling, punctuation, and expression, as well as legible handwriting, are expected of all applicants for admission; and failure in any of these particulars will be taken into account at the examination" (34). The 1873–1874 catalogue includes, for the first time, a formal requirement in English composition: "Each candidate will be required to write a short English Composition," which would be evaluated for spelling, punctuation, grammar, and expression. In the 1877–1878 catalogue, the criterion of paragraph division was added. The 1881–1882 catalogue states that a candidate for admission was also required to correct "specimens of bad English."

Other scholars have already made several points about the institution of this exam: for example, that it indicates that a new student was matriculating at Harvard and that, from Harvard's perspective at least, secondary schools had failed to educate "him" properly. Kitzhaber himself refers to this examination as the *beginning* of the "debilitation of rhetoric." As he explains, the examination placed more and more emphasis upon correctness; more and more attention was thus being placed on the evaluation of deficiencies that the rhetoric course was being refashioned to address. Thus, rhetoric became a course important for students to take "only insofar as it could eliminate mechanical errors for freshman writing." The deficiencies the examination was designed to reveal were the same deficiencies the freshman rhetoric course was designed to rectify. As the scope of rhetoric began to narrow, as rhetoric became transformed into rhetoric/composition, its connection with remediation increased.

Kitzhaber obviously tries to associate the beginning of composition with the (beginning of the) decline of rhetoric, a move that has important implications for a consideration of teaching. Turning to Kitzhaber's discussion of Barrett Wendell (another kind of beginning) reveals these implications. A former undergraduate of Hill's, Wendell taught at Harvard from 1888 to 1917. While Kitzhaber is more critical of Hill (for the role he played in "rhetoric's debilitation") than he is of Wendell, because Wendell was apparently interested in larger units of rhetoric like the paragraph, he is nonetheless troubled by Wendell's effort to render the subject of rhetoric/composition teachable through its reduction to a trivium consisting of "unity, coherence and mass." As Kitzhaber explains, "Like Unity-Coherence-Emphasis—or any other set of static abstractions concerning writing—they substitute mechanical for organic conceptions and therefore distort the real nature of writing. It was this trivium and the dominance it acquired as a teaching practice that had much to do with maintaining the stereotyped character of composition instruction for at least three decades" (139). This trivium, we all know, is the instructional model that modern historians of composition refer to as "current traditional."

Wendell's image has undergone significant rehabilitation in recent years, but Kitzhaber himself seems remarkably oblivious, or insensitive, to the challenges faced by Wendell as he struggled to transform a method of rhetorical instruction into a method for writing instruction. What, for Kitzhaber, seems narrow-minded or uninventive, might appear, if examined from a different perspective (especially Wendell's), the well-intentioned effort of a teacher trying to figure out how to graft an old methodology onto a new subject matter. To understand Wendell's effort in this way—as a pedagogical struggle—requires the adopting of a perspective which seems to elude Kitzhaber: "the pedagogical perspective."

In terms of the "conditions of imposability," Kitzhaber demonstrates the importance of asking how historical investigation is related to matters of disciplinary authority. While Kitzhaber was not really an "elitist" scholar, his emphasis on an "elitist" institution like Harvard gives rise to several important questions. Who is authorized to tell the story of a discipline's emergence and development? Who gets to tell the story? Why should others not get to tell the story? And who is able to hear it? Furthermore, Kitzhaber's work demonstrates the methodological and theoretical difficulties involved in writing a story of disciplinary beginning. Kitzhaber refers to a particular course, emerging at a particular moment, at a particular institution, as constituting a "beginning" of a new program of study; but having identified that moment, he finds himself looking "ahead" of it for antecedents, precedents, figures of parentage: his "beginning" is ultimately an arbitrary and unstable point. Finally, Kitzhaber's example raises questions about the designation of exemplarity, its hows and whats. How was Kitzhaber constructed as an exemplary figure? What is at stake in such a construction? What is he presented as an example of? If nothing else, the questions highlight the fact that the name "Kitzhaber" within composition studies has become as powerful a signifier as that of "Harvard" itself.

EASE AND DIFFICULTY IN THE PEDAGOGICAL PERSPECTIVE

I want to open up another beginning, that of "the pedagogical perspective." My turning to pedagogy, to teaching in disciplinary histories, is inspired in part by Mariolina Salvatori's book, *Pedagogy: Disturbing History, 1819–1929,* in which she writes: "In twenty years of professional life, I have been struck over and over again either by a wide-spread, peculiar, and unrestrained hubris on the part of the academy toward pedagogues and things pedagogical—in which case what pedagogy and pedagogues do, can do, should do, is defined for them; or by a lack of knowledge about and understanding of what even the terms mean" (1). In her book (a book which is cited in many essays in this collection and which, like Brereton's book, presents a wonderful archive), Salvatori provides an analysis of the cultural history of the term "pedagogy" and also constructs an instructional history that reveals the contributions made by early normal school professors to the theorization of pedagogy as "reflexive praxis." Salvatori wants to "disturb" totalizing narratives of these professors' work, narratives that represent pedagogy as overly reliant on methods severed from larger philosophical considerations. She seeks to reclaim for "pedagogy" its early origins as an epistemological field: as she says elsewhere, "I want to reclaim pedagogy as a 'philosophical science'" ("Pedagogy: From" 30).

Salvatori's work on pedagogy has provided this collection with numerous "precedents." For example, she has defined pedagogy in a way that has allowed these contributors to speak of teaching without having to sever theory from practice or practice from theory. As she defines it, pedagogy is "a theory and practice of knowing that makes manifest its own theory and practice by continuously reflecting on, deconstructing, and getting to know one's theory and practice." Opposed to pedagogy is what she calls "didactics," defined as a "concept of teaching and learning—in whatever discipline—that programmatically invalidates teachers' and students' critical reflexivity on the act of knowing, and promotes the reduction of somebody else's method of knowing into a sequential schematization of that method" (31). Pedagogy brings theory and practice into reciprocal relationship, makes this relationship visible, so it can be studied and transformed. In contrast, didactics disengages practice from theory and theory from practice, reducing the latter to a model that teachers are said simply to reproduce (the work of teaching as a serious intellectual endeavor is thus disparaged).

What Salvatori sees as the reciprocity and reflexivity within pedagogy gave our contributors a way to sidestep some of the "conditions of imposability" generated by Kitzhaber. For example, they could "disturb" discrete institutional narratives without having to wrestle with the unwieldy distinction drawn between rhetoric/composition. Admittedly, this distinction and its many associations (most dominant is the association of rhetoric with theory and composition with practice) might be too deeply entrenched in our field to be avoided altogether—and perhaps the distinction no longer really matters. Yet shifting the terms from rhetoric/composition to the teaching of writing is useful, opening up new possibilities, as in my discussion of Kitzhaber's representation of Wendell. If we reframe Wendell's challenge, speak of it not in terms of bad teaching and the debilitation of rhetoric but as a struggle to teach an emerging subject with a preexisting methodology, then we can speak not of decline but of mismatch: we can proceed more positively. In addition, reading history through the "pedagogical perspective" also allowed our contributors to sidestep the limitations of terms such as "current traditional," which emphasize reproduction and efface the innovation that is always apparent when one reads locally.[5]

This "pedagogical perspective"—and Salvatori's project—has also served this collection by encouraging the contributors to disturb the histories they inherited from their institutions by looking at actual practices and asking new questions about them. More often than not, these questions engaged them in an examination not of easy pedagogy, but difficult pedagogy. Building upon Salvatori's definition of pedagogy, sometimes the "theory/practice" enactment goes relatively smoothly; sometimes it hits a wall. Our efforts as disciplinary historians might be better served if we examined these difficult moments not as evidence of failure, but as an effort to contend with the diverse and often competing expectations of students, teachers, institutions, and culture. Instead of taking at face value an institution's claim that it attempted to incorporate those of a "humbler background" (or for that matter, women) we might ask (as several of these contributors to this collection have done, in different ways) how these students understood and represented to themselves and to others their own desire to become part of higher education. Did they see themselves as being co-opted by some dominant force, or were they strategically assenting to hegemonic educational structures for their own individual purposes? What can be learned about their perception of teaching and learning through their writing assignments, diaries, and notes? Is the teaching of grammatical correctness inevitably stultifying, or does the teaching of such practices strike us as stultifying because we do not yet understand the conditions of its difficulty? In reflecting on such questions in a diverse range of ways, this collection presents itself, unlegitimately, as a sustained and rich narrative about teaching. In constructing disciplinary history from "the pedagogical perspective," it offers those already seated in the parlor and those standing at the door a new kind of beginning.

Notes

1. The word "event" has various definitions. Most interesting, in this context, may be provided by Michel de Certau, who refers to an event as a heavily coded trope that "reads" or allegorizes the past. He cautions, "try as we may to describe an event in order to determine 'what happened there,' we must realize that events are often our own mental projections bearing strong ideological and even political imprints" (38). In other words, an "event" is a constructed occasion assigned a particular significance. This collection is an "event" in that it offers a perspective on past "events." It is also an event in that, if it does it work well, it will alter present histories and provide a resource for future histories.

2. Said's book, first published in 1975, is one of the theoretical texts of the 1970s and 1980s that compositionists might want to revisit, because it allows us to rethink some of the terms we use quite loosely, terms like "beginning." The chapter titles include "Beginning Ideas," "A Meditation on Beginnings," "The Novel as Beginning Intention," and "Beginning with a Text." My comments are derived primarily from his preface.

3. I use "discourse" here in the sense developed by many that a discourse is a series of rules, stipulated as well as secret, determining what could be discussed, how, and by whom.

4. The chapters that follow these three are: Chapter IV. "Rhetoric, 1850–1900 (Definitions, Relations, Scope)"; Chapter V. "Subject Matter and Logic"; Chapter VI. "The Forms of Discourse"; Chapter VII. "The Communicative Function of Rhetoric"; Chapter VIII. "The Paragraph"; Chapter IX. "Style"; Chapter X. "Diction, Usage, Grammar"; Chapter XI. "The Shift from Theoretical to Practical Rhetoric"; Chapter XII. "Conclusion."

5. This kind of shift might provide another way to interpret the entire "current traditional" model. Rather than see it as a linear duplication of Wendell's trivium, it would be promising to determine within it a series of pedagogical challenges.

Afterword

Jean Ferguson Carr

The archive gives rise to particular practices of reading. If you are a historian, you nearly always read something that was not intended for your eyes: you are the reader impossible-to-be-imagined. . . . Historians read for what is *not there*: the silences and the absences of the documents always speak to us.

CAROLYN STEEDMAN

As much as and more than a thing of the past, before such a thing, the archive should *call into question* the coming of the future.

JACQUES DERRIDA

THE EPIGRAPHS FROM Steedman and Derrida raise the complicated relationship of past, present, and future represented by a book of archival readings. Working with archives calls for, as Steedman argues, "particular practices of reading"—ways of piecing together fragments, of paying attention to traces and small details, of investigating unfamiliar languages and values.

The archival critic makes documents "speak"—bringing forward and into visibility what has been forgotten or buried from view. Archival work confirms what was speculation or assumption; it counters prejudices and reopens foreclosures. Such attention to the past pressures critics to reflect on and articulate the investments of the present, those ways of telling history or of making distinctions that shape teaching and learning, that frame disciplinary practices and values. And, as Derrida proposes, archival work pressures the "coming of the future," suggesting new avenues for research and inquiry, jostling settled patterns to make way for new connections or threads.

The contributors to *Local Histories* traverse the past, present, and future in suggestive and challenging ways. They invite readers to rethink assumptions about the history of instruction, assumptions overly conditioned by particular archives and programs, circles drawn with too narrow a compass around too fixed a point. A history of U.S. instruction rendered from a small sample of leading textbooks, or from the narratives and figures of schools like Harvard or Andover, is thus enriched, complicated, and refigured. By focusing on what seems to be the periphery, the history of dominant texts and leading institutions are both altered and enhanced: their influences and determining practices are newly engaged in complex relationship with a wider range of institutions, regions, levels of instruction, and demographics of students. The many "local" histories thus fashion a richer, more fluid and permeable national history.

These chapters model energetic and cautious approaches to archives, recognizing that there are many gaps between what documents pronounce and what teachers and students do. Contributors note the problems of what is missing, of what was never valued enough to be collected or itemized. This admirable scholarly caution about the extent and use of archives is matched by expansive and inventive notions of the kinds of "evidence" that shape a history of teaching and learning. The contributors creatively reread materials saved for different kinds of purposes, those materials Steedman calls the "mad fragmentations that no one intended to preserve and that just ended up there" (68). Consider, for example, the value of composition exercises, preserved perhaps as signs of handwriting, which can now be reread for what they offer to understandings of rhetorical performance or student resistance. University archives offer many examples of "miscellaneous" documents, records, and books, materials preserved for their associative or collegiate connections rather than for their official status as historical record. Such materials often serve as significant evidence of what was taught, read, examined, or celebrated. These chapters work to reconstruct the relationship of students and teachers, investigating the gaps between what a teacher says or does and how students act on such prompts. They suggest the complications of reading the evidence of textbooks, teacher memoirs, curricula, pedagogical practices, programs, or disciplinary structures to complicate what it means (or meant) to "learn" in particular locations, situations, and times.

In 1897, the historian Gabriel Compayré argued that "pedagogy is a complex affair, and there are many ways of writing its history." He proposed that a "useful and eminently practical" history might study "not the great writers on education and their doctrines, not the great teachers and their methods, but pupils themselves." This historian of pedagogy would "relate in minute detail . . . the manner in which a great or a good man has been educated." The chapters in *Local Histories* attempt to write such an enlarged history, one that traces out many situated pupils, investigating their curricula, their assignments, or their material circumstances. The authors search not just for the "great or good man," but for differently situated students, the ordinary and the extraordinary, the local and the representative. They invite modern readers to rethink the questions and habits of mind they bring to pedagogical situations and documents, and, in the process, encourage such readers to carry on their own situated reflections on teaching and learning.

Many of the contributors to *Local Histories*, following what is a common gesture in archival studies, note the importance of serendipity—finding a particular document, following a stray recommendation, opening the right box on the right day to discover something powerful or illuminating. Serendipity is a compelling aspect of a story researchers recall: the moment of discovery or "luck" when fragments appeared to connect, when effects found causes, or when a search uncovered an "origin." Indeed, much of the pleasure and skill of archival work is the ability to be open to illumination, to what a document can frame or call into question. The tension between planned rigor and the luck of the moment is a valuable insight for archival researchers: it encourages them to return to their archives with competing questions, with refreshed eyes and interests, to pay attention to the remnant or the out of place.

But all archivists know the labors involved in making (allowing for) such "luck." Archival work is patient, attentive to the accumulation of details; it is time-consuming, responsive to the need to gather multiple kinds of evidence. At the beginning of an archival project, the researcher reads in a wide and widening circle, following cues from one text to another, tracing back through footnotes or biographical entries the errant "stuff" of the past. The circle gathers in the expected and the unexpected, those materials often juxtaposed and used to inform each other and those newly queried, brought from other kinds of inquiries to inform a project. The archivist shapes a project, becomes knowledgeable, and learns how to read pronouncements shaped by different times and places, framed by different education or cultural values and habits. As Coleridge wrote about his own projects, "The razor's edge becomes a saw to the armed vision."

Local Histories is shaped by such knowledgeable labor, by thoughtful preparation, and by openness to serendipity, to newness and surprise. Its historians are saturated with the complex material history of education, even as they insist on the ways that history is inflected by the local, by the figures and locations in which students and teachers met and corresponded.

Works Cited, Secondary Sources

Adams, Charles Francis, et al. "Report of the Committee on Composition and Rhetoric (1897)." Salvatori. *Pedagogy*. 101–26.

Adams, John L., and Katherine H. Adams. "The Paradox Within: Origins of the Current-Traditional Paradigm." *Rhetoric Society Quarterly* 7 (1987): 421–31.

Adams, Katharine H. *A Group of Their Own: College Writing Courses and American Women Writers, 1880–1940*. Albany: SUNY P, 2001.

Altenbaugh, Richard J., and Kathleen Underwood. "The Evolution of Normal Schools." Goodlad, Soder, and Sirotnik 136–86.

Applebee, Arthur N. *Tradition and Reform in the Teaching of English: A History*. Urbana, IL: NCTE, 1974.

Atwater, Caleb. "Extract from *Essay on Education* (1841)." Salvatori, *Pedagogy* 114–20.

Arnold, Matthew. *Culture and Anarchy*. Ed. Samuel Lipman. New Haven: Yale UP, 1993.

Bain, Alexander. *English Composition and Rhetoric*. New York: D. Appleton and Co., 1866.

Barthes, Roland. "The Discourse of History." *The Rustle of Language*. Trans. Richard Howard. New York: Hill & Wang, 1987. 127–40.

Bay Area Paul Robeson Centennial Committee, Inc. "Paul Robeson Chronology: 1958–1976." 2000. April 20, 2001 <http://www.bayarearobeson.org/Chronology.htm>.

Berkenkotter, Carol, and Thomas Huckin. *Genre Knowledge in Disciplinary Communication: Cognition/Culture/Power*. Hillsdale, NJ: Erlbaum, 1994.

Berlin, James A. *Rhetoric and Reality: Writing Instruction in American Colleges, 1900–1985*. Carbondale: Southern Illinois UP, 1987.

———. *Rhetorics, Poetics, and Cultures: Refiguring College English Studies*. Urbana: NCTE, 1996.

———. "Richard Whately and Current-Traditional Rhetoric." *College English* 42.1 (Sept. 1980): 10–17

———. *Writing Instruction in Nineteenth-Century American Colleges*. Carbondale: Southern Illinois UP, 1984.

Bernard, Jessie. *Academic Women*. University Park: Pennsylvania State UP, 1964.

Board of Regents of Normal Schools. *Reports of Proceedings of Annual Meeting, 1868–1905*. Madison: State of Wisconsin, 1868–1905.

Bond, Horace Mann. *Education for Freedom: A History of Lincoln University, Pennsylvania*. Lincoln University: Lincoln UP, 1976.

Borrowman, Merle L. *Teacher Education in America: A Documentary History*. New York: Teachers College P, 1965.

Boyden, Albert. "Genera; View of the Work of the Normal School in Massachusetts." *Paris Exposition of 1900. The Public Schools of Massachusetts, USA. Eight Educational Monographs*. Boston: Wright and Potter, 1900.

Brereton, John C. *The Origins of Composition Studies in the American College, 1875–1925.* Pittsburgh: U of Pittsburgh P, 1995.

Brint, Steven, and Jerome Karabel. *The Diverted Dream: Community Colleges and the Promise of Educational Opportunity in America, 1900–1985.* New York: Oxford UP, 1989.

Brown, Robert T. *The Rise and Fall of the People's Colleges: The Westfield Normal School 1839–1914.* Westfield: Institute for Massachusetts Studies, Westfield State College Library, 1988.

Burns, Lee. "The Beginnings of Butler College." *Butler Alumnal Quarterly* 15.1 (April 1926): 3–12.

Bush, John. "Gil Scott-Heron." Excerpted from *All Music Guide 1997.* April 16, 2001 <http://authors.aalbc.com/gil-scot.htm>.

Buss, Helen. Introduction. *Working in Women's Archives: Researching Women's Private Literature and Archival Documents.* Ed. Helen Buss and Marlene Kadar. Waterloo, Ontario: Wilfrid Laurier UP, 2001.

Campbell, JoAnn. "Controlling Voices: The Legacy of English A at Radcliffe College, 1883–1917." *College Composition and Communication* 43 (Dec. 1992): 472–85.

———. "Freshman (*sic*) English: A Nineteenth-Century Wellesley 'Girl' Negotiates Authority." *Rhetoric Review* 15 (1996): 110–27.

———. "'A Real Vexation': Student Writing in Mount Holyoke's Culture of Service, 1837–1865." *College English* 59.7 (Nov. 1997): 767–88.

Campbell, Karlyn Kohrs. "Consciousness Raising: Linking Theory, Criticism, and Practice." *Rhetoric Society Quarterly* 32.1 (Winter 2002): 45–64.

———. Introduction. *Man Cannot Speak for Her.* Ed. Karlyn Kohrs Campbell. Vol. 2. New York: Greenwood, 1989. ix–xxviii.

Carr, Jean Ferguson, Stephen L. Carr, and Lucille M. Schultz. *Archives of Instruction: Nineteenth-Century Rhetorics, Readers, and Composition Books in the United States.* Carbondale: Southern Illinois UP, 2005.

Carver, Elvira. *How to Teach Geography: A Plan for an Elementary and a Scientific Course.* Boston: n.p., 1887.

Clark, Burton. "The Cooling Out Function in Higher Education." *American Journal of Sociology* 65 (1960): 569–76.

Clark, Gregory, and S. Michael Halloran, eds. *Oratorical Culture in Nineteenth-Century America: Transformations in the Theory and Practice of Rhetoric.* Carbondale: Southern Illinois UP, 1993.

Clark, Kate Upson. "Our Boys' Politics." Published Address. *Semi-Centennial and Other Exercises of the State Normal School, at Westfield, Mass., June 25, 1889.* Boston, n.p.: 1889. 45–51.

Clifford, Geraldine Joncich. "Man/Woman/Teacher: Gender, Family, and Career in American Educational History." Warren 293–343.

Cogan, Frances B. *All-American Girl: The Ideal of Real Womanhood in Mid-Nineteenth-Century America.* Athens: U of Georgia P, 1989.

Cohen, Arthur M., and Florence B. Brawer. *The American Community College.* 3rd ed. San Francisco: Jossey-Bass, 1996.

Cohen, David. "Practice and Policy: Notes on the History of Instruction." Warren 393–407.

Coleridge, Samuel Taylor. *Biographia Literaria.* Vol. I. 1817. New York: E. P. Dutton, 1906. vii.

Compayré, Gabriel. *The History of Pedagogy*, trans. W. H. Payne. Boston: D. C. Heath, 1897.

Connors, Robert J. "The Abolition Debate in Composition: A Short History." *Composition in the Twenty-First Century*. Ed. Lynn Z. Bloom, Donald A. Daiker, and Edward M. White. Carbondale: Southern Illinois UP, 1996. 47–63.

———. *Composition-Rhetoric: Backgrounds, Theory, and Pedagogy*. Pittsburgh: U of Pittsburgh P, 1997.

———. "Dreams and Play: Historical Method and Methodology." *Methods and Methodology in Composition Research*. Ed. Gesa Kirsch and Patricia A. Sullivan. Carbondale: Southern Illinois UP, 1992. 15–36.

———. "Historical Inquiry in Composition Studies." *Writing Instructor* 4 (1984): 157–67.

———. "Personal Writing Assignments." *College Composition and Communication* 38 (May 1987): 166–83.

———. "The Rise and Fall of the Modes of Discourse." *College Composition and Communication* 37.2 (1981): 444–56.

———. "Writing the History of Our Discipline." *An Introduction to Composition Studies*. Ed. Erika Lindemann and Gary Tate. New York: Oxford UP, 1991. 49–71.

Conway, Kathryn. "Woman Suffrage and the History of Rhetoric at the Seven Sisters Colleges, 1865–1919." Lunsford 203–26.

Corbett, Edward P. J. *Classical Rhetoric for the Modern Student*. 4th ed. Oxford: Oxford UP, 1999.

Corcoran, Sister Catherine Theresa. "Vida Dutton Scudder: The Progressive Years." Diss. Georgetown U, 1973.

Creek, Herbert L. "Forty Years of Composition Teaching." *College Composition and Communication* 6:1 (Feb. 1955): 4–10.

Crowley, Sharon. *Composition in the University*. Pittsburgh: U of Pittsburgh P, 1998.

———. *The Methodical Memory: Invention in Current-Traditional Rhetoric*. Carbondale: Southern Illinois UP, 1990.

———. "Review of *Rhetoric in American Colleges, 1850–1900*." *College Composition and Communication* 42 (1991): 514–16.

De Certau, Michel. *The Writing of History*. Trans. Tom Conley. New York: Columbia UP, 1988.

DeGenaro, William. "Class Consciousness and the Junior College Movement: Creating the Docile Worker." *jac: A Journal of Composition Theory* 21 (2001): 499–520.

———. "Social Utility and Needs-Based Education: Writing Instruction at the Early Junior College." *Teaching English in the Two-Year College* 28 (2000): 129–40.

Derrida, Jacques. *Archive Fever: A Freudian Impression*. 1995. Trans. Eric Prenowitz. Chicago: U Chicago P, 1996.

Dewey, John. *The School and Society*. Chicago: U of Chicago P, 1967.

Dickinson, John W. *The Limits of Oral Training*. Syracuse: n.p., 1890.

———. *Rhetoric and Principles of Written Composition*. Boston: Emerson College of Oratory, 1901.

Diener, Thomas, ed. *Growth of an American Invention: A Documentary History of the Junior and Community College Movement*. New York: Greenwood, 1986.

Douglas, Wallace. "Rhetoric for the Meritocracy: The Creation of Composition at Harvard." *English in America.* Ed. Richard Ohmann. Hanover, NH: Wesleyan UP, 1976. 97–132.

Dunn, Patricia A., and Kenneth Lindblom. "Why Revitalize Grammar?" *English Journal* 92.3 (2003): 43–50.

———. "Developing Savvy Writers by Analyzing Grammar Rants." *Language in the Schools.* Ed. Kristin Denham and Ann Lobeck. Mahwah, NJ: Lawrence Erlbaum, 2005. 191–207.

Dyson, Michael Eric. "I Saw That Dream Turn into a Nightmare: From Color-Blindness to Black Compensation." *I May Not Get There With You: The True Martin Luther King, Jr.* By Dyson. New York: Free Press, 2000.

Eells, Walter Crosby. *The Junior College.* Boston: Houghton Mifflin, 1931.

Fitzgerald, Kathryn. "A Rediscovered Tradition: European Pedagogy and Composition in Nineteenth-Century Midwestern Normal Schools." *College Composition and Communication* 53 (2001): 224–50.

Flake, Floyd. H. "Event Transcript: October 26, 1999, Mayors' Education Summit ." Center for Civic Innovation, The Manhattan Institute. Jan. 3, 2007 <http://www.manhattan-institute.org/html/mayors_ed_summit_1.htm>.

Flynt, Suzanne L. *The Allen Sisters: Pictorial Photographers, 1885–1920.* Deerfield, MA: Pocumtuck Valley Memorial Association, 2002.

Foner, Philip S. *The Voice of Black America.* New York: Simon and Schuster, 1972. Rpt. at Robert L. Ivie, "The American Dream: Democracy: Rhetorical Texts." February 22, 2007 <http://www.indiana.edu/~ivieweb/mlkad.html>.

Foucault, Michel. "What is an Author?" *language counter-memory, practice: Selected essays and interviews by Michel Foucault.* Trans. Donald F. Bouchard and Sherry Simon. Ed. Donald F. Bouchard. Ithaca: Cornell UP, 1977. 124–42.

Fowler, William Chauncey. *English Grammar.* 1855. Rev. and enlarged. New York: Harper and Brothers, 1877.

Fraser, James. "Agents of Democracy: Urban Elementary School Teachers and the Conditions of Teaching." Warren 118–56.

Frye, John H. "Expansion or Exclusion: A Question of Intent." *Community College Review* 22 (1995): 27–28.

———. *The Vision of the Public Junior College, 1900–1940.* New York: Greenwood, 1992.

Gage, John T. Introduction. *Rhetoric in American Colleges, 1850–1900.* By Albert R. Kitzhaber. Dallas: Southern Methodist UP, 1990.

Gannett, Cinthia. *Gender and the Journal.* Albany: SUNY Press, 1992.

Garbus, Julie. "Service-Learning, 2002." *College English* 64 (2002): 547–65.

Gelley, Alexander, ed. *Unruly Examples: On the Rhetoric of Exemplarity.* Palo Alto: Stanford UP, 1995.

Genung, John F. *The Practical Elements of Rhetoric.* Boston: Ginn and Co., 1886.

———. *The Study of Rhetoric in the College Course.* Boston: D. C. Heath and Co., 1887.

Gerson, Carole. "Locating Female Subjects in the Archives." *Working in Women's Archives: Researching Women's Private Literature and Archival Documents.* Ed. Helen M. Buss and Marlene Kadar. Ontario: Wilfred Laurier UP, 2001. 7–22.

Gilson, Mary. *What's Past is Prologue.* New York: Harper and Brothers, 1940.

Ginzburg, Carlo. *The Cheese and the Worms: The Cosmos of a Sixteenth-Century Miller.* Trans. John and Anne Tedeschi. New York: Penguin, 1982.

Goodlad, John I., Roger Soder, and Kenneth A. Sirotnik, eds. *Places Where Teachers Are Taught*. San Francisco: Jossey-Bass, 1990.

Goodspeed, Thomas Wakefield. *A History of The University of Chicago 1891–1916*. Chicago: U of Chicago P, 1916.

———. *The Story of the University of Chicago 1890–1925*. Chicago: U of Chicago P, 1925.

Gordy, J. P. *Rise and Growth of the Normal-School Idea in the United States*. Washington, DC: GPO, 1891.

Gould, Stephen Jay. *The Mismeasure of Man*. New York: Norton, 1981.

Graff, Gerald. *Professing Literature: An Institutional History*. Chicago: U of Chicago P, 1987.

Greenbaum, Leonard. "The Tradition of Complaint." *College English* 31: 2 (Nov. 1969): 174–76.

Griffin, Gail. "Alma Mater." *Profession 90*. New York: Modern Language Association of America, 1990: 37–42.

Guindon, Francis X. *Fitchburg State College: A Record of Leadership*. Fitchburg, MA: Fitchburg State College, 1990.

Hagarty, Laura Dunbar. "English." *Normal Instructor* (June 1910).

Halloran, S. Michael. "From Rhetoric to Composition: The Teaching of Writing in America to 1900." Murphy, *Short* 151–82.

Harmon, Sandra D. "'The Voice, Pen and Influence of Our Women Are Abroad in the Land': Women and the Illinois State Normal University, 1857–1899." Hobbs 84–102.

Harper, Charles A. *Development of the Teachers College in the United States with Special Reference to the Illinois State Normal University*. Bloomington, IL: McKnight and McKnight, 1935.

Harper, William Rainey. "The Associate Degree." *University Record* 5 (1900–1901): 12–13. Rpt. in Diener 50–52.

———. "Changes Affecting the Small College Which May Be Expected and Which Are to Be Desired." *Journal of Proceedings and Addresses of the Thirty-Ninth Meeting Held at Charleston, South Carolina, July 7–13, 1900*. Chicago: The Association, 1900. 80–84, 86–87. Rpt in Diener 53–59.

———. "The High School of the Future." *School Review* 11 (1903): 1–3.

———. *The Trend in Higher Education*. Chicago: U of Chicago P, 1905.

Harris, Joseph. *A Teaching Subject: Composition Since 1966*. Upper Saddle River: Prentice Hall, 1997.

Heath, Shirley Brice. "The Essay in English: Readers and Writers in Dialogue." *Dialogue and Critical Discourse: Language, Culture, Critical Theory*. Ed. Michael Macovski. New York: Oxford UP, 1997. 195–214.

Helscher, Thomas P. "The Subject of Genre." *Genre and Writing: Issues, Arguments, Alternatives*. Ed. Wendy Bishop and Hans Ostrom. Portsmouth, NH: Heinemann, 1997. 27–36.

Herbst, Jurgen. *And Sadly Teach: Teacher Education and Professionalism in American Culture*. Madison: U of Wisconsin P, 1989.

———. "Teacher Preparation in the Nineteenth Century: Institutions and Purposes." Warren 213–36.

Hobbs, Catherine, ed. *Nineteenth Century Women Learn to Write*. Charlottesville: U of Virginia P, 1995.

Hofstader, Richard, and C. DeWitt Hardy. *The Development and Scope of Higher Education in the United States*. New York: Columbia UP, 1952.

Horner, Winifred. *Nineteenth-Century Scottish Rhetoric: The American Connection*. Carbondale: Southern Illinois UP, 1993.

Horowitz, Helen. *Campus Life: Undergraduate Cultures from the End of the Eighteenth Century to the Present*. Chicago: U of Chicago P, 1988.

Hurwitz, Ruth Sapin. "Coming of Age at Wellesley." *Menorah Journal* 12 (Oct. 1935): 210–30.

"Interview with Calvin Morris: The Pilgrimage of Jesse Jackson." *Frontline*. WGBH Boston. 1998. Feb. 22, 2007 <http://www.pbs.org/wgbh/pages/frontline/jesse/interviews/morris.html>.

Johnson, Nan. *Gender and Rhetorical Space in American Life, 1866–1910. Studies in Rhetorics and Feminisms*. Carbondale: Southern Illinois UP, 2002.

———. *Nineteenth-Century Rhetoric in North America*. Carbondale: Southern Illinois UP, 1991.

Johnson, William R. "Teachers and Teacher Training in the Twentieth Century." Warren 237–56.

Joliet Junior College. "History of Joliet Junior College." August 29, 2000 <http://www.jjc.cc.il.us/Admin/History.html>.

Jolliffe, David. "Writers and Their Subjects: Ethnologic and Chinese Composition." *A Rhetoric of Doing*. Ed. Stephen P. Witte, Neil Nakadate, and Roger D. Cherry. Carbondale: Southern Illinois UP, 1992.

Kirkpatrick, Doris. *The City and the River*. Fitchburg, MA: Fitchburg Historical Society, 1971.

Kitzhaber, Albert R. *Rhetoric in American Colleges, 1850–1900*. Dallas: Southern Methodist UP, 1990. (Diss. University of Washington, 1953.)

Kolodny, Annette. "Inventing a Feminist Discourse: Rhetoric and Resistance in Margaret Fuller's *Woman in the Nineteenth Century*." Lunsford 137–66.

Knight, Adeline. "Spots of Weakness in Training." *Education* 10 (Sept. 1889): 11–21.

Knotts, Laura. "Normal School English, As Based Upon the Work in the State Normal School at Lowell, Mass." *Paris Exposition of 1900: The Public Schools of Massachusetts, U.S.A. Eight Educational Monographs*. Boston: Wright and Potter, 1900.

Labaree, David F. "Career Ladders and the Early Public High School Teacher: Studying Inequality and Opportunity." Warren 157–89.

LaCapra, Dominick. *Rethinking Intellectual History: Texts, Contexts, Language*. Ithaca: Cornell UP, 1983.

Levering, Julia Henderson. *Historic Indiana*. New York: G. P. Putnam's Sons, 1909.

Levin, Robert A. "Reoccurring Themes and Variations." Goodlad, Soder, and Sirotnik 40–83.

Lewiecki-Wilson, Cynthia, and Jeff Sommers. "Professing at the Fault Lines: Composition at Open Admissions Institutions." *College Composition and Communication* 50 (1999): 438–62.

Lindblom, Kenneth, and Patricia A. Dunn. "Cooperative Writing 'Program' Administration at Illinois State University: The Committee on English of 1904–05 and the Influence of Professor J. Rose Colby." *Historical Studies of Writing Program Administration: Individuals, Communities, and the Formation of a Discipline*. Ed. Barbara L'Eplattenier and Lisa Mastrangelo. West Lafayette, IN: Parlor Press, 2004. 37–70.

Logan, Shirley Wilson. *"We Are Coming": The Persuasive Discourse of Nineteenth-Century Black Women*. Carbondale, Southern Illinois UP, 1999.

Lunsford, Andrea A. ed. *Reclaiming Rhetorica: Women in the Rhetorical Tradition*. Pittsburgh: U of Pittsburgh P, 1995.

Maher, Jane. *Mina P. Shaughnessy: Her Life and Work*. Urbana: NCTE, 1997.

Manchester, O. L., David Felmley, J. Rose Colby, Manfred J. Holmes, John A. H. Keith, and William T. Bawden, eds. *Semi-Centennial History of the Illinois State Normal University 1857–1907*. Normal: Illinois State Normal University, 1907. Feb. 27, 2007 <http://www.mlb.ilstu.edu/ressubj/subject/isuhist/jubilee/home.htm>.

Mann, Horace. *A Few Thoughts on the Powers and Duties of Woman: Two Lectures*. Syracuse: Hall, Mills, 1853.

Marbury, Elizabeth. "Education of Woman." *Education* 8 (Dec. 1887): 236.

March, Francis Andrew. *A Comparative Grammar of the Anglo-Saxon Language*. 1869. New York: Harper, 1873.

——. "Craik's English of Shakespeare." *North American Review* 105 (1867): 302–8.

——. *Method of Philological Study of the English Language*. New York: Harper, 1865.

——. "Methods of Teaching English in the High School." *Address and Journal of Proceedings of the National Education Association, Session of the Year 1872* (1873): 240–44.

March, Francis Andrew, and Francis A. March, Jr. *A Thesaurus-Dictionary of the English Language*. Philadelphia: Historical Publishing, 1902.

Marshall, Helene E. *Grandest of Enterprises: Illinois State Normal University, 1857–1857*. Normal: Illinois State Normal U, 1956.

Matthews, Glenna. *The Rise of Public Woman: Woman's Power and Woman's Place in the United States, 1630–1970*. New York: Oxford UP, 1992.

McGrath, Dennis, and Martin B. Spear. *The Academic Crisis of the Community College*. Albany: SUNY P, 1991.

McLachlan, James. "The Choice of Hercules: American Student Societies in the Early 19th Century." *The University in Society*. Ed. Lawrence Stone. Vol. 2. Princeton: Princeton UP, 1974. 449–94.

Miller, Carolyn. "Genre as Social Action." *Quarterly Journal of Speech* 70 (May 1984): 151–67.

Miller, Susan. "Classical Practice and Contemporary Basics." Murphy, *Rhetorical* 46–57.

——. "Is There a Text in This Class?" *Freshman English News* 1 (1982): 20–24.

——. *Textual Carnivals: The Politics of Composition*. Carbondale: Southern Illinois UP, 1991.

Minto, William. *A Manual of English Prose Literature: Biographical and Critical*. Boston: Ginn, 1889.

Mirtz, Ruth M. "The Territorial Demands of Form and Process." *Genre and Writing: Issues, Arguments, Alternatives*. Ed. Wendy Bishop and Hans Ostrom. Portsmouth, NH: Heinemann, 1997. 190–98.

Murphy, James J., ed. *The Rhetorical Tradition and Modern Writing*. New York: MLA, 1982.

——, ed. *A Short History of Writing Instruction: From Ancient Greece to Twentieth-Century America*. Davis, CA: Hermagoras, 1990.

National Education Association. *Report of Committee on Normal Schools*. Chicago: U of Chicago P, 1899.

Nesbit, Robert C. *Wisconsin: A History*. Madison: U of Wisconsin P, 1973.

Newkirk, Thomas. "Octalog: The Politics of Historiography." *Rhetoric Review* 7 (1988): 5–57.

Newman, Samuel P. *A Lecture on a Practical Method of Teaching Rhetoric*. Boston: Hilliard, Gray, 1830.

———. *A Practical System of Rhetoric*. New York: Gould and Newman, 1839.

———. *A Practical System of Rhetoric or the Principles and Rules of Styles Inferred from Examples of Writing: To Which Is Added a Historical Dissertation on Style*. New York: Mark H. Newman, 1851.

Noble, Harriet. *Literary Art: A Handbook for Its Study*. Terre Haute: Inland Publishing, 1897.

"Normal Commencement." *Westfield Times and News-Letter*. June 22, 1887.

"The Normal School: Address to the Graduates." *Western Hamden Times*. January 24, 1877.

North, Stephen M. *The Making of Knowledge in Composition: Portrait of an Emerging Field*. Portsmouth: Boynton/Cook, 1987.

Ogren, Christine A. "Where Coeds Were Co-educated: Normal Schools in Wisconsin, 1870–1920." *History of Education Quarterly* 5 (Spring 1995): 1–26.

Oliver, Mark. "Martin Luther King." *Guardian Unlimited*, January 21, 2002. February 22, 2006 <http://www.guardian.co.uk/netnotes/article/0,,637107,00.html>.

Paine, Charles. *The Resistant Writer: Rhetoric as Immunity, 1850 to the Present*. Albany: SUNY P, 1999.

Palmieri, Patricia Ann. *In Adamless Eden: The Community of Women Faculty at Wellesley*. New Haven: Yale UP, 1995.

Powell, Arthur G. *The Uncertain Profession: Harvard and the Search for Educational Authority*. Cambridge: Harvard UP, 1980.

Ratcliff, James L. "The Excitement of Discovery and the Perils of Premature Conclusions." *Community College Review* 22 (1995): 29–34.

———. "Seven Streams in the Historical Development of the Modern American Community College." *A Handbook on the Community College in America: Its History, Mission, and Management*. Ed. George Baker. Westport, CT: Greenwood P, 1994. 3–16.

———. "Should We Forget William Rainey Harper?" *Community College Review* 13 (1986): 12–19.

Ricks, Vickie. "'In an Atmosphere of Peril': College Women and their Writing." Hobbs 59–83.

Ringel, Paul Joseph. "The Introduction and Development of Manual Training and Industrial Education in the Public Schools of Fitchburg, MA, 1893–1928." Diss. Teachers College, Columbia U, 1980.

Robbins, Sarah. *Managing Literacy, Mothering America: Women's Narratives on Reading and Writing in the Nineteenth-Century*. Pittsburgh: U of Pittsburgh P, 2004.

Rothermel, Beth Ann. "A Sphere of Noble Action: Gender, Rhetoric, and Influence at a Nineteenth-Century Massachusetts State Normal School." *Rhetoric Society Quarterly* 33 (2003): 35–64.

Rouse, P. Joy. "Cultural Models of Womanhood and Female Education: Practices of Colonization and Resistance." Hobbs 230–47.

Rudolph, Frederick. *Curriculum: A History of the American Undergraduate Course of Study since 1636*. San Francisco: Jossey-Bass, 1977.

Rury, John, and Glenn Harper. "The Trouble with Co-education: Mann and Women at Antioch, 1853–1860." *History of Education Quarterly* 26 (1986): 481–502.

Russell, David R. *Writing in the Academic Disciplines, 1870–1990: A Curricular History*. Carbondale: Southern Illinois UP, 1991.

Said, Edward W. *Beginnings: Intention & Method*. Baltimore: Johns Hopkins UP, 1975.

Salvatori, Mariolina Rizzi, ed. *Pedagogy: Disturbing History, 1819–1929*. Pittsburgh: U of Pittsburgh P, 1996.

———. "Pedagogy: From the Periphery to the Center." *Reclaiming Pedagogy: The Rhetoric of the Classroom*. Ed. Patricia Donahue and Ellen Quandahl. Carbondale: Southern Illinois UP, 1989. 17–34.

———. "Pedagogy in the Academy." Salvatori, *Pedagogy* 233–51.

Salvatori, Mariolina Rizzi, and Patricia Donahue. "English Studies in the Scholarship of Teaching." *Disciplinary Styles in the Scholarship of Teaching and Learning: Exploring Common Ground*. Ed. Mary Taylor Huber and Sherwyn P. Morreale. Washington, DC: American Association for Higher Education and the Carnegie Foundation for the Advancement of Teaching, 2002. 69–86.

Schultz, Lucille M. "Letter-Writing Instruction in 19th Century Schools in the United States." *Letter Writing as a Social Practice*. Ed. David Barton and Nigel Hall. Philadelphia: John Benjamins, 2000. 109–30.

———. *The Young Composers: Composition's Beginnings in Nineteenth Century Schools*. Carbondale: Southern Illinois UP, 1999.

Scudder, Vida Dutton. *On Journey*. London: Dent, 1937.

———. *The Privilege of Age*. New York: Dutton, 1939.

———. *Social Ideals in English Letters*. Boston: Houghton, 1923.

Severo, Richard. "James Farmer, Civil Rights Giant in the 50s and 60s, Is Dead at 79." *New York Times*, July 10, 1999, natl. ed.

Sharer, Wendy Beth. "Rhetoric, Reform, and Political Activism in United States Women's Organizations, 1920–1930." Diss. Pennsylvania State U, 2001.

Shaughnessy, Mina. *Errors and Expectations*. New York: Oxford UP, 1977.

Shor, Ira. *Critical Teaching and Everyday Life*. Chicago: U of Chicago P, 1987.

———. "Our Apartheid: Writing Instruction and Inequality." *Journal of Basic Writing* 16 (1997): 91–104.

Steedman, Carolyn. *Dust: The Archive and Cultural History*. 2001. New Brunswick, NJ: Rutgers UP, 2002.

Stewart, Donald. "Harvard's Influence on English Studies: Perceptions from Three Universities in the Early Twentieth Century." *College Composition and Communication* 43 (1992): 455–71.

———. "Two Model Teachers and the Harvardization of English Departments." Murphy, *Rhetorical* 118–30.

Storr, Richard J. *Harper's University: The Beginnings; A History of the University of Chicago*. Chicago: U of Chicago P, 1966.

Tonkovich, Nicole. "Rhetorical Power in the Victorian Parlor: *Godey's Lady's Book* and the Gendering of Nineteenth-Century Rhetoric." Clark and Halloran 158–83.

Tyack, David. "The Future of the Past: What Do We Need to Know About the History of Teaching?" Warren 408–21.

Veysey, Laurence R. *The Emergence of the American University*. Chicago: U of Chicago P, 1965.

Warren, Donald, ed. *American Teachers: Histories of a Profession at Work*. New York: Macmillan, 1989.

Watt, William. *An American Rhetoric*. New York: Holt, Rinehart, and Winston, 1952.

———. "Freshman English and Variations." *Lafayette Alumni Quarterly* 34.14 (April 1964): 5–7.

Wattenbarger, James L., and Allen A. Witt. "Origins of the California System: How the Junior College Movement Came to California." *Community College Review* 22 (1995): 17–25.

Weber, Samuel. *Institution and Interpretation*. 2nd ed. Palo Alto: Stanford UP, 2001.

Weidner, Heidemarie Z. "Coeducation and Jesuit 'Ratio Studiorum' in Indiana: Rhetoric and Composition Instruction at Nineteenth-Century Butler and Notre Dame." Diss. U of Louisville, 1991.

Welsch, Kathleen A. "Nineteenth-Century Composition: The Relationship Between Pedagogical Concerns and Cultural Values in American Colleges, 1850–1890." Diss. U of Pittsburgh, 1994.

Whately, Richard. *Elements of Rhetoric*. New York: Sheldon, 1832.

Woods, William F. "The Reform Tradition in Nineteenth-Century Composition Teaching." *Written Communication* 2 (1985): 377–90.

Woody, Thomas. *A History of Women's Education in the United States*. New York: Octagon, 1966 (rpt. of 1929 ed.).

Wozniak, John Michael. *English Composition in Eastern Colleges, 1850–1940*. UP of America, Washington, DC, 1978.

Wright, Elizabethada A., and S. Michael Halloran. "From Rhetoric to Composition: The Teaching of Writing in America to 1900." Murphy, *Short* 213–46.

Wyman, Mark. *Wisconsin Frontier*. Bloomington: Indiana UP, 1998.

Contributors

WILLIAM P. BANKS is assistant professor of composition and rhetoric and director of the First-Year Writing Studio at East Carolina University. His essays have appeared in *Computers and Composition, College English, Teaching English in the Two-Year College,* and *Dialogue: A Journal for Writing Specialists.* His current book project investigates the rhetorical strategies of queer writers and activists, and explores the implications these strategies may have on undergraduate writing students.

JEAN FERGUSON CARR writes and teaches in composition, women's studies, and literary studies, focusing on nineteenth-century American constructions of literacy and letters. She is coeditor of the Pittsburgh Series in Composition, Literacy, and Culture, and has edited two volumes of the works of Emerson. Her publications include "Writing as a Woman: Dickens, *Hard Times,* and Feminine Discourses" (*Dickens Studies Annual,* 1989), "The Polemics of Incomprehension: Mother and Daughter in *Pride and Prejudice*" (in *Tradition and the Talents of Women,* 1990), and "Cultural Studies and Curricular Change" (*Academe,* November 1990).

WILLIAM DeGENARO, assistant professor of rhetoric and composition at the University of Michigan–Dearborn, teaches courses in writing and working-class studies. The editor of *Who Says: Working-Class Rhetoric, Class Consciousness, and Community* (2007), he has published articles and reviews in *College English, Teaching in the Two-Year College, jac,* and *The Community College Journal of Research and Practice.* Much of his scholarship focuses on the intersections of literacy, social class, and higher education in the United States.

PATRICIA DONAHUE is professor of English at Lafayette College in Easton, Pennsylvania, where she serves as the director of the College Writing Program. She has published articles and reviews in the *WAC Journal, Pedagogy, Reader, College English,* and *College Composition and Communication.* In 2003, she was selected as a Carnegie Scholar by the Carnegie Foundation for the Advancement of Teaching for her work on reading across the curriculum. In 2004, she coauthored *The Elements (and Pleasures) of Difficulty,* with Mariolina Salvatori.

BIANCA FALBO is associate professor of English at Lafayette College where she teaches composition and literature and is codirector of the College Writing Program. Her research includes work on pedagogy, the history of reading and writing practices, and nineteenth-century literary culture. Recent articles have appeared in *Reader: Essays in Reader-Oriented Theory, Criticism, Pedagogy; Composition Studies;* and *Romantic Textualities: Literature and Print Culture, 1780–1840.*

KATHRYN FITZGERALD is an associate professor at Utah State University, specializing in composition and rhetoric and English education. She has coauthored two composition textbooks,

The Student Writer (1991), and *Conversations in Context* (1998). She has published several articles on the history of composition, including the 2002 Braddock Award winning "A Rediscovered Tradition: European Pedagogy and Composition in Nineteenth-Century Midwestern Normal Schools" (*CCC*, December 2001).

JULIE GARBUS is assistant professor of English at the University of Northern Colorado, where she directs the Writing Center and teaches composition and rhetoric. A recipient of a Rising Scholar's Award from the Kellogg Foundation for Higher Education and the Public Good, she has published articles about composition history and service-learning in *College English* and *Rhetoric Society Quarterly*.

PATRICE K. GRAY, professor and chair of the English Department at Fitchburg State College, teaches undergraduate and graduate courses in writing, composition theory and practice, and creative nonfiction. A frequent presenter at several national conferences in composition, communication, and teaching, she has published her work in the *Journal of Student-Centered Learning* and in *Teaching Effectiveness*.

JEFFREY L. HOOGEVEEN is associate professor at Lincoln University, where he teaches composition and is the administrator of the Writing Program. He has published *The Role of Students in the History of Composition* (2003) and, with David Blakesley, *The Thomson Handbook: A Writer's Reference for the Digital Age* (2006). He is currently working on *Understanding Visual Culture*.

KENNETH LINDBLOM is associate professor of English and director of English Teacher Education at Stony Brook University (SUNY). His essays have appeared in *Rhetoric Review*, *English Journal*, *Journal of Pragmatics*, and several edited collections. He currently edits a regular column for *English Journal*, entitled "Teaching English in the World," and served as guest editor of *English Journal*'s November 2006 issue devoted to "Teaching English After 9/11."

GRETCHEN FLESHER MOON is professor of English and director of the Writing Center at Willamette University in Salem, Oregon. She is a founding member of the CCC special interest group on Composition in the Small College/University and has written on teaching writing in liberal arts colleges. Her current book project examines the uses of literacy by women who kept diaries on the Overland Trail.

RISË QUAY, assistant professor of composition at Central Oregon Community College, is currently finishing doctoral work in English studies at Illinois State University with a focus on composition pedagogy and adult literacy.

BETH ANN ROTHERMEL is associate professor of English at Westfield State College in Westfield, Massachusetts. She teaches graduate and undergraduate courses in composition, rhetoric, and writing pedagogy, and coordinates the first-year writing program. She has done field research on the teaching of writing in Sweden, publishing her findings in *Multicultural Education* and in the Dutch language-arts journal *Spiegel*.

MARIOLINA RIZZI SALVATORI teaches and does research in hermeneutics, composition literacy, and pedagogy at the University of Pittsburgh. She is the author of numerous book chapters; of articles in *College English*, *College Composition and Communication*, *Reader*, and many other publications; of *Pedagogy: Disturbing History, 1819–1929* (1996); and, with Patricia Donahue, of *The Elements (and Pleasures) of Difficulty* (2004). In 1999 she was selected as a Carnegie Scholar for her work on "Pedagogy of Difficulty." She is the former editor of *Reader*, with Paul Kameen.

HEIDEMARIE Z. WEIDNER, professor of English at Tennessee Technological University, teaches undergraduate and graduate courses in composition and rhetoric as well as upper-level German. From 1993–2001, she directed the composition program at TTU. Her research and publications focus on the nineteenth-century history of rhetoric and composition as well as composition pedagogy. Since 2000 she has been chief editor of the national creative nonfiction journal, *Under the Sun.*

KATHLEEN A. WELSCH is associate professor of English at Clarion University of Pennsylvania where she directs the Writing Center and teaches composition, rhetoric, and writing pedagogy. She has had articles published in the teachers' guide to *Ways of Reading: An Anthology for Writers, Teaching/Writing in the Late Age of Print* (2003), the *Writing Lab Newsletter*, and *CCC* and has edited a collection of memoirs, *Those Winter Sundays: Female Academics and Their Working-Class Parents* (2004).

Index